SEXUAL HARASSMENT: ANALYSES AND BIBLIOGRAPHY

SEXUAL HARASSMENT: ANALYSES AND BIBLIOGRAPHY

V.P. ARGOS AND TATIANA SHOHOV
COMPILERS

Nova Science Publishers, Inc.
Commack, New York

Editorial Production:	Susan Boriotti
Office Manager:	Annette Hellinger
Graphics:	Frank Grucci and Jennifer Lucas
Information Editor:	Tatiana Shohov
Book Production:	Donna Dennis, Patrick Davin, Christine Mathosian, Tammy Sauter and Lynette Van Helden
Circulation:	Maryanne Schmidt
Marketing/Sales:	Cathy DeGregory

Library of Congress Cataloging-in-Publication Data
available upon request

ISBN 1-56072-711-X

Copyright © 1999 by Nova Science Publishers, Inc.
     6080 Jericho Turnpike, Suite 207
     Commack, New York 11725
     Tele. 516-499-3103   Fax 516-499-3146
     e-mail: Novascience@earthlink.net
     e-mail: Novascil@aol.com
     Web Site: http://www.nexusworld.com/nova

Printed in the United States of America

CONTENTS:

1) General...1

2) Sexual Harassment in the Workplace...53

3) Sexual Harassment in the Military..75

4) Laws and Legislation on Sexual Harassment...81

5) Sexual Harassment in Education...97

6) Psychological Aspects of Sexual Harassment...141

7) Health Care..151

Subject Index...169

Author Index..173

1) GENERAL

[A] [Sexualization in therapeutic relations].
[Article in Norwegian]
Sudmann T
Senter for kvinne, Universitetet i Bergen.

[A] "Nagging" questions : feminist ethics in everyday life/ edited by Dana E. Bushnell.
Lanham, Md. : Rowman & Littlefield, c1995.
x, 402 p. ; 23 cm.
Series: New feminist perspectives series.
LC Call No.: BJ1395 .N34 1995
ISBN: 0847680061 (alk. paper)
084768007X (pbk. : alk. paper)
Includes bibliographical references and index.
Introduction : philosophy and feminism / Dana E. Bushnell -- Feminism and autonomy /
John Christman -- Oppression and Victimization : choice and responsibility / Susan
Wendell -- Right-wing women : causes, choices, and blaming the victim / Anita M.
Superson -- Sexual harassment, the acquiescent plaintiff, and the "unwelcomeness"
requirement / Melinda A. Roberts -- Women, equality, and the military / Judith Wagner
DeCew -- New reproductive technologies / Susan Sherwin -- Markets in women's
reproductive labor / Debra Satz -- Privacy and reproductive liberty / Anita L. Allen –
Coerced birth control and sexual discrimination / Lenore Kuo -- Is IVF research a threat to
women's autonomy? / Mary Anne Warren -- To be or not to be a woman : anorexia
nervosa, normative gender roles, and feminism / Mary Briody Mahowald -- Women and
the knife : cosmetic surgery and the colonization of women's bodies / Kathryn Pauly
Morgan -- Beauty's punishment : how feminists look at pornography / Edward Johnson --
Feminine masochism and the politics of personal transformation / Sandra Lee Bartky.
Subjects: Feminist ethics. Feminist theory.
Source: DLC DLC GZM YHM MTH

[A] "Sexgate," the sisterhood, and Mr. Bumble
Podhoretz, Norman
Commentary.v. 105 no6 June 1998 p. 23-36.
The recent sex scandals involving President Bill Clinton illustrate how feminism has
become simply another wing of the Democratic Party. Feminists introduced the concept of
sexual harassment into the mainstream of American culture. Nonetheless, they were
dismissive of both Paula Jones's claims that Clinton had made an unwelcome sexual

advance on her and the Monica Lewinsky case because both work against the Democrats' interests. The writer discusses a number of factors that have spread confusion about feminism, the law of sexual harassment, and the principles of conservatism.

[A] "Some gorgeous gams"
American Journalism Review.v. 15 Oct. 1993 p. 13.
A number of extracts taken from a diary kept at the journal's request by a 22-year-old female reporter on a daily newspaper in northwest Indiana. The extracts detail episodes of sexual harassment experienced by the journalist.

[A] A language game approach to narrative analysis of sexual harassment law in Meritor v. Vinson
Myrsiades, Linda
College Literature.v. 25 Winter 1998 p. 200-30.
Part of a special issue on law, literature, and interdisciplinarity. The writer applies narrative analysis to sexual harassment law to construct an interpretation that accounts for the different voices that speak, both in terms of the themes they give voice to and those they close off. Using the work of Jean Francois Lyotard, she develops an understanding of language game theory as a framework for narrative analysis. With reference to this theory, she discusses the case of Meritor v. Vinson. She finds that this approach enables an appreciation of the frequent interchangeability of positions within and among games, the heterogeneity that makes up presumably singular voices, and the ambiguity that characterizes much of the context of games.

[A] A mighty baptism : race, gender, and the creation of American Protestantism / edited by Susan Juster and Lisa MacFarlane.
Ithaca, N.Y. : Cornell University Press, 1996.
x, 288 p. : ill. ; 24 cm.
LC Call No.: BR515 .M53 1996
ISBN: 0801430240 (alk. paper)
0801482127 (pbk. : alk. paper)
Includes bibliographical references and index.
Introduction : "a sperit in de body" / Susan Juster and Lisa MacFarlane -- To slay the beast : visionary women in the early republic / Susan Juster -- "Ethiopia shall stretch forth her hands unto God" : Laura Kofey and the gendered vision of redemption in the Garvey Movement / Barbara Bair -- Resurrecting man : desire and "The damnation of Theron Ware" / Lisa MacFarlane -- Ministerial misdeeds : the Onderdonk trial and sexual harassment in the 1840s / Patricia Cline Cohen -- "The women have had charge of the church work long enough" : the Men and the Religion Forward Movement of 1911-1912 and the masculinization of middle-class Protestantism / Gail Bederman -- "Theirs the sweetest songs" : women hymn writers in the nineteenth-century United States / Mary De Jong -- The uses of the supernatural : toward a history of Black women's magical practices / Yvonne Chireau -- "It's a spirit in me" : spiritual power and the healing work of African American women in slavery / Sharla Fett -- Reading, writing, and the race of mother

figures : Shakers Rebecca Cox Jackson and Alonzo Giles Hollister / Etta Madden --
"When we were no people, then we were a people" : evangelical language and the Free
Blacks of Philadelphia in the early republic / Stephen Hum -- The governing spirit :
African American writers in the antebellum city on a hill / John Ernest.
Subjects: Protestant churches -- United States -- History. United States -- Church history.
Sex role -- Religious aspects -- Christianity -- History.United States -- Race relations.
Afro-Americans -- Religion.
Source: DLC DLC GDC UKM SNN

[A] A no-win situation
Shepard, Alicia C
American Journalism Review.v. 16 July/Aug. 1994 p. 26-9.
The allegations leveled by Paula Corbin Jones against President Clinton posed a no-win
situation for the media. At a press conference on February 11, Jones accused Clinton of
sexual harassment, claiming that she was traumatized by the alleged 1991 incident but that
she did not file a complaint for fear that she would lose her job as a clerk for a state
agency. The article traces press reactions to Jones's claims.

[A] A rose by any other name might smell as sweet, but it wouldn't come in dozens on
Valentine's Day: how sexual harassment got its name
Lawrence, Jennifer
Journal of American Culture.v. 19 Fall 1996 p. 15-23.
The writer examines narration as argument, using the Anita Hill/Clarence Thomas
hearings as the narrative, especially the opening statements, Hill's substantive claims of
sexual harassment, and Thomas' "rebuttal" to these charges as he is questioned afterward.
In understanding the Hill/Thomas hearings as narrative, she steps outside the bounds of
traditionally defined stories, examining the no-man's land between reality and fiction. She
explores how American culture might read the issues that appeared in the texts of the
hearings, hoping to come to a new understanding of what the hearings meant.

[A] A secret no more
Weaver, Carolyn
WJR.v. 14 Sept. 1992 p. 23-7.

[A] A warm gesture
JAMA.v. 267 Feb. 5 1992 p. 743.

[A] Access denied
Augmented Title: women avoid computer science as a profession
Grossman, Wendy M
Scientific American.v. 279 no2 Aug. 1998 p. 38.
According to statistics compiled by Tracy K. Camp, then at the University of Alabama,
the number of undergraduate degrees in computer science awarded to women has been
gradually declining. She notes that this trend runs counter to other science and engineering

fields, which have increased their recruitment of women. Proposed reasons for the decline include male-orientated computer games during the 1980s, unsociable hours in programming jobs, a lack of role models, the unappealing image of the hacker, gender discrimination, and the perceived high rate of sexual harassment in the computer industry.

[A] Adelson, Melissa.
Shifting identifications and antediluvian politics in Anita Hill's "15 minutes" / by Melissa Adelson.
Amherst, Mass. : [s.n.], 1992.
73 leaves ; 29 cm.
Local Call No: DIV III SS92 .A3
Typescript.
A Division III examination in the School of Social Science, Hampshire College, May 1992. Chairperson, Margaret Cerullo.
Includes bibliographical references.
Subjects: Hill, Anita, Sexual harassment of women.
Source: HAM HAM

[A] Am J Psychiatry 1995 Mar;152(3):478; discussion 479
Sexual harassment.
Feldman-Schorrig S
Comments: Comment on: Am J Psychiatry 1994 Jan;151(1):10-7

[A] Am J Psychiatry 1995 Mar;152(3):478; discussion 479
Sexual harassment.
Bursztajn HJ
Publication Types: Comment Letter
Comments: Comment on: Am J Psychiatry 1994 Jan;151(1):10-7

[A] Am J Psychiatry 1995 Mar;152(3):478-9
Sexual harassment.
Klein J
Publication Types: Comment Letter
Comments: Comment on: Am J Psychiatry 1994 Jan;151(1):10-7

[A] Apes of wrath
Augmented title: comparing male aggression against females in primates and humans
Smuts, Barbara
Discover.v. 16 Aug. 1995 p. 35-7.
A deeper understanding of male aggression against females in other species could shed light on the same problem among humans. Among primate species whose males practice intimidation and sexual coercion on females, two key factors appear to be the social relationships that females form with other females and with males. In "female bonded" species, such as vervet monkeys, macaques, and olive baboons, females form alliances

against aggressive males. In some primate species, females also use relationships with males to help protect themselves against sexual coercion. Given that male alliances are much more highly developed in humans than in other primates, women need to form alliances with one another on an unprecedented scale to avoid sexual coercion.

[A] Arch Sex Behav 1998 Dec;27(6):561-80
Sexual harassment: identifying risk factors.
O'Hare EA, O'Donohue W
Department of Psychology, Northern Illinois University, DeKalb 60115, USA. A new model of the etiology of sexual harassment, the four-factor model, is presented and compared with several models of sexual harassment including the biological model, the organizational model, the sociocultural model, and the sex role spillover model. The risk factors most strongly associated with sexual harassment were an unprofessional environment in the workplace, sexist atmosphere, and lack of knowledge about the organization's formal grievance procedures.

[A] Aten Primaria 1998 Apr 30;21(7):467-70
[Sexual harassment: assessment and follow-up].
[Article in Spanish]
Cancelo-Hidalgo MJ, Monte-Mercado JC, Viuda de la Garcia E, Calleja Garcia E, Gomez N, Ruiz Diana D, Alvarez de los Heros JI
Centro de Planificacion Familiar de Guadalajara, Hospital General Universitario de Guadalajara, Universidad de Alcala de Henares.

[A] Backlash
Barstow, Anne L
Journal of Feminist Studies in Religion.v. 10 Spring 1994 p. 107-9.
Part of a roundtable discussion on the issue of backlash. The writer discusses the views expressed by conservative politicians and their evangelical allies at the Republican Convention of 1992. She notes that the penalties imposed by some men on women who speak up--isolation, sexual harassment, and physical violence--began to occur more often with the entrance of the New Right men in politics. Although the 1992 Republican platform was rejected by the voters, she states, the religious Right is attacking again in its attempts to stop the sexual revolution and destroy the women's rights that went with it. She contends that part of their motivation is the desire to control women, but part is also their fear that if they do not control women, then women will control them.

[A] Behav Sci Law 1998 Spring;16(2):237-63
Emotional maltreatment in adolescents' everyday lives: furthering sociolegal reforms and social service provisions.
Levesque RJ
Criminal Justice Department, Indiana University, Bloomington 47405-2601, USA. rlevesqu@indiana.edu
The article examines sociolegal responses to adolescent victimization, particularly

responses to the emotional dimensions of their violent personal relationships. The investigation reveals how the legal system generally fails to recognize youth's emotional maltreatment. Responses tend to consider emotional maltreatment as subordinate and secondary to some legally prohibited sexual and physical assaults.

[A] BMJ 1999 Mar 27;318(7187):846-50
Lifetime prevalence, characteristics, and associated problems of non-consensual sex in men: cross sectional survey.
Coxell A, King M, Mezey G, Gordon D
Department of Psychiatry and Behavioural Sciences, Royal Free and University College Medical School, London NW3 2PF.
Objective: To identify the lifetime prevalence of non-consensual sexual experiences in men, the relationship between such experiences as a child and as an adult, associated psychological and behavioural problems, and help received. Almost 3% of men in England report non-consensual sexual experiences as adults. Medical professionals need to be aware of the range of psychological difficulties in men who have had such experiences. They also need to be aware of the relationship between sexual experiences in childhood and adulthood in men.

[A] Boureau, Alain.
Le droit de cuissage : la fabrication d'un mythe (XIIIe-XXe siècle) / Alain Boureau.
Paris : Albin Michel, c1995.
325 p. ; 23 cm.
Series: L'Evolution de l'humanité, 0755-1843.
LC Call No.: JC116.S5 B68 1995
ISBN: 2226076344 : 140F
Includes bibliographical references (p. [291]-305) and index.
Subjects: Jus primae noctis. Feudalism. Sexual harassment -- History.
Source: CU CUY DLC SRT MTH

[A] Boureau, Alain.
Uniform Droit de cuissage. English.
The lord's first night : the myth of the droit decuissage / Alain Boureau ; translated by Lydia G. Cochrane.
Chicago : University of Chicago Press, 1998.
viii, 300 p. ; 24 cm.
LC Call No.: JC116.S5 B6813 1998
ISBN: 0226067432 (pbk. : alk. paper)
0226067424 (alk. paper)
Includes bibliographical references (p. [243]-268) and index.
"Chronological bibliography of works and documents relating to the droit de cuissage": p. [277]-288.
Subjects: Jus primae noctis. Feudalism. Sexual harassment -- History.
Source: DLC DLC

[A] British Broadcasting Corporation
Sexual harassment [(Videocassette)]
London, 1990

[A] Brock, David, 1962-
The real Anita Hill : the untold story / David Brock.
New York : Free Press ; Toronto : Maxwell Macmillan
Canada ; New York : Maxwell Macmillan International, c1993.
ix, 438 p. ; 25 cm.
LC Call No.: KF8745.T48 B76 1993
ISBN: 0029046556 : $24.95
Includes bibliographical references (p. 389-424) and index.
Subjects: Thomas, Clarence, 1948-. Hill, Anita. Judges -- United States -- Selection and
appointment. Sexual harassment of women -- United States.
Source: DLC DLC MTH

[A] Brock, David, 1962-
The real Anita Hill : the untold story / with a new afterword by David Brock.
New York : Free Press ; Toronto : Maxwell Macmillan
Canada ; New York : Maxwell Macmillan International, c1994.
ix, 452 p. ; 24 cm.
LC Call No.: KF8745.T48 B76 1994
ISBN: 0029046564 : $12.95
Includes bibliographical references (p. 403-438) and index.
Subjects: Thomas, Clarence, 1948-. Hill, Anita. Judges -- Selection and appointment --
United States. Sexual harassment of women -- United States.
Source: DLC DLC AMH

[A] Bull Am Acad Psychiatry Law 1996;24(3):387-92
Factitious sexual harassment.
Feldman-Schorrig S
UCLA School of Medicine, USA. schorrig@ucla.edu
Among those claims that trivialize true sexual harassment is a type that the author has
come to recognize as factitious (i.e., prompted by the lure of victim status). Women who
file factitious sexual harassment cases usually voice their allegations in a very convincing
manner and, in the presence of contradictory findings, present a diagnostic challenge.
Forensic clinicians must be able to recognize factitious sexual harassment in order to bring
objectivity to these complex cases.

[A] Can a woman harass a man? Toward a cultural understanding of bodies and power
Bordo, Susan, 1947
Philosophy Today.v. 41 Spring 1997 p. 51-66.
The writer discusses the current definitions of sexual harassment through an analysis of

recent prominent court cases, magazine articles, advertising, and motion pictures, and her own experience of harassment. She focuses on how the ideology of masculinity frames the question of sexual harassment, insisting that current discourse on the subject is wide of the mark. She contends that harassers should be seen as gender bullies and that harassment should be understood as the willful reduction or dismissal of one subjectivity by another.

[A] CDS Rev 1998 Sep;91(6):44-5
Is physical harassment sexual harassment?
Sfikas EM
Bell, Boyd & Lloyd, Illinois, USA.

[A] Changing perceptions of public space on the New York rapid transit system
Hood, Clifton
Journal of Urban History.v. 22 Mar. 1996 p. 308-31.
An examination of the relationship between New York's rapid transit system and public space between 1880 and 1920. The writer argues that during this period, the city's huge rapid transit system had a unique effect on perceptions of public space. Using first-person accounts of transit riders' experiences and other sources, he shows how the subways and elevated railways became socially contested terrain where several million riders competed to use and define the meaning of urban space. He points out that the city's rapid transit system was defined at different times in its history as a realm of technological novelty; as a setting of such urban problems as noise, pollution, crowding, and sexual harassment; as a netherworld occupied by the poor; and as a prison that teemed with criminals.

[A] Ciresi, Rita.
Pink slip / Rita Ciresi.
New York : Delacorte Press, 1999.
353 p. ; 24 cm.
LC Call No.: PS3553.I7 P5 1999
ISBN: 038532362X
Subjects: Italian Americans -- New York (State) -- Fiction. Italian Americans -- Connecticut -- New Haven -- Fiction. Children of Holocaust survivors -- Fiction. AIDS (Disease) -- Patients -- Fiction. Sexual harassment -- Fiction. Gay men Fiction.
Source: DLC DLC

[A] Clode, Dianne.
Sexual harassment in the federal government : an update.
[Washington, D.C.] : U.S. Merit Systems Protection Board, [1988]
vii, 49, 12 p. : ill., 1 form ; 28 cm.
Local Call No: JK721 .U572 1981
MS 1.2 Se9/2
"A report to the President and the Congress of the United States by the U.S. Merit Systems Protection Board"--Cover.
"Updates the findings of an earlier study by the Board... issued in 1981"--P. [iii]

Shipping list no.: 88-421-P.
"June 1988"--Cover.
Includes bibliographical references.
Subjects: Sexual harassment -- United States. Civil service -- United States – Personnel management. United States -- Officials and employees -- Attitudes.
Other authors: United States. Merit Systems Protection Board.
Source: NSA NSA SLU UDI GPO SNN

[A] Color, class & country : experiences of gender / edited by Gay Young & Bette J. Dickerson.
London ; Atlantic Highlands, N.J., USA : Zed Books, 1994.
252 p. ; 22 cm.
LC Call No.: HQ1206 .C68 1994
ISBN: 185649179X : $49.95 (U.S.)
1856491803 (pbk.) : $15.00 (U.S.)
Includes bibliographical references and index. Gendered reproduction of race-ethnicity and social class. "Becoming somebody" : aspirations, opportunities, and womanhood / Wendy Luttrell -- Chicanos in white collar occupations : work and the gendered construction of race-ethnicity / Denise A. Segura -- Urban women's work in three social strata : the informal economy of social networks and social capital / Larissa Lomnitz -- Gender and challenges to the construction of social class and race-ethnicity. "I'm not your maid. I am the housekeeper" : the restructuring of housework and work relationships in domestic service / Mary Romero -- Fighting sexual harassment : a collective labour obligation / Stan Gray -- Ethnic identity and feminism : views from leaders of African American women's associations / Bette J. Dickerson -- Race, class, gender and US state welfare policy : the nexus of inequality for African American families / Rose Brewer. Reproduction of and challenges to gender relations : cases and comparisons at the national level. Gender inequality around the world : comparing fifteen nations in five world regions / Lucia Fort, Mona Danner, and Gay Young -- The state, gender policy, and social change : an analysis from Turkey / Nüket Kardam -- Work intensity and time use : what do women do when there aren't enough hours in a day? / Maria Sagrario Floro – Gender stratification and vulnerability in Uganda / Christine Obbo -- Challenges to white western middle class gender analysis and agendas. "Lifting as we climb" : how scholarship by and about women of color has shaped my life as a white feminist / Kathryn B. Ward -- The place of the WID discourse in global feminist analysis : the potential for a "reverse flow" / Vidyamali Samarasinghe -- Difference, diversity, and divisions in an agenda for the women's movement / Elizabeth Fox-Genovese.
Subjects: Women -- Social conditions. Feminism. Social classes. Ethnic groups. Race.
Other titles: Color, class, and country.
Source: DLC DLC UKM WEA MTH

[A] Conceptualizing sexual harassment as discursive practice (book review)
Keaveney, Madeline M., reviewer
Women's Studies in Communication.v. 19 Fall 1996 p. 355-7.

This book discusses sexual harassment as a discursive practice because, in spite of progress, a great deal of ground remains to be covered for an understanding of the dynamics of sexual harassment. The essays collected here look at the topic from a multiplicity of perspectives. This volume is must reading for anyone interested in learning about and understanding sexual harassment.

[A] Conceptualizing sexual harassment as discursive practice / edited by Shereen G. Bingham.
Westport, Conn. : Praeger, 1994.
viii, 206 p. ; 25 cm.
LC Call No.: HQ1237 .C657 1994
ISBN: 0275945936 (alk. paper)
Includes bibliographical references and index.
Introduction : framing sexual harassment--defining a discursive focus of study / Shereen G. Bingham -- Saying it makes it so : the discursive construction of sexual harassment / Julia T. Wood – Gender socialization and communication : the inscription of sexual harassment in social life / Elizabeth Grauerholz -- The context(s) of sexual harassment power, silences, and academe / Charles Conrad and Bryan Taylor -- Hegemony and harassment : a discursive practice / Robin P. Clair -- Anita Hill on trial : a dialectical analysis of a persuasive interrogation / Claudia L. Hale, Leda M. Cooks, and Sue DeWine -- Talk about sexual harassment : women's stories on a woman's story / Janette Kenner Muir and Kathryn Mangus -- (Un)becoming "voices" : representing sexual harassment in performance / Della Pollock -- Sexual harassment as information equivocality : communication and requisite variety / Gary L. Kreps -- Secrets of the corporation : a model of ideological positioning of sexual harassment victims / Dana M. Kaland and Patricia Geist -- Particularities and possibilities : reconceptualizing knowledge and power in sexual harassment research / Karen A. Foss and Richard A. Rogers -- Epilogue : research on sexual harassment--continuing the conversation / Shereen G. Bingham.
Subjects: Sexual harassment of women. Sexual harassment.
Source: DLC DLC VET UKM UCX

[A] Confronting sexual harassment (book review)
Brandenburg, Judith Berman; Franke, Ann H., reviewer

[A] Confronting sexual harassment (book review)
Brandenburg, Judith Berman; Moser, Rita M., reviewer
Journal of College Student Development.v. 40 no1 (Jan./Feb. 1999) p. 109-10.

[A] Constructing and reconstructing gender : the links among communication, language, and gender / edited by Linda A.M. Perry, Lynn H. Turner, Helen M. Sterk.
Albany : State University of New York Press, c1992.
ix, 310 p. : ill. ; 24 cm.
Series: SUNY series in feminist criticism and theory.
LC Call No.: P96.S48 C64 1992

P96.S48 C64 1992
ISBN: 0791410099 : $49.50
0791410102 : $16.95
"Selected readings from the 10th and 11th Annual Meetings of the Organization for the Study of Communication, Language, and Gender"--P. ix. Includes bibliographical references and index. The possibility of a liberating narrative : Woman on the edge of time as radical, mythic, moral argument / Dana L. Cloud -- Gender orientation scales : an empirical assessment of content validity / T. Joan Fecteau, Jullane Jackson, and Kathryn Dindia -- Gender, ethnicity, and the politics of oral interpretation / Lisa Merrill -- Rhetoric and women : the private and the public spheres / Lesley Di Mare -- Women negotiating : assertiveness and relatedness / Steven Hartwell, Roger C. Pace, and Renata Hutak -- Discourse on women's bodies : advertising in the 1920s / Margaret A. Hawkins and Thomas K. Nakayama -- Mind, body, and language :when a woman notices her humanity / Margret S. Crowdes -- Rhythm, gender, and poetic language / Elizabeth Fay. Six readers reading six photographs / Rebecca Bryant Lockridge -- Speaking metaphorically : cultural enactment of community among women / Denice A. Yanni -- Genderlect, powerlect, and politeness / Nancy Hoar -- A comparison of male-female interaction norms regarding new ideas / Marjorie A. Jaasma -- The tu/vous dilemma : gender, power, and solidarity / Alice H. Deakins -- Power and subordinate evaluations of male and female leaders / Belle Rose Ragins -- Sex, romance, and organizational taboos / Patrice M. Buzzanell -- Teasing and sexual harassment : double-bind communication in the workplace / J.K. Alberts -- Men communicating with women : self-esteem and power / Mary Monedas -- Writing in the borderlands : the poetic prose of Gloria Anzaldúa and Susan Griffin / Diane P. Freedman. Gender in communication : within and across cultures / Margaret Riley -- An investigation of gender differences in Brazilian versus American managers' perceptions of organizational stressors / Ana Rossi, William R. Todd-Mancillas, and Barbara Apps -- Conflict scripts of men and women / Judi Beinstein Miller -- Competition and collaboration : male and female communication patterns during dyadic interactions / Mary-Jeanette Smythe and Bill Huddleston -- Enacting feminism in the teaching of communication / Judith K. Bowker and Pamela Regan Dunkin -- God's wife : some gender reflections on the Bible and biblical interpretation / John J. Schmitt -- Effecting labor reform through stories : the narrative rhetorical style of Mary Harris "Mother" Jones / Mari Boor Tonn.
Subjects: Communication -- Sex differences. Language and languages -- Sex differences.
Other authors: Organization for the Study of Communication, Language, and Gender.
Source: DLC DLC PMC AMH

[A] Contemp Longterm Care 1998 Sep;21(9):69-70
Rewriting the rules. Ten steps to avoiding sexual harassment liability.
Lyncheski JE, Brown JB

[A] Cornell, Drucilla
The imaginary domain: abortion, pornography & sexual harassment
New York; London: Routledge, 1995
xii,292p; 24cm

Bibliography: p275-283. - Includes index
Subjects: Women--Legal status, laws, etc., Equality before the law, Sex differences, Abortion, Pornography, Sexual harassment

[A] Court of appeal : the Black community speaks out on the racial and sexual politics of Clarence Thomas vs. Anita Hill / edited by Robert Chrisman and Robert L. Allen.
Edition: 1st Ballantine Books ed.
New York : Ballantine Books, c1992.
xliii, 290 p. ; 21 cm.
Local Call No: E185.86 .C589 1992
ISBN: 034538136X
On cover: Edited by the Black scholar.
Subjects: Hill, Anita. Thomas, Clarence, 1948-. United States. Supreme Court -- Officials and employees -- Selection and appointment. Judges -- United States -- Selection and appointment. Afro-American men -- Social conditions. Afro-American women -- Social conditions. Sexual harassment of women -- United States.
Other titles: Black scholar.
Source: NPL NPL ECL OCL AMH

[A] Critical issues in victimology : international perspectives / Emilio C. Viano, editor.
New York : Springer Pub. Co., c1992.
xii, 260 p. : ill. ; 24 cm.
LC Call No.: HV6250.25 .C75 1992
ISBN: 0826172504
Includes bibliographies and indexes.
Victimization and its context. Victims, crime, and social context / Augusto Balloni -- The news media and crime victims : the right to know versus the right to privacy / Emilio C. Viano -- The trauma of victimization. Traumatized populations : roles and responsibilities of professionals / Lenore E.A. Walker -- An empirical investigation of the coping strategies used by victims of crime : victimization redefined / Rosa Casarez-Levison -- Victims of violent crime and their coping processes / Otmar Hagemann -- Victims of violence in everyday life : considerations about a qualitative research / Patrizia Faccioli and Simonetta Simoni -- Familial violence in India : the dynamics of victimization / Ranjana S. Jain -- An analysis of cases involving elderly homicide victims and offenders / Peter C. Kratcoski -- The child victim. Analysis of child abuse and neglect court cases in three cities in Turkey / Esin Konanç, Sezen Zeytinoæglu, and Seyda Kozcu -- Aftereffects of childhood abuse and incest / Irving Kaufman. The victimology of children : a transpersonal conceptual treatment model / Carol L. Bryant -- Mental health professionals' treatment of child abuse : why professionals may not report / Seth C. Kalichman, Mary E. Craig, and Diane R. Follingstad -- The trauma of false allegations of sexual abuse / Michael Robin -- Sexual harassment and assault. Sexual harassment of students : victims of the college experience / Richard B. Barickman, Michele A. Paludi, and Vita Carulli Rabinowitz -- Sexual assault in Canada : a social and legal analysis / Rita Gunn and Candice Minch -- Preventing rape : how people perceive the options of defending oneself

during an assault / Lita Furby, Baruch Fischhoff, and Marcia Morgan -- The adolescent
sexual offender : victim and perpetrator / Carol B. DiCenso -- Society's reaction to
victimization. Police reactions to victims of burglary / Joop W. van den Bogaard and Oene
Wiegman -- The victim and the failure to report the crime in Italy / Paola Violante. (cont.)
Implementation of federal legislation to aid victims of crime in the United States / Mario
Thomas Gaboury -- Assessing restitution's impact on recidivism : a review of the
evaluative research / Thomas C. Castellano.
Subjects: Victims of crimes.
Source: DLC DLC WEA

[A] Cyber abuse
Clark, Robert
New Scientist.v. 150 Apr. 20 1996 p. 58.
One problem that is not often referred to in the Internet censorship debate is that of cyber
abuse. This occasionally takes the form of pornography being displayed on screens in
public computer rooms, which is a form of sexual harassment. However, a more frequent
and even less controllable problem is that of unwanted E-mail. This is usually irritating in
content, but it may sometimes be vicious and personally targeted racial or sexual abuse.
This E-mail arrives whether a person wants it or not. The victims of this new
psychopathology are understandably traumatized by it.

[A] Debating sexual correctness : pornography, sexual harassment, date rape and the
politics of sexual equality / edited and with an introduction by Adele M. Stan.
New York, NY : Delta, c1995.
xlviii, 286p; 21 cm.
LC Call No.: HQ1237.5.U6 D43 1995
ISBN: 0385313845,
0385312210
Subjects: Sexual harassment of women -- United States. Acquaintance rape -- United
States. Pornography -- United States. Feminist theory -- United States.
Source: DLC DLC JBO MTH

[A] Dedication to hunger (book review)
Heywood, Leslie; Herndl, Diane Price, reviewer
American Literary History.v. 10 no4 Winter 1998 p. 771-85.
In this book, Heywood argues that much of (white male) modernist literature is dominated
by an "anorexic logic." Inspired by her own experiences of rape, sexual harassment, and
anorexia, she writes to expose the role of this anorexic logic in making other women suffer
and in perpetuating an intellectual and cultural ideal in which the feminine is viewed as
"fat" to be "cut.".
Source: DLC DLC HAM
Subjects: Sexual harassment. Sexual harassment of women. Feminist theory

[A] Despite the positive rhetoric about women's sports, female athletes face a culture of

sexual harassment
Heywood, Leslie
The Chronicle of Higher Education.v. 45 no18 (Jan. 8 1999) p. B4-B5.
The writer discusses the issue of sexual harassment in sports and the discrepancy that
exists between the increasing equality and respect for female athletes on one hand and the
behavior within the athletics culture that demonstrates profound disrespect for female
competitors on the other.

[A] Distorted images (book review)
Borrowdale, Anne; Dowell, Susan, reviewer
Scottish Journal of Theology.v. 47 no1 1994 p. 97-101.
In Distorted Images: Christian Attitudes to Women, Men and Sex, Anne Borrowdale
focuses on the denigration that underlies sexual violence in all its forms from sexual
harassment to battering, rape, child abuse, and pornography. She demolishes the "victim-
blaming" rationalizations that serve to mask the harsh reality that these are predominantly
crimes committed against females by males in a male-controlled world..

[A] Dominant and muted discourses in popular representations of feminism
Augmented title: review article
Wood, Julia T
The Quarterly Journal of Speech.v. 82 May 1996 p. 171-85.
The writer reviews three books on the subject of feminism. They are Fire with Fire: The
New Female Power and How to Use It, by Naomi Wolf; The Morning After: Sex, Fear,
and Feminism, by Katie Roiphe; and Who Stole Feminism? How Women Have Betrayed
Women, by Christina Hoff Sommers. He finds that what unifies these books is the thesis
that women should adopt an Emersonian self-reliance to avoid sexual violence and
discrimination. He examines the ways in which larger cultural narratives frame and
invigorate the claims and ideological premises these books advance but that are not
warranted by the evidence and arguments they present. He offers alternative premises that
are obscured by these three books, inviting in the process a fuller engagement than has
often existed between the popular and academic writers who discuss feminism.

[A] Eisaguirre, Lynne, 1951-
Sexual harassment : a reference handbook / Lynne Eisaguirre.
Santa Barbara, Calif. : ABC-CLIO, c1993.
xiv, 217 p. : ill. ; 24 cm.
Series: Contemporary world issues.
LC Call No.: KF4758 .E36 1993
ISBN: 0874367239 (acid-free paper)
Includes bibliographical references and index.
Introduction -- Chronology -- Biographical sketches -- Facts and statistics -- Directory of
organizations -- Selected print resources -- Selected nonprint resources.
Subjects: Sex discrimination -- Law and legislation – United States. Sex discrimination --

United States.
Source: DLC DLC IAC OBE MLX MTH

[A] Eisaguirre, Lynne, 1951-
Sexual harassment : a reference handbook / Lynne Eisaguirre.
Edition: 2nd ed.
Santa Barbara, Calif. : ABC-CLIO, c1997.
xvi, 285 p. : ill. ; 24 cm.
Series: Contemporary world issues.
LC Call No.: KF4758 .E36 1997
ISBN: 0874369711 (alk. paper)
Includes bibliographical references and index.
Subjects: Sex discrimination -- Law and legislation – United States.
Sex discrimination -- United States.
Source: DLC DLC C#P

[A] Female foraging responses to sexual harassment in the solitary bee Anthophora
plumipes
Stone, Graham N
Animal Behaviour.v. 50 Aug. 1995 p. 405-12.
A study examined attempts by males of the solitary bee Anthophora plumipes Pallas
(Apoidea: Anthophoridae) to mate with foraging females at flowers of comfrey,
Symphytum orientale. Females could experience attempted copulation at rates greater than
once every 3 s, which markedly reduced their rate of visiting flowers and consequently
extended the period needed to provision nest cells. Assessment of sugar rewards per flower
and handling times implied that male harassment halved the rate of reward for females
from exposed outer flowers. The mating system corresponded to scramble competition
polygyny.

[A] Feminist accused of sexual harassment (book review)
Gallop, Jane, 1952 ; Schilb, John, 1952 , reviewer
College English.v. 61 no3 (Jan. 1999) p. 340-6.

[A] Feminist accused of sexual harassment (book review)
Gallop, Jane, 1952 ; Bruner, Belinda, reviewer
Feminist Teacher.v. 11 no1 (Spring/Summer 1997) p. 55-60.

[A] Feminist jurisprudence / edited by Patricia Smith.
New York : Oxford University Press, 1993.
xii, 628 p. ; 24 cm.
LC Call No.: K644.Z9 F457 1993
ISBN: 0195073975 (alk. paper)
Includes bibliographical references. Equality and difference : the case of pregnancy /
Herma Hill Kay -- Will equality require more than assimilation, accommodation, or

separation from the existing social structure? / Nadine Taub and Wendy W. Williams --
The family and the market : a study of ideology and legal reform / Frances E. Olsen -- The
emergence of feminist jurisprudence : an essay / Ann C. Scales -- Reconstructing sexual
equality / Christine A. Littleton -- Sexual harassment : its first decade in court / Catharine
A. MacKinnon -- Rape / Susan Estrich -- The criminal justice system's responses to
battering : understanding the problem, forging the solutions / Kathleen Waits -- Justice
engendered / Martha Minow -- Legality and empathy / Lynne N. Henderson -- Black
women and the Constitution : finding our place, asserting our rights / Judy Scales-Trent --
Reproductive freedom / Deborah L. Rhode. Reproductive laws, women of color, and low-
income women / Laurie Nsiah-Jefferson – Unraveling compromise / Frances Olsen --
Rethinking sex and the Constitution / Sylvia A. Law – Market inalienability / Margaret
Jane Radin – Pornography and the tyranny of the majority / Elizabeth Wolgast -- Against
the male flood : censorship, pornography, and equality / Andrea Dworkin -- Brief amici
curiae of feminist anticensorship task force et al., in American Booksellers Association v.
Hudnut / Nan D. Hunter and Sylvia A. Law -- Jurisprudence and gender / Robin West --
Deconstructing gender / Joan C. Williams -- The pragmatist and the feminist / Margaret
Jane Radin -- Sapphire bound! / Regina Austin -- Feminist critical theories / Deborah L.
Rhode -- Toward feminist jurisprudence / Catherine A. MacKinnon.
Subjects: Women -- Legal status, laws, etc. Sex discrimination against women. Sex and
law. Feminist theory. Feminism.
Source: DLC DLC PMC UKM

[A] First or right?
Kirtz, William
The Quill (Chicago, Ill.).v. 86 no2 Mar. 1998 p. 25.
The writer cites the opinions of a number of journalists on the media's coverage of
allegations of sexual harassment brought against President Clinton. Among the journalists
whose opinions are noted are Mark Jurkowitz, Marvin Kalb, and Bill Kovach.

[A] Flowers, Ronald B.
The victimization and exploitation of women and children : a study of physical, mental,
and sexual maltreatment in the United States / by R. Barri Flowers.
Jefferson, N.C. : McFarland & Co., c1994.
xiv, 240 p. : ill. ; 24 cm.
LC Call No.: HV6250.4.W65 F55 1994
ISBN: 0899509789 (lib. bdg. : alk. paper)
Includes bibliographical references (p. 227-230) and index.
Pt.1. Family dynamics and child victimization : Child abuse and neglect -- Domestic
violence – Runaways and throwaways -- Missing and abducted children. **Pt.2.** The
sexploitation of children : The sexual abuse and exploitation of children -- Incest and child
molestation -- Statutory rape and other sex crimes -- The prostitution of children – Child
pornography. **Pt.3.** Violence and victimized children : Violent crimes against children --
School violence and victimization. Pt.4. The violent victimization of women : Violent
crimes against women -- Rape and sexual assault of women -- Battered women. Pt.5. The

sexploitation of women : The prostitution of women -- Pornography and violence against women -- Sexual harassment and stalking. Pt.6. Protecting women and children from violence and exploitation : Responding to the victimization and sexual exploitation of children and women.
Subjects: Women -- Crimes against -- United States. Children -- Crimes against -- United States. Abused women -- United States. Child abuse -- United States. Wife abuse -- United States. Child Abuse. Spouse Abuse. Violence. Women. Sex Offenses.
Source: DLC DLC UKM NLM MZN AMH

[A] Ford, Laura Christian, 1948-
Liberal education and the canon : five great texts speak to contemporary social issues / Laura Christian Ford.
Edition: 1st ed.
Columbia, SC, USA : Camden House, c1994.
293 p. ; 24 cm.
LC Call No.: LC1011 .F65 1994
ISBN: 1571130136 (cloth : acid-free paper)
1571130594 (paper : acid-free paper)
Includes bibliographical references (p. [271]-282) and index.
Sexual harassment--Rape--Homophobia--Abortion--The right to die--The death penalty.
Subjects: Education, Humanistic -- United States. Canon (Literature) Criticism -- United States. Education, Higher -- Social aspects -- United States. Social problems in literature.
Source: DLC DLC CWS MTH

[A] Fortschr Med 1999 Feb 28;117(6):44-5
[Sexual harassment: there is no specific symptomatic. Interview].
[Article in German]
Grundhuber L
Publication Types: Interview

[A] From data to public policy: affirmative action, sexual harrassment, domestic violence, and social welfare/ edited by Rita J. Simon
Lanham, Md.; London: University Press of America, c1996
xi, 185p; 24cm
Includes bibliographical references and index
Published in association with: Women's Freedom Network
Subjects: Policy sciences, Social policy, Affirmative action programs, Sexual harassment, Family violence, Sex role

[A] Gardner, Carol Brooks.
Passing by : gender and public harassment / Carol Brooks Gardner.
Berkeley : University of California Press, c1995.
xiii, 256 p. ; 24 cm.
LC Call No.: HQ1237.5.U6 G37 1995

ISBN: 0520081870 (cloth : acid-free paper)
0520202155 (paper : acid-free paper)
Includes bibliographical references (p. 241-252) and index.
Subjects: Sexual harassment of women -- Indiana -- Indianapolis. Invective -- Indiana -- Indianapolis. Etiquette -- Indiana -- Indianapolis. Women -- Crimes against -- Indiana -- Indianapolis.
Source: DLC DLC UKM MTH

[A] Garner, Helen, 1942-
The first stone : some questions about sex and power / Helen Garner.
New York : Free Press, 1997.
237 p. ; 22 cm.
LC Call No.: HQ1237.5.A8 G37 1997
ISBN: 0684835061
Originally Sydney : Pan Macmillan, 1995.
Subjects: Sexual harassment of women -- Australia – Melbourne (Vic.) -- Case studies. Man-woman relationships -- Case studies. Power (Social sciences) -- Case studies. Feminism -- Australia.
Source: DLC DLC

[A] Gender / edited by Carol C. Gould.
Atlantic Highlands, N.J. : Humanities Press International, 1997.
xx, 485 p. ; 23 cm.
Series: Key concepts in critical theory.
LC Call No.: HQ1075 .G455 1997
ISBN: 0391037919
Includes bibliographical references and index.
Subjects: Sex role. Sex differences. Sexual harassment. Feminist theory.
Source: DLC DLC SNN

[A] Gender violence and women's human rights in Africa / Center for Women's Global Leadership.
New Brunswick, New Jersey : The Center, 1994.
iv, 42 p. : ill. ; 22 cm.
Local Call No: HV6250.4.W65 G47 1994
Includes bibliographical references.
Subjects: Women -- Crimes against -- Africa. Human rights -- Africa. Sexual harassment of women -- Africa.
Other authors: Center for Women's Global Leadership.
Source: PBU PBU AMH

[A] Georgie Porgie: Sexual harassment in everyday life. [Pandora Press Focus]
London, 1987

[A] Getting Serious about Sexual Harassment.
Lumsden, Linda S.

[A] Guppies that don't get it
Augmented title: feeding of females inhibited by males attempting copulation
Discover.v. 16 July 1995 p. 24.
Researchers studying guppies in Trinidad's upper Tunapuna River have discovered that
female guppies are so plagued by unwanted male sexual advances that their feeding is
seriously inhibited. Behavioral ecologist Anne Magurran of the University of St. Andrews
in Scotland and colleague Benoni Seghers of Oxford have found that whereas female
guppies usually respond to male overtures only if they are virgins or have just given birth,
males spend roughly half their time attempting to mate. Magurran and Seghers discovered
this form of sexual harassment by placing female Poecilia reticulata guppies in pools with
and without males. In the pool containing males, the amount of time the females spent
feeding dropped by one-fourth.

[A] Harassment hinders women's care and careers
Cotton, Paul
JAMA.v. 267 Feb. 12 1992 p. 778-9+.

[A] Harassment linked to fraud, lawsuit alleges
Cotton, Paul
JAMA.v. 267 Feb. 12 1992 p. 783-4.

[A] Hartel, Lynda Jones.
Sexual harassment : a selected, annotated bibliography / Lynda Jones Hartel and Helena
M. VonVille.
Westport, CT : Greenwood Press, 1995.
x, 158 p. ; 24 cm.
Series: Bibliographies and indexes in women's studies,
0742-6941 ; no. 23.
LC Call No.: Z7164.S46 H37 1995 HQ1237.5.U6
Local Call No: HQ1237.5.U6 H37 1995
ISBN: 0313290555 (alk. paper)
Includes indexes.
Subjects: Sexual harassment of women -- United States -- Bibliography. Sexual
harassment of women -- Law and legislation -- United States -- Bibliography. Sexual
harassment -- United States -- Bibliography. Sexual harassment -- Law and legislation –
United States -- Bibliography.
Source: DLC DLC SNN

[A] Help Yourself: A Manual for Dealing with *Sexual Harassment.*
Lebrato, Mary T., Ed.

This manual provides an overview of *sexual harassment* and what can be done about it. Although it deals with laws in California, its general sections and sections of federal laws could be used by persons in any state. The guide contains 12 chapters. They include information on the advantages and disadvantages of these options and what may be expected in the pursuit of a particular course of action. These chapters discuss documenting the experience, which is critical regardless of which avenue is pursued, remedies, the use of the criminal justice system, the employment complaint system, the military service complaint system, and the prison complaint system. The manual concludes with a comprehensive bibliography and resource list and extensive appendixes containing sample forms from various complaint agencies and current federal and California law and regulations. (KC)

[A] Herbert, Carrie M. H.
Talking of silence: the sexual harrassment of schoolgirls/ Carrie M.H. Herbert
London: Falmer, 1989
[vii],200p; 23cm
Includes bibliography
Subjects: Child molesting--Great Britain, Girls--Great Britain, Sexual harassment--Great Britain, Sex crimes--Great Britain

[A] Heterophobia: sexual harassment and the future of feminism
Patai, Daphne, 1943
Rowman & Littlefield, 1998. 276 p.

[A] Heywood, Leslie.
Dedication to hunger : the anorexic aesthetic in modern culture / Leslie Heywood.
Berkeley : University of California, c1996.
xvi, 243 p. : ill. ; 24 cm.
LC Call No.: PN771 .H43 1996
ISBN: 0520201175 (alk. paper)
Includes bibliographical references (p. 203-238) and index.
Missing persons: the black hole of the feminine in Jean Rhys. Rhys's life: booze and black holes--The "Problem with no name" (reprise): the constitution of female subjectivity in the black hole--Jean Rhys, sexual harassment and the academy: manifestations of the "First Death", or "Clipping your students wings--Beyond negation (?): Wide Sargasso Sea.
Subjects: Literature, Modern -- History and criticism. Anorexia nervosa in literature. Women in literature.
Source: DLC DLC IAY CDS AMH

[A] High-tech challenge: attracting women readers to cyberspace
Resnick, Rosalind
American Journalism Review.v. 16 Oct. 1994 p. 14-15.
While women make up about half of all newspaper readers, fewer than 20 percent of the users of the major online services, on which many papers have launched electronic

editions, are female. Conventional wisdom has it that women are too busy juggling work and family to log on, but it may be that the confrontational male discourse that is common to the Internet and the sexual harassment that women encounter there play a larger role. The article discusses a number of methods being employed by papers to attract more female readers online.

[A] Ideology or Experience: A Study of *Sexual Harassment.*
Saperstein, Aron; And Others
Sex Roles: A Journal of Research; v32 n11-12 p835-42 Jun 1995

[A] Italian lessons in sexual favours
Pacitti, Domenico
The Times Higher Education Supplement.no1296 (Sept. 5 1997) p. 10.
A voluntary resistance group at the University of Bari in Italy is promoting the country's first national forum on the problem of sex and power relationships in universities. The forum is an attempt to reveal and resist the supposedly rampant male chauvinism in universities and has the support of the university's rector, equal opportunities commissions, and the local town council.

[A] J Christ Nurs 1996 Spring;13(2):32-4
Handling harassment.
Conway J, Conway S

[A] J Healthc Prot Manage 1998-99 Winter;15(1):118-22
Sexual harassment: what every security manager needs to know.
Costello R
SUNY Albany, NY, USA.
Security directors are responsible for protecting against sexual harassment and ultimately may be civilly liable for any violations, says the author. His goals here are to highlight an often-overlooked topic, provide the reader with a basic understanding of sexual harassment, give a background of its growth since 1991, help security managers identify and prevent sexual harassment, and provide resources for further investigation.

[A] J Health Risk Manag 1997 Fall;17(4):53-5
Sexual harassment may be insidious and may continue after termination. Smith v. St. Louis University.
West JC

[A] J Ky Med Assoc 1998 Nov;96(11):437-8
Sexual harassment.
Publication Types: News

[A] J Pers Soc Psychol 1994 Oct;67(4):699-712
Sexually aggressive men's perceptions of women's communications: testing three

explanations.

Malamuth NM, Brown LM

Department of Communication, University of Michigan, Ann Arbor.

The authors tested three explanations of findings that sexually aggressive men perceive women's communications differently than less aggressive men. The first suggests that aggressors are incompetent in decoding women's negative emotions. The second posits that they fail to make subtle distinctions between women's friendliness and seductiveness and between assertiveness and hostility. The third explanation contends that sexual aggressors use a suspicious schema and therefore discount the veridicality of women's communications.

[A] J Pers Soc Psychol 1995 May;68(5):768-81

Attractiveness of the underling: an automatic power --> sex association and its consequences for sexual harassment and aggression.

Bargh JA, Raymond P, Pryor JB, Strack F

Department of Psychology, New York University, New York 10003, USA.

One characteristic of men who sexually harass is that they are not aware that their actions are inappropriate or a misuse of their power (L. F. Fitzgerald, 1993a). We investigated the existence and automaticity of a mental association between the concepts of power and sex, and its consequences for sexual harassment tendencies. For men likely to sexually aggress, but not other participants, attraction ratings of a female confederate were significantly higher in the power priming than the neutral priming condition.

[A] Journalese; Anita Hill explosion also hit the press

Monroe, Bill

WJR.v. 13 Dec. 1991 p. 6.

[A] Kuhlmann, Ellen

Gegen die sexuelleBelästigung am Arbeitsplatz: juristische Praxis und Handlungsperspektiven/ Ellen Kuhlmann Pfaffenweiler: Centaurus-Verl.-Ges., c1996 ix, 157p; 21cm (pbk)

Series Aktuelle Frauenforschung; Bd. 24

Subjects: Sexual harassment, Sexual harassment of women

[A] Law Hum Behav 1998 Feb;22(1):33-57

The reasonable woman standard: a meta-analytic review of gender differences in perceptions of sexual harassment.

Blumenthal JA

Psychology Department, Harvard University, Cambridge, MA 02138, USA.

jeremy@wjh.harvard.edu

Courts and legislatures have begun to develop the "reasonable woman standard" (RWS) as a criterion for deciding sexual harassment trials. This standard rests on assumptions of a "wide divergence" between the perceptions of men and women when viewing social-sexual behavior that may be considered harassing. In discussing legal implications of the present findings, earlier claims are echoed suggesting caution in establishing the reasonable woman standard, and one alternative to the RWS, the "reasonable victim standard," is discussed.

[A] Law Hum Behav 1998 Feb;22(1):59-79
Are men sexually harassed? If so, by whom?
Waldo CR, Berdahl JL, Fitzgerald LF
University of Illinois at Urbana-Champaign, USA. cwaldo@psg.ucsf.edu
Research on sexual harassment has recently expanded to include examination of men's experiences. The results indicate that men experience potentially sexually harassing behaviors from other men at least as often as they do from women; however, men in all samples reported relatively few negative reactions to these experiences. Future research should examine the predictors and outcomes of such situations to clarify the meaning of such behavior for male targets.

[A] LeMoncheck, Linda.
Sexual harassment : a debate / Linda LeMoncheck and Mane Hajdin.
Lanham : Rowman & Littlefield Publishers, Inc., c1997.
x, 239 p. ; 24 cm.
Series: Point/counterpoint.
LC Call No.: HQ1237 .L46 1997
ISBN: 0847684245 (alk. paper)
0847684253 (pbk. : alk. paper)
Includes bibliographical references and index.
Subjects: Sexual harassment of women, Sexual harassment.
Other authors: Hajdin, Mane.
Source: DLC DLC SNN

[A] Mate choice in the polymorphic African swallowtail butterfly, Papilio dardanus: male-like females may avoid sexual harassment
Cook, S. E; Vernon, Jennifer G; Bateson, Melissa
Animal Behaviour.v. 47 Feb. 1994 p. 389-97.
The effect of the polymorphic wing color pattern in females of the African swallowtail butterfly (Papilo dardanus subsp. tibullus) on male behavior was studied. The black and white Batesian mimic morph hippocoonides was protected against predation but not against male harassment. The black and yellow (trimeni) and black and yellow with orange wing patches (lamborni) male-like morphs were protected against male harassment but not against predation. It is suggested that the 3 genetically distinct morphs are stably maintained by different frequency-dependent selective advantages.

[A] Mazza, Cris.
Is it sexual harassment yet? : short fiction / by Cris Mazza. 1st ed.
Boulder : Fiction Collective Two ; [New York, N.Y.] :
Distributed by Talman Co., c1991.

223 p. ; 23 cm.
Series: On the edge ; #1.
LC Call No.: PS3563.A988 I8 1991
ISBN: 0932511333 (cloth) : $18.95
0932511341 (paper) : $8.95
Subjects: Short stories -- United States lcsh.
Source: DLC DLC AMH

[A] McCaghy, M. Dawn.
Sexual harassment : a guide to resources / M. Dawn McCaghy.
Boston, Mass. : G.K. Hall, c1985.
xvi, 181 p. ; 25 cm.
Series: Women's studies publications.
LC Call No.: Z7963.E7 M427 1985 HD6060.3
Local Call No: HD6060.3 .M427 1985
ISBN: 0816186693 (alk. paper)
Includes indexes.
Bibliography: p. xiii-xvi.
Subjects: Sexual harassment of women -- United States -- Bibliography.
Sexual harassment of women -- Bibliography.
Source: DLC DLC OCL

[A] Med Econ 1999 Apr 12;76(7):252, 255-60
Sexual harassment: prevention is the best defense.
Preston SH

[A] Med Health R I 1996 Dec;79(12):422-5
Preventing and responding to sexual harassment and sexual assault.
Hogan K, Mark Y, Paranjpe R

[A] Mich Med 1998 Dec;97(12):14-6
MSMS adopts "model" harassment policy.
Cuzydlo C

[A] Ministerial misdeeds: the Onderdonk trial and sexual harassment in the 1840s
Cohen, Patricia Cline
Journal of Women's History.v. 7 Fall 1995 p. 34-57.
The case of the Right Reverent Benjamin T. Onderdonk, who was brought to trial in 1844 on nine counts of "immoralities and impurities" committed against episcopal women, is discussed. The Onderdonk controversy has all the hallmarks of what today would be classified as a case of sexual harassment. Lacking a concept of sexual harassment to frame the issues, however, commentators on both sides of the case were perplexed and at odds about how to interpret Onderdonk's intimate touches. In the end, only one interpretative

strategy worked: use of racist stereotypes to distil and simplify the complex issues with which Episcopalians struggled.

[A] MLO Med Lab Obs 1994 Dec;26(12):7
Is it harassment, or just 'horsing around'?
Hendrix BB
Northside Hospital, St. Petersburg, FL.

[A] Mod Healthc 1992 Sep 28;22(39):34
Groups: VA failing to address sexual harassment, assaults.
Weissenstein E
Publication Types: News

[A] Mod Healthc 1996 Oct 14;26(42):2-3, 6
ACHE survey response spurs expedited sexual harassment policy.
Burda D
Publication Types: News

[A] Modleski, Tania, 1949-
Old wives' tales, and other women's stories / Tania Modleski.
New York : New York University Press, c1998.
x, 238 p. : ill. ; 23 cm.
LC Call No.: PS152 .M63 1998
ISBN: 0814755933 (acid-free paper)
0814755941 (pbk. : acid-free paper)
Includes bibliographical references (p. 213-224) and indexes.
Introduction: feminist criticism today: notes from Jurassic Park -- Breaking silence, or an old wives' tale: sexual harassment and the legitimation crisis -- Axe the piano player -- My life as a romance reader -- My life as a romance writer -- The white Negress and the heavy-duty dyke -- Doing justice to the Subjects: the work of Anna Deavere Smith -- Do we get to lose this time? revising the Vietnam War film -- A woman's gotta do-- what a man's gotta do? cross-dressing in the Western -- Something else besides a mother: reflections of a feminist on the death of her mother. Portions of some chapters have been previously published in slightly different form.
Subjects: American literature -- 20th century -- History and criticism -- Theory, etc.
Feminism and literature -- United States -- History -- 20th century. Women and literature -- United States -- History -- 20th century. Feminism -- United States -- History -- 20th century. Feminist criticism -- United States.
Source: DLC DLC C#P

[A] Morewitz, Stephen John, 1954-
Sexual harassment & social change in American society/ Stephen J. Morewitz
San Francisco: Austin & Winfield, 1996
498p; 22cm

Includes bibliographical references (p. [443]-465) and indexes
Cover Sexual harassment and social change in American society
Subjects: Sexual harassment of women--United States Sexual harassment--United States--
History

[A] Morris, Celia, 1935-
Bearing witness : sexual harassment and beyond--everywoman's story / Celia Morris.
Boston : Little, Brown and Co., c1994.
326 p. ; 24 cm.
LC Call No.: HQ1237.5.U6 M67 1994
ISBN: 0316584223 : $21.95 ($27.95 Canada)
Includes bibliographical references (p. [307]-317) and index.
Anita Hill sparks a revolution -- Verbal sexual harassment -- The laying on of hands --
Putting up with it -- Falling into the trap -- Extortion -- Blowing the whistle -- Congress
and the Nations's Capital -- The military -- The home -- Understanding how we got here --
The hazards of counting on other women -- The makings of a cultural revolution -- Women
who ground their lives in helping other women -- A new day.
Subjects: Sexual harassment of women -- United States.
Source: DLC DLC OFA MLX UKM

[A] Most of us haven't got a clue!
Augmented title: guidelines for avoiding accusations of sexual harassment
Gerardi, Robert J
Contemporary Education.v. 68 (Summer 1997) p. 254-5.
Part of a special issue on education's Right and Left. The writer describes how he was
accused and cleared of sexual harassment. He outlines some lessons the experience has
taught him.

[A] No safe haven : male violence against women at home, at work, and in the community
/ Mary P. Koss ... [et al.]. 1st ed.
Washington, D.C. : American Psychological Association, c1994.
xviii, 344 p. ; 24 cm.
LC Call No.: HV6626.2 .N62 1994
ISBN: 1557982376 (hard)
1557982449 (pbk.)
Includes bibliographical references (p. 259-315) and indexes.
Subjects: Women -- Crimes against -- United States. Abused women -- United States.
Abusive men -- United States. Conjugal violence -- United States. Sexual harassment of
women -- United States. Rape -- United States.
Other authors: American Psychological Association.
Source: DLC DLC VET NLM SNN

[A] Nurs Spectr (Wash D C) 1995 Jun 26;5(13):8-9

Dealing with sexual harassment.
Prochaska SJ Jr

[A] Nurs Times 1999 Mar 3-9;95(9):64-6
High time for justice.
Sayce L
Lambeth, Southwark and Lewisham Health Action Zone, London.

[A] Nursing 1996 Jul;26(7):62
Dealing with sexual harassment.
Gomez-Preston C, Reisfeld R

[A] Nursing 1997 Apr;27(4):65
Handling inappropriate sexual behavior
336):72-8
Perils of being a plaintiff: impressions of a forensic psychiatrist.
Halleck SL
University of North Carolina, School of Medicine, Chapel Hill 27599-7160, USA.
The stresses of litigation for defendants are obvious. Less attention generally is given to the problems experienced by plaintiffs. Some examples are presented of plaintiffs in personal injury cases who experienced adverse reactions to the process of litigation. These experiences are not uncommon, and often the patient's condition is worse even after a case is settled.

[A] October
Mattick, Paul
Arts Magazine.v. 66 Jan. 1992 p. 17-18.

[A] On oestrous advertisement, spite and sexual harassment
Radwan, Jacek
Animal Behaviour.v. 49 May 1995 p. 1399-400.
Arguments made by Pagel in his article on estrus advertisement in primates in Animal Behaviour 1994;47:1333-41 are disputed. The writer refutes Pagel's assumption that all females have the same value for males, as well as Pagel's usage of the notion spite. However, the central proposition of Pagel's model that male Old World monkeys may use sexual swelling for the assessment of female quality is not criticized.

[A] Othello goes to Washington: cultural politics and the Thomas/Hill affair
Russo, Peggy Anne
Journal of American Culture.v. 17 Winter 1994 p. 15-22.
A discussion of Senator Alan Simpson's allusion to Shakespeare's Othello during the investigation of Judge Clarence Thomas. This reference was a feeble bid to lend sympathy and tragic stature to Thomas, who was being investigated for the alleged sexual harassment of Anita Hill. Familiarity with Othello led some to view Simpson's reference

with amused contempt because the lines he quoted belong to Iago rather than Othello. Nevertheless, the allusion worked more effectively than many of the other analogies employed during the investigation.

[A] Other thoughts on harassment
Bier, John Allan; Weinstein, Bruce D
Journal of the American Dental Association.v. 126 Mar. 1995 p. 286+.
The writer criticizes Bruce Weinstein's July 1994 article "Sexual Harassment: Identifying it in Dentistry" on 2 counts. On the question of why sexual harassment is predominantly inflicted on women by men, he asserts that Weinstein fails to acknowledge the innate human behavior of male advance/female response. On the question of male earning power, he suggests that Weinstein does not allow for such factors as pregnancy, delivery, child rearing, and homemaking. Weinstein responds to the criticisms.

[A] PC playhouse: on David Mamet's Oleanna
Silverthorne, Jeanne
Artforum.v. 31 Mar. 1993 p. 10-11.

[A] Phelps, Timothy M.
Capitol games : Clarence Thomas, Anita Hill, and the story of a Supreme Court nomination / Timothy M. Phelps, Helen Winternitz.
New York : Hyperion, c1992.
xvii, 458 p. ; 25 cm.
LC Call No.: KF8745.T48 P48 1992
ISBN: 1562829165 : $24.95 ($27.95 Can.)
Includes bibliographical references (p. [435]-437) and index.
Subjects: Thomas, Clarence, 1948-. Hill, Anita. United States. Supreme Court. Judges -- United States -- Selection and appointment. Sexual harassment of women -- United States.
Other authors: Winternitz, Helen.
Source: DLC DLC MTH

[A] Phelps, Timothy M.
Capitol games : the inside story of Clarence Thomas, Anita Hill, and a Supreme Court nomination / Timothy M. Phelps, Helen Winternitz.
1st HarperPerennial ed.
New York : HarperPerennial, 1993.
xiv, 464 p. ; 21 cm.
Local Call No: KF8745.T48 P48 1993
ISBN: 0060975539 (pbk.) : $14.00
Reprint. Originally published in 1992 by Hyperion.
"With a new epilogue by the authors"--Cover.
Includes bibliographical references (p. [442]-444) and index.
Subjects: Thomas, Clarence, 1948-. Hill, Anita. United States. Supreme Court. Judges -- Selection and appointment -- United States. Sexual harassment of women -- United States.

Other authors: Winternitz, Helen.
Source: PMD PMD AMH

[A] Plast Reconstr Surg 1997 Mar;99(3):910-2
Discrimination on the basis of gender.
Luce EA
Division of Plastic Surgery, University Hospitals of Cleveland, Ohio, USA.

[A] Prison deaths spotlight how boards handle impaired, disciplined physicians
Skolnick, Andrew A
JAMA.v. 280 no16 Oct. 28 1998 p. 1387-90.
Several recent deaths of prison inmates have led to calls for medical licensing boards to be more vigilant in protecting patients from physicians who commit offenses. Physicians who commit offenses often do not have their licenses revoked but are subjected to licensure restrictions that lead them into jobs in correctional settings, where rising inmate populations have sorely stressed medical staffing and care. The medical licensing boards need to provide stronger safeguards to guard the profession, protect the public from the relatively small proportion of problem physicians, and ensure that these physicians are properly disciplined.

[A] Provider 1996 Feb;22(2):59-61
Safely handling a harassment complaint.
Vaccaro PL, Bryant M

[A] Psychiatr Clin North Am 1995 Mar;18(1):139-53
Sexual abuses.
Abel GG, Rouleau JL
Behavioral Medicine Institute of Atlanta, Emory University School of Medicine, Georgia, USA.
The sexual abuses described in this article are occurring so frequently that they constitute a public health problem. Superficially they appear to be quite dissimilar because they involve individuals of different ages, different settings, and different power relationships. Basic to each of them, however, is an absence of consent by the victim and the misuse of power by the perpetrator in order to accomplish the abuse.

[A] Qld Nurse 1996 Nov-Dec;15(6):13
Sexual harassment? It couldn't happen to me!

[A] Qld Nurse 1997 Jan-Feb;16(1):10-1
Sexual harassment.

[A] Race, gender, and power in America : the legacy of the Hill-Thomas hearings / edited by Anita Faye Hill, Emma Coleman Jordan.
New York : Oxford University Press, 1995.

xxxii, 302 p. ; 25 cm.
LC Call No.: KF8745.T48 R32 1995
ISBN: 0195087747
Includes bibliographical references. "She's no lady, she's a nigger": abuses, stereotypes, and realities from the middle passage to capitol (and Anita) Hill / Adele Logan Alexander -- The Hill-Thomas hearings--what took place and what happened: white male domination, black male domination, and the denigration of black women / A. Leon Higginbotham, Jr. -- The power of false racial memory and the metaphor of lynching / Emma Coleman Jordan -- The crisis of gender relations among African Americans / Orlando Patterson -- The message of the verdict: a three-act morality play starring Clarence Thomas, Willie Smith, and Mike Tyson / Charles R. Lawrence -- Stopping sexual harassment: a challenge for community education / Robert L. Allen -- The people vs. Anita Hill: a case for client-centered advocacy / Charles J. Ogletree, Jr. -- From the senate judiciary committee to the country courthouse: the relevance of gender, race, and ethnicity to adjudication / Judith Resnik -- Sexual harassment law in the aftermath of the Hill-Thomas hearings / Susan Deller Ross -- Anita Hill and the year of the woman / Eleanor Holmes Norton -- The most riveting television: the Hill-Thomas hearings and popular culture / Anna Deavere Smith -- Marriage and patronage in the empowerment and disempowerment of African American women / Anita Faye Hill.
Subjects: Thomas, Clarence, 1948-. Hill, Anita. United States. Supreme Court -- Officials and employees -- Selection and appointment. Sexual harassment of women -- Law and legislation -- United States.
Source: DLC DLC LUL IPL ZYF MTH

[A] Race-ing justice, en-gendering power: essays on Anita Hill, Clarence Thomas and the construction of social reality/ edited by Toni Morrison
London: Chatto & Windus, 1993
xxx, 475p; 23cm
Originally New York : Pantheon, c1992
Subjects: "Thomas, Clarence, 1948-, Hill, Anita, Women's rights--United States, Judges--United States--Selection and appointment, Afro-Americans--Social conditions, Racism--United States, Sexism--United States, Sexual harassment of women--Law and legislation--United States, United States--Law and legislation, Thomas-Hill scandal--United States--Political history--Bush administration, 1989-1993

[A] Raising aggression to an art form
Angier, Natalie
New York Times (Late New York Edition).Oct. 10 1995 p. C5.
Some anthropologists and primatologists theorize that male harassment of females is more elaborate among humans than in any other primate species. Among other primates, females may cooperate to resist aggressive males. Human males in many cultures, by contrast, cooperate to circumscribe women's sexuality and their ability to earn a living.

[A] Raising Expectations: Institutional Responsibility and the Issue of *Sexual Harassment*.

Diehl, Lesley A.
Initiatives; v57 n3 p1-10 May 1996
Sexual harassment defined as a gender neutral action aided by a power differential cannot explain the complex nature of *sexual harassment*, occurrence of peer *harassment*, or campus policies that address the issue when it occurs. *Sexual harassment* needs to be understood as a complex phenomenon determined by the interaction of power, gender, and climate in our culture. (FC)

[A] Real people: when I say stop, I mean stop! (videotape review)
Augmented title: video review
Shaver, Susan, reviewer
Book Report.v. 17 no5 (Mar./Apr. 1999) p. 91.
Real People: When I Say Stop, I Mean Stop! ($99.95), from Sunburst Communications, is a 30-minute video that examines many sensitive areas of teen dating, pressure of peers, and relationships, through candid discussions among teens, teacher-led classroom discussions, and role playing.

[A] Real world: when I say stop, I mean stop! (videotape review)
Augmented title: video review
McCaffrey, Susan, reviewer
School Library Journal.v. 45 no2 (Feb. 1999) p. 57.
Real World: When I Say Stop, I Mean Stop! ($99.95), from Sunburst, is a 30-minute video for students in grades 7-12 that deals with the very sensitive issues of sexual pressure and harassment in the lives of young people. It offers a starting point to help young people become aware of these issues and handle them in a safe and mature way. Viewers will relate to the program's fast pace and to the diverse and credible actors.

[A] Rethinking sexual harassment
Fox Genovese, Elizabeth, 1941
Partisan Review.v. 64 Summer 1997 p. 366-74.
The writer discusses sexual harassment policies. She states that many people are coming to suspect that the prevailing sexual harassment policies and laws demand a fresh look. She states that there is much to recommend the position of equity feminists such as Christina Hoff, Cathy Young, and Katie Roiphe, beginning with a basic notion of fairness. In their view, she notes, women who cling to the status of victim demean themselves. Gender feminists, on the other hand, she argues, are seeking to reshape the workplace to conform to the sensibilities of the most "feminine" women workers and are using claims of sexual harassment as their weapon.

[A] Rethinking sexual harassment/ edited by Clare Brant and Yun Lee Too
London: Pluto, 1994
xii,292p; 25cm
Includes Index and Bibliography.
Subjects: Sexual harassment, Sexual harassment of women, Feminist theory

[A] Revolution 1997 Winter;7(4):51
Sexual harassment? Yes, please.
Vietenthal P
Warren Memorial Hospital, Front Royal, Virginia, USA.
[A] Revolution 1998 Spring;8(1):80-1
I'm sorry, was that sexual harassment?
Barnts AL

[A] RN 1996 Feb;59(2):61-4
If you're sexually harassed.
Wolfe S

[A] Sabbath's theater (book review)
Roth, Philip; Bellow, Janis Freedman, reviewer
Partisan Review.v. 62 Fall 1995 p. 699-708+.
In Sabbath's Theater, Philip Roth invites readers to inhabit a world bereft of love where all real feeling is with the dead. It is a book about the end of things, where grief, malice, and the itch for a fight is all that is left. We are introduced to a "hero" who has turned his longtime mistress into a whore; been "publicly disgraced for the gross sexual harassment of a girl forty years his junior"; and all the while sponged on his wife, driving her to drink and eventually into a psychiatric institution.

[A] Salk Institute investigated after claims of inhumane research
Dalton, Rex
Nature.v. 394 no6695 Aug. 20 1998 p. 709.
A civil court in San Diego, California, has heard of great deficiencies in animal research at the Salk Institute. Teresa J. Sylvina, who was hired by the institute to correct these problems, is suing the institute for wrongful termination, retaliation, defamation, and sexual harassment. The research difficulties included severe disease among the animals and failed surgical techniques, and the problems at one stage threatened a major NIH cancer grant, according to Sylvina. Sylvina's claims have prompted federal authorities to investigate animal research at the Salk Institute, as well as questionable NIH billing practices.

[A] Sekushuariti / Inoue Teruko, Ueno Chizuko, Ehara Yumiko hen ; Amano Masako hensh⁻u ky⁻oryoku.
T⁻oky⁻o : Iwanami Shoten, 1995.
vii, 256 p. : ill. ; 19 cm.
Series: Nihon no feminizumu = Feminism in Japan ; 6.
LC Call No.: HQ18.J3 S44 1995
ISBN: 4000039067
Includes bibliographical references.
Subjects: Sexual orientation -- Japan. Sexual harassment -- Japan. Sex oriented

businesses -- Japan. Feminism -- Japan.
Series Entry: Nihon no feminizumu ; 6.
Source: DLC DLC MTH

[A] Sex, power, conflict : evolutionary and feminist perspectives / edited by David M.
Buss, Neil M. Malamuth.
New York : Oxford University Press, 1996.
vi, 339 p. ; 24 cm.
LC Call No.: HQ801.83 .S49 1996
ISBN: 0195103572 (pbk.)
0195095812 (cloth)
Includes bibliographical references (p. 316-318) and indexes.
Subjects: Man-woman relationships. Acquaintance rape. Dating violence. Family
violence. Sexual harassment. Sex (Psychology) Genetic psychology. Feminist theory.
Source: DLC DLC UKM

[A] Sexual harassment / Carol Wekesser, senior editor ; Karin L. Swisher, book editor ;
Christina Pierce, assistant editor.
San Diego, CA : Greenhaven Press, c1992.
208 p. ; ill. ; 25 cm.
Series: Current controversies.
LC Call No.: HD6060.3 .S47 1992
ISBN: 1565100204 (pbk. : acid-free paper)
1565100212 (lib. bdg. : acid-free paper)
Includes bibliographical references (p. 201-202) and index.
Is sexual harassment a serious problem? -- What causes sexual harassment? -- How can
sexual harassment be reduced? -- Can broad legal definitions of sexual harassment be
effectively used in the courts? Subjects: Sexual harassment of women -- United States.
Sexual harassment of women -- Law and legislation -- United States.
Source: DLC DLC OCL MLX SNN

[A] Sexual harassment : women speak out / edited by Amber Coverdale Sumrall & Dena
Taylor ; with introductions by Andrea Dworkin & Margaret Randall ; cartoons chosen by
Roz Warren.
Freedom, CA : Crossing Press, 1992.
viii, 321 p. : ill. ; 23 cm.
LC Call No.: HQ1237.5.U6 S49 1992
ISBN: 0895945452 (Cloth)
0895945444 (Paper)
"Resources": p. 318-321.
Subjects: Sexual harassment of women -- United States – Case studies.
Source: DLC DLC IAF AMH

[A] Sexual harassment and confessional poets

Creamer, Elizabeth
The Kenyon Review.ns16 Fall 1994 p. 139-52.

[A] *Sexual Harassment* Bibliography.
This annotated bibliography lists 56 resources on *sexual harassment*. The resources are divided into two categories. Section I contains resources on *sexual harassment* of women in nontraditional occupations (NTOs). The annotations are categorized as follows: books/journal articles, hearings, news articles, NTO training curricula, legal commentaries, and court cases. Section II contains general *sexual harassment* resources.

[A] Sexual harassment is about bullying, not sex
Bordo, Susan, 1947
The Chronicle of Higher Education.v. 44 no34 (May 1 1998) p. B6.
Society has made a major mistake in equating sexual harassment with sexual gestures and overtures. Sexual harassment involves the action of gender bullies trying to bring women down to size and to restore a balance of power in which they were on top.

[A] Sexual harassment policies and computer-based training
Wellbrock, Richard D
Community College Review.v. 26 no4 (Spring 1999) p. 61-8.
[A] Sexual harassment/ Hazel Houghton-James London: Cavendish Publishing, c1995
xviii,228p; 22cm (pbk)
Subjects: Sexual harassment of women--Great Britain. Sexual harassment of women--Law and legislation--Great Britain. Sex discrimination in employment--Law and legislation -- Great Britain. Equal rights--England—1995. England--Equal rights--1995

[A] Sexual harassment/ producer Chris Oxley; director Cathy Elliott
[London]: Laurel Productions for Channel Four, 1996
1 videocassette (60min)
Series Cutting edge
Subjects: 658.386
Sexual harassment – videocassette.
Work environment - videocassette

[A] Sexual harassment: contemporary feminist perspectives/ edited by Alison M. Thomas and Celia Kitzinger
Buckingham: Open University Press, 1997
x,208p
Includes index
Subjects: Sexual harassment

[A] Sexual harassment: contemporary feminist perspectives/ edited by Alison M. Thomas and Celia Kitzinger
Buckingham: Open University Press, 1997

x,208p; 23cm (pbk)
Includes index
Subjects: Sexual harassment

[A] *Sexual Harassment*: Frankly, What Is It?
Pierce, Patricia A.
Journal of Intergroup Relations; v20 n4 p3-12 Win 1993-94
Reviews federal definitions of *sexual harassment* and traces some court cases to show that *sexual harassment* encompasses verbal, visual, or mental *harassment* that can be overt or implied. Some actions employers might take to prevent and stop *sexual harassment* are suggested. (SLD)

[A] Sexual harassment: looking deeper
Nursing 94.v. 24 Nov. 1994 p. 30+.
A male nurse who has become the target of an HIV-positive male patient's overt sexual advances asks whether he has an ethical right to refuse care for the patient on the basis of sexual harassment. It is recommended that the situation should be discussed with a trusted friend, coworker, or member of the clergy, while maintaining the patient's confidentiality. If the nurse still feels that he has to refuse to care for this patient, the record should show that it is on the basis of his relentless, unwanted behavior and not on the basis of his gender or HIV status.

[A] Sexual harassment: stop it now (videotape review)
Augmented title: video review
O'Donnell, Teresa Blankenbeker, reviewer
School Library Journal.v. 44 (Feb. 1998) p. 62-3.
Sexual Harassment: Stop It Now ($99), from Ragamuffin Movies, is a 28:56-minute video dealing with sexual harassment via the dramatized stories of three different teenagers. The program is well produced and suitable for grades 7-12. It is a recommended purchase for all libraries serving junior and senior high school students.

[A] Sexual harassment: to protect, empower
Thistlethwaite, Susan Brooks, 1948
Christianity and Crisis.v. 51 Oct. 21 1991 p. 328-30.

[A] Sexual harassment: why even bees do it
Angier, Natalie
New York Times (Late New York Edition).Oct. 10 1995 p. C1+.
Researchers have observed harassment-type sexual behavior in a variety of animal species, ranging from insects to apes. Such behavior may range from persistent advances to violent assaults that cause females to miscarry or die. The writer discusses the reasons why such behavior occurs, female resistance strategies, and the differences between social and biological definitions of sexual harassment.

[A] Sexualidad y confesion (book review)
Sarrion Mora, Adelina; Nieto, Jose C., reviewer
The Sixteenth Century Journal.v. 26 Summer 1995 p. 492-3.
Sexualidad y Confesion: La solicitacion ante el Tribunal del Santo Oficio (Siglos XVI-XIX), by Adelina Sarrion Mora, studies the sexual harassment that mostly women suffered while confessing their sins to priests and friars in Spain between the 16th and 19th centuries. Mora handles this topic with both tact and care, using ample documentation from the former Inquisition archives of Cuenca in Castile.

[A] Siegel, Deborah L.
Sexual harassment : research and resources ; a report-in-progress, November 1991 / prepared by the National Council for Research on Women ; [compiled and written by Deborah L. Siegel ; edited by Susan A. Hallgarth and Mary Ellen S. Capek]
Edition: 1st ed.
New York, NY : National Council for Research on Women, c1991.
30 p. : ill. ; 28 cm.
Local Call No: HD6060.3 .S53 1991
ISBN: 1880547104
Includes bibliographical references (p. 26-29)
Subjects: Sexual harassment of women -- United States.
Other authors: Hallgarth, Susan A. and Capek, Mary Ellen S.
Other authors: National Council for Research on Women (U.S.)
Source: AZU AZU IAC MTH

[A] Soc Work 1998 Jan;43(1):55-64
Teenage peer sexual harassment: implications for social work practice in education.
Fineran S, Bennett L
School of Social Work, Boston University, MA 02215, USA. sfineran@bu.edu
Peer sexual harassment is an often overlooked problem for both girls and boys in the educational environment. This article provides a historical framework for defining peer sexual harassment as a sex discrimination issue and a description of peer sexual harassment as a potential mental health issue. The article also reviews the limited empirical research on teenage peer sexual harassment, which has consistently revealed that nearly four of five adolescents are the targets of sexual harassment by their peers. Finally, the authors explore a theoretical context in which to understand sexual harassment and the implications for social work practice in education.

[A] Speech & equality : do we really have to choose? / edited by Gara LaMarche ; foreword by Norman Dorsen.
New York : New York University Press, c1996.
xi, 164 p. ; 22 cm.
LC Call No.: KF4772 .S64 1996

ISBN: 0814750915 (cloth : alk. paper)

0814751059 (pbk. : alk. paper)

Includes bibliographical references (p. 151-162)

Abortion clinic protests / David Cole, Sylvia Law, Catherine Albisa -- Hate crimes/hate speech / Ira Glasser, Martin Redish, Randall Kennedy -- Workplace harassment / Susan Deller Ross, Deborah Ellis, Wendy Kaminer.

Subjects: Freedom of speech -- United States. Abortion services -- Law and legislation -- United States. Hate speech -- United States. Sexual harassment -- Law and legislation -- United States.

Source: DLC DLC ZYF UKM AMH

[A] Strout, Elizabeth

Amy and Isabelle : a novel / Elizabeth Strout. 1st ed.

New York : Random House, c1998.

303 p. ; 25 cm.

LC Call No.: PS3569.T736 A8 1998

ISBN: 0375501347

Subjects: Teenage girls -- New England -- Fiction. Single mothers -- New England -- Fiction. Illegitimate children -- New England -- Fiction. Mothers and daughters -- New England -- Fiction. High school teachers -- New England -- Fiction. Sexual harassment in education -- New England -- Fiction. Sexual ethics for teenagers -- New England--Fiction. Sexual consent -- New England--Fiction. New England--Fiction. Domestic fiction. lcsh.

Source: DLC DLC C#P QUE CLE SNN

[A] Subtle sexism: current practice and prospects for change/ [edited by] Nijole V. Benokraitis

Thousand Oaks, Calif.: Sage Publications, c1997

xiv, 338p; 24cm

Includes bibliographical references and index

Subjects: Sexism, Sexual harassment of women

[A] Targets, effects, and perpetrators of sexual harassment in newsrooms

Brown, Cindy M; Flatow, Gail M

Journalism and Mass Communication Quarterly.v. 74 Spring 1997 p. 160-83.

Results of a random sample survey of Indiana journalists concerning targets, perpetrators, and effects of sexual harassment are used to test two theoretical models that have been formulated to explain sexual harassment--the sociocultural model and the organizational model. Both models are grounded in a conception of power differences between harassed and harasser. Survey responses show both models have explanatory power.

[A] The abuse of power in intimate relationships

Dziech, Billie Wright

The Chronicle of Higher Education.v. 44 no28 (Mar. 20 1998) p. B4-B5.

The current President Clinton-Monica Lewinsky scandal recalls recent campus debates about intimate relationships between individuals with different levels of power and whether those relationships can be truly consensual. Many colleges and universities ignore the problem of consent in their policies on sexual harassment, whereas some issue stern warnings against consensual relationships. However, almost none has banned consensual relationships completely.

[A] The Best of the rest (book review)
Stepp, Carl Sessions, reviewer
American Journalism Review.v. 15 Oct. 1993 p. 67.
The Best of the Rest: Non-Syndicated Newspaper Columnists Select Their Best Work, edited by Sam G. Riley, is a collection of works from 77 non-syndicated columnists. The range of subject matter is immense, covering subjects as diverse as okra, the death penalty, and sexual harassment. If the book is stiffly priced, it is also inspirational and instructive..

[A] The case against Anita Hill
Augmented title: review article
Eastland, Terry
Commentary.v. 96 Aug. 1993 p. 39-44.
David Brock's bestselling book The Real Anita Hill: The Untold Story may be bringing about another shift in public opinion on the Anita Hill-Clarence Thomas affair. The controversial book argues, on the basis of some impressive evidence, that Hill was not telling the truth when she claimed that Thomas had sexually harassed her while he was serving as her boss. Brock shows that Hill did not come forward to make her accusation to the Senate Judiciary Committee, as was originally claimed, but was "drawn forward" by staffers who opposed Thomas's nomination to the Supreme Court. He also casts doubt on the credibility of Hill's corroborating witnesses and points out discrepancies in her sworn testimony and public statements that call her own truthfulness into question. Finally, he debunks the claim that Hill was a Republican and a supporter of Robert Bork. None of this evidence proves conclusively that Hill lied, but it suggests that Thomas should be vindicated of her charges.

[A] The difference race makes: sexual harassment and the law in the Thomas/Hill hearings
Baker Fletcher, Karen
Journal of Feminist Studies in Religion.v. 10 Spring 1994 p. 7-15.
The writer explores the complex interaction of racial and gender representations in the Senate committee hearings of Clarence Thomas and Anita Hill. She explains that the positive legacy of the hearings is that they forced the nation to face the reality of sexual harassment in the workplace in an unprecedented way. The problem, she states, is that African-Americans in the modern era have been used as means for working out ethical questions regarding human rights in American culture, with little genuine regard to their actual personhood. She states that the roots of sexual harassment will be dealt with only when white Americans confront and reject their myths about black sexuality and only when black Americans recognize harassment as a problem in their own communities.

[A] The modern academy raging in the dark: misreading Mamet's political incorrectness in Oleanna
Badenhausen, Richard
College Literature.v. 25 no3 Fall 1998 p. 1-19.
David Mamet's Oleanna should be seen as primarily about the difficulties of acquiring and controlling language, particularly in the specialized environment of the academy. Because this acquisition relies on a student-teacher relationship that is unequal, its participants would benefit from coming to some agreement about how power will be exercised during their association. The play ends tragically, however, because both characters refuse to define those boundaries and fail to grasp the complexities of language while ignoring its subversive power.

[A] The personal you: sexual harassment
Horosko, Marian
Dance Magazine.v. 67 Apr. 1993 p. 62-3.

[A] The politics of gender, language and hierarchy in Mamet's Oleanna
MacLeod, Christine
Journal of American Studies.v. 29 Aug. 1995 p. 199-213.
A discussion of David Mamet's play Oleanna. The narrow critical preoccupation with sexual harassment, political correctness, and beleaguered masculinity in the play has obscured a wider and more challenging dramatic engagement with issues of power, hierarchy, and the control of language. For the two protagonists of Oleanna, a change in social relations can only be figured in terms of reversal, retaliation, and the combative substitution of one domination for another.

[A] The Post and Paula Jones
Shepard, Alicia C
American Journalism Review.v. 16 July/Aug. 1994 p. 30-1.
On May 4, three months after Paula Corbin Jones appeared at a press conference to level accusations at President Clinton, the Washington Post ran a highly detailed story of what Jones and her corroborators said had taken place three years before. Post reporter Michael Isikoff, who covered the press conference and then conducted further research, felt that he had a piece that was ready to go to print earlier, but his editors disagreed over how to handle the story. On March 16, Isikoff was suspended for two weeks for insubordination and abusive behavior toward an editor following a shouting match that was related to the handling of the story. Conservatives began accusing the Post of covering up the charges against Clinton. According to Post Executive Editor Leonard Downie Jr., the paper had not spiked the story but was waiting until it was ready to go to press. Two weeks after the story appeared, Isikoff quit the Post. He is now employed by Newsweek as an investigative reporter.

[A] The press and the Thomas feeding frenzy

Sabato, Larry J
The Quill (Chicago, Ill.).v. 79 Nov./Dec. 1991 p. 10.

[A] The queen of America goes to Washington city: Harriet Jacobs, Frances Harper, Anita
Hill
Berlant, Lauren, 1957
American Literature.v. 65 Sept. 1993 p. 549-74.
Part of a special issue on nation, race, and gender. The writer examines the relationship
between sexuality and citizenship in Harriet A. Jacobs's Incidents in the Life of a Slave
Girl (1861), Frances E. W. Harper's Iola Leroy (1892), and the testimony of Anita Hill.
She argues that these black women take their individual losses as exemplary of larger ones,
namely the failure of the law and the nation to protect the sexual dignity of women from
the hybrid body of patriarchal official and sexual privilege. She explains that they resist
further submission to a national sexuality that blurs the line between the disembodied
entitlements of liberal citizenship and the places where bodies experience the sensation of
being dominated.

[A] The rector and the deaconess: women, the church, and sexual harassment in early-
twentieth-century English Canada, a case study
Knowles, Norman
Journal of Canadian Studies.v. 31 Summer 1996 p. 97-114.
This paper examines the events surrounding an incident of sexual harassment involving a
young deaconess and the rector of a Halifax parish at the time of the First World War.
Based on the correspondence of the principal figures involved in the case and the church
officials who later investigated the affair, the paper provides a rare and intimate look into
sexual impropriety within the middle class, the construction of gender relations and the
ambivalence and ambiguity that surrounded women's role and position within the Church
at the beginning of the twentieth century.

[A] The VA is charged with fostering sexual harassment
RN.v. 55 Dec. 1992 p. 14-15.

[A] Thinking through (book review)
Bannerji, Himani; Wylie, Herb, reviewer
Canadian Literature.no152/153 Spring/Summer 1997 p. 251-3.
This volume contains a varied series of essays that drives home the necessity to theorize
race, gender, and class not as independent considerations but as necessarily interconnected.
The author's exploration shifts from the theoretical, sociological discourse of the early
essays to a more personal voice in the later essays, in which she contemplates the position
of the emigre, considers her experiences a a part-time instructor in York University's
Atkinson College, and applies her theorizing of the race/gender/class nexus to a case of
sexual harassment.

[A] To your health!

Hamilton, Linda H
Dance Magazine.v. 70 Nov. 1996 p. 56-60.
The results of a mail survey relating to the health concerns and other problems that dancers may have while training on the job. Topics discussed are weight, body image, eating problems, exercise, illness, mood disorders, substance abuse, sexual behavior, and sexual harassment. Practical suggestions for problems relating to these topics are given.

[A] Transforming a rape culture / edited by Emilie Buchwald, Pamela R. Fletcher, Martha Roth.
Minneapolis, MN : Milkweed Editions, 1993.
xiv, 467 p. : ill. ; 24 cm.
LC Call No.: HV6556 .T73 1993
ISBN: 0915943069 (acid-free paper) : $23.95
Includes bibliographical references and indexes.
Are we really living in a rape culture? -- I want a twenty-four-hour truce during which there is no rape / Andrea Dworkin --Fraternities and the rape culture / Chris O'Sullivan -- Erotica vs. pornography / Gloria Steinem --Twenty years later : the unfinished revolution / Peggy Miller & Nancy Biele -- "I just raped my wife! What are you going to do about it, pastor?" : the church and sexual violence / Carol J. Adams -- Conversations of consent : sexual intimacy without sexual assault / Joseph Weinberg & Michael Biernbaum -- The language of rape / Helen Benedict -- I thought you didn't mind / Elizabeth Powell -- Clarence, William, Iron Mike, Tailhook, Senator Packwood, Spur Posse, Magic ... and us / Michael S. Kimmel -- Creating redemptive imagery : a challenge of resistance and creativity / Sandra Campbell -- How rape is encouraged in American boys and what we can do to stop it / Myriam Miedzian -- On becoming anti-rapist / Haki R. Madhubuti -- Raising girls for the 21st century / Emilie Buchwald -- Religion and violence : the persistence of ambivalence / Joan H. Timmerman -- Making rape an election issue / John Stoltenberg -- The date rape play : a collaborative process / Carolyn Levy -- Outside in : a man in the movement / Richard S. Orton -- Training for safehouse / Claire Buchwald -- Model for a violence-free state / Susan J. Berkson --Commodification of women : morning, noon, and night / Sarah Ciriello --Civil rights antipornography legislation : addressing the harm to women / Steven Hill & Nina Silver -- In the wake of Tailhook : a new order for the Navy / Barbara Spyridon Pope -- No laughing matter : sexual harassment in K-12 schools / Nan Stein -- The veils / Louise Erdrich -- The lie of entitlement / Terrence Crowley -- Seduced by violence no more / Bell Hooks -- Radical heterosexuality ... or how to love a man and save your feminist soul / Naomi Wolf -- comin to terms / Ntozake Shange -- In praise of insubordination, or, what makes a good woman go bad? / Inés Hernandex-Avila -- A woman with a sword : some thoughts on women, feminism, and violence / D.A. Clarke -- Transforming the rape culture that lives in my skull / Martha Roth -- Up from brutality : freeing black communities from sexual violence / W.J. Musa Moore-Foster -- Whose body is it, anyway? : transforming ourselves to change a rape culture / Pamela R. Fletcher -- The not yet spoken / Susan Griffin.
Subjects: Sexual harassment of women. Rape. Women -- Crimes against.
Source: DLC DLC SLC PGC OBE OCL

[A] Trip's cinch (play review)
King, Robert L., reviewer
The North American Review.v. 279 July/Aug. 1994 p. 46-7.
Phyllis Nagy's Trip's Cinch is a long one-act play about sexual harassment. At the start,
Val Greco, an English professor, interviews Benjamin Trip, who may have exploited Lucy
Parks. For a new book, Greco attempts to recreate what happened between them, to catch
the tone and intent of their coded discourse, and to not rely on transcripts. The audience is
given a jury's limited knowledge, the truth of literal transcript, with the result that the
emotional and ethical truths slip away.

[A] U.S. Supreme Court trends
Richardson, L. Anita
Social Education.v. 62 no6 (Oct. 1998) p. 371-6.
A selection of 1997 U.S. Supreme Court decisions are presented with teaching tips and
resources. The court cases concern sexual harassment, the Line Veto Act of 1996,
attorney-client privilege, the Americans with Disabilities Act, the National Endowment for
the Arts, public broadcasters' editorial discretion, the legality of no-knock entries into
property, the constitutionality of Chicago's anti-gang loitering ordinance, and Colorado's
statutory requirements for ballot initiatives.

[A] United States. Congress. Senate. Committee on the Judiciary Uniform Nomination of
Judge Clarence Thomas to be Associate Justice of the Supreme Court of the United States.
October 11, 12, and 13, 1991
The complete transcripts of the Clarence Thomas--Anita Hill hearings: October 11, 12, 13,
1991/ edited by Anita Miller; preface by Nina Totenberg
Chicago, Ill.: Academy Chicago Publishers, c1994 480p; 23cm
Clarence Thomas--Anita Hill hearings
Subjects: "Thomas, Clarence, 1948- Hill, Anita United States. Supreme Court
Judges--Selection and appointment--United States Sexual harassment of women--United
States

[A] United States. Congress. Senate. Committee on the Judiciary.
The complete transcripts of the Clarence Thomas—Anita Hill hearings, October 11, 12,
13, 1991 / preface by Nina Totenberg ; edited by Anita Miller.
Chicago, IL : Academy Chicago Publishers, 1994.
480 p. : ill. ; 23 cm.
LC Call No.: KF8745.T48 U55 1994
ISBN: 0897334086 : $22.50
Subjects: Thomas, Clarence, 1948-. Hill, Anita. United States. Supreme Court. Judges --
Selection and appointment -- United States. Sexual harassment of women -- United States.
Source: DLC DLC CNO AMH

[A] United States. Congress. Senate. Committee on the Judiciary.

Sexual harassment hearing compilation [videorecording] / Senate Judiciary Committee.
[West Lafayette, Ind.] : Purdue University, Public
Affairs Video Archives, [1991?]
1 videocassette (122 min.) : sd., col. ; 1/2 in.
Local Call No: KF8745.T48 U56 1991
Title from videocassette label.
Caption title from original C-SPAN broadcast: Thomas confirmation hearing.
"Made available by Purdue University under an agreement with C-SPAN."
"91-10-11-1000-4 4706-22538"--Cassette.
Compilation of testimony of Clarence Thomas and Anita Hill appearing before the Senate
Judiciary Committee at the October 1991 Confirmation hearing for Supreme Court
nominee Thomas.
VHS.
Subjects: Thomas, Clarence, 1948-. Hill, Anita. United States. Supreme Court -- Officials
and employees -- Selection and appointment. Sexual harassment of women -- United
States.
Other authors: Thomas, Clarence, 1948-. Hill, Anita.
Public Affairs Video Archives. C-SPAN (Television network)
Other titles: Thomas confirmation hearing.
Source: EMU EMU MTH
Control No.: 25266515

[A] United States. Congress. Senate. Select Committee on Ethics.
Documents related to the investigation of Senator Robert Packwood / Select Committee on
Ethics, United States Senate, One Hundred Fourth Congress, first session.
Washington : U.S. G.P.O. : For sale by the U.S.
G.P.O., Supt. of Docs., Congressional Sales Office, 1995.
10 v. : ill. ; 29 cm.
Series: S. prt. ; 104-30.
LC Call No.: KF4961.P34 U55 1995
ISBN: 016047535X (v.1) : $43.00
"104th Congress, 1st session. Committee print."
Distributed to some depository libraries in microfiche.
Shipping list no.: 95-9060-P.
Includes bibliographical references.
Subjects: Packwood, Bob. United States. Congress. Senate -- Expulsion. United States.
Congress. Senate -- Discipline. Misconduct in office -- United States. Political corruption -
- United States. Sexual harassment of women -- United States.
Source: DUSS DLC MTH

[A] United States. General Accounting Office.
DOD service academies : update on extent of sexual harassment: report to Congressional
requesters / United States General Accounting Office.
Washington, D.C. : The Office ; Gaithersburg, MD (P.O. Box 6015, Gaithersburg 20884-

6015) : The Office [distributor, 1995]
34 p. : ill. ; 28 cm.
LC Call No.: U408.3 .U54 1995
Cover title.
"March 1995."
Includes bibliographical references.
"GAO/NSIAD-95-58."
"B-259415"--P. 1.
Availability: 153897 GAO (202) 512-6000 (Voice); (301) 258-4066 (Fax)
Subjects: Military education -- United States -- Evaluation. Sexual harassment in universities and colleges -- United States -- Evaluation. Sexual harassment of women -- United States.
Source: DGAO DLC SNN

[A] United States. National Institute of Justice
Civil rights and criminal justice: primer on sexual harassment/ by Paula N. Rubin
Washington: National Institute of Justice, 1995
10p; 28cm
Series Research in Action
Subjects: QWUHb (QWUH)

[A] United States. National Institute of Justice. Research in Action
Civil rights and criminal justice: primer on sexual harassment/ by Paula N. Rubin
Washington: U.S. Department of Justice, 1995
5p; 28cm
Subjects: QWUHb (QWUH)

[A] Universal truth and multiple perspectives: controversies on sexual harassment
Chamallas, Martha
Etc..v. 49 Fall 1992 p. 285-91.

[A] Villains and victims: "sexual correctness" and the repression of feminism
Willis, Ellen
Salmagundi.no101/102 Winter/Spring 1994 p. 68-78.
The writer examines the distortion in the public conversation about feminism. She states that one of the great successes of the anti-feminist reaction is that there is at present no socially legitimate public language in which women can directly and explicitly express anger at the "mundane kinds of sexism." Feelings of anger and frustration, she explains, are channelled into campaigns against such issues as date rape and sexual harassment, which have become relatively acceptable metaphors for a larger, and largely inexpressible, set of feminist concerns. She argues that the complexities and contradictions of male-female relations are flattened to caricatures of villains and victims.

[A] Violence against women : philosophical perspectives / edited by Stanley G. French,

Wanda Teays, Laura M. Purdy.
Ithaca, N.Y. : Cornell University Press, 1998.
ix, 260 p. ; 23 cm.
LC Call No.: HV6250.4.W65 V565 1998
ISBN: 0801434416 (cloth : alk. paper)
0801484529 (pbk. : alk. paper)
Includes bibliographical references (p. 235-256) and index.
Subjects: Women -- Crimes against. Sexual harassment of women. Sexual abuse victims.
Family violence.
Source: DLC DLC C#P

[A] Violence Vict 1998 Fall;13(3):203-16
Measuring sexual harassment: development and validation of the Sexual Harassment
Inventory.
Murdoch M, McGovern PG
Section General Internal Medicine, Minneapolis Veterans Affairs Medical Center, USA.
Sexual harassment is a pervasive and damaging public health problem, yet the natural
history is poorly understood, and research in this area has tended to focus on prevalence
reporting. We describe the development and initial validation results of a survey tool, the
Sexual Harassment Inventory, that may be helpful in future epidemiologic research.
Routine use of this or some other standardized measurement tool would help clarify our
understanding of the natural history and health costs of sexual harassment.

[A] Vocalizations of female red-winged blackbirds inhibit sexual harassment
Birks, Sharon M; Beletsky, Les D
Wilson Bulletin.v. 99 Dec. 1987 p. 706-7.

[A] Wade, Brent, 1959-
Company man : a novel / by Brent Wade.
1st Anchor Books ed.
New York : Anchor Books/Doubleday, 1993.
219 p. ; 21 cm.
LC Call No.: PS3573.A313 C6 1993
ISBN: 0385425635 : $9.50 ($12.00 Can.)
Subjects: Afro-American executives -- Fiction. Afro-American gays -- Fiction. Corporate
culture -- Fiction. Baltimore (Md.) -- Fiction. Sexual harassment -- Fiction. Detective and
mystery stories. gsafd.
Source: DLC DLC OCL AMH

[A] What is sexual harassment? / Karin Swisher, book editor.
San Diego, Calif. : Greenhaven Press, c1995.
91 p. ; 23 cm.
Series: At issue series.
An opposing viewpoints series.

LC Call No.: HQ1237 .W48 1995
ISBN: 1565102665 : $7.95
Includes bibliographical references and index.
Subjects: Sexual harassment.
Series Entry: Opposing viewpoints series (Unnumbered)
At issue (San Diego, Calif.)
Source: DLC DLC SNN

[A] Who stole feminism? (book review)
Sommers, Christina Hoff; Wood, Julia T., reviewer
The Quarterly Journal of Speech.v. 82 May 1996 p. 171-85.
In Who Stole Feminism? How Women Have Betrayed Women, Christina Hoff Sommers
argues that "gender feminists" have used faulty research to justify exaggerated claims
about the extent of rape, sexual harassment, and sexism in education. Her strong, recurring
praise of liberal feminism does not grant voice to alternative discourses that criticize
liberal feminism for having benefited middle-class white women and done little for women
of other races and classes.

[A] Why Anita Hill lost
Garment, Suzanne
Commentary.v. 93 Jan. 1992 p. 26-35.
The opponents of Supreme Court nominee Clarence Thomas contributed to their defeat
when they brought Anita Hill's sexual harassment charges into the open for a public face-
off before the Judiciary Committee that resembled a criminal trial. The majority of
Americans found Thomas more credible than Hill, and their opinions were based largely on
Hill's testimony. Hill's ambitiousness and capacity for self protection, qualities about
which she was not entirely candid, probably led many people to reject her description of
herself as a victim of sexual harassment.

[A] Wilcox, Diane Michelfelder.
Applied ethics in American society / Diane Michelfelder Wilcox, William H. Wilcox ;
under the general editorship of Robert C. Solomon.
Fort Worth : Harcourt Brace College Publishers, c1997.
xi, 783 p. ; 24 cm.
Local Call No: BJ1031 .W45 1997
ISBN: 0155028596
Includes bibliographical references.
Moral theory -- Abortion -- Euthanasia – Death penalty -- Distributive justice: Welfare
and world hunger -- Discrimination and affirmative action -- Animals and the environment
-- Freedom of expression-- Gay rights and sexual harassment – Privacy issues: Griswold v.
Connecticut. [The book] offers instructors and students a well-balanced anthology for
ethics courses of all kinds. Applied ethics, Social problems, Introduction to ethics, and
Moral problems are just some of the courses that might use this up-to-date collection of
readings on the most hotly debated issues of our time. The book also includes important

readings in moral theory, providing students with the necessary framework to evaluate positions. The book juxtaposes several different viewpoints on [various] social issues. -Back cover. This book is primarily intended for undergraduates taking philosophy courses that address contemporary moral problems. -Pref.
Subjects: Applied ethics. United States -- Social conditions.
Other authors: Wilcox, William H. and Solomon, Robert C.
Source: RFB RFB UKM AMH

[A] Wise, Sue, 1953-
Georgie Porgie : sexual harassment in everyday life / Sue Wise and Liz Stanley.
London ; New York : Pandora, 1987.
xii, 235 p. ; 20 cm.
Series: Pandora Press focus.
LC Call No.: HD6060.3 .W57 1987
ISBN: 0863580181 (pbk.) : £5.95 ($9.95 U.S.)
Includes index and bibliography: p. [209]-230.
Subjects: Sexual harassment of women. Sex role in the work environment.
Sex discrimination in employment.
Other authors: Stanley, Liz, 1947-
Source: DLC DLC AMH

[A] Women and philosophy / consulting editor, Janna Thompson.
Bundoora, Vic. : Australian Association of Philosophy, [1986]
147 p. ; 24 cm.
Local Call No: HQ1233 .W65 1986
ISBN: 095925451X
"Australasian Journal of Philosophy, Supplement to
Volume 64; June 1986."--Spine.
Includes bibliographical references.
Rousseau and Wollstonecraft: nature vs. reason/Moira Gatens --Gender and essence in Aristotle/Gareth B. Matthews --Rawls, women and the priority of liberty/Karen Green --Can a feminist be a liberal?/Marion Tapper --Simple equality is not enough/Lorraine Code --Mill on women and human development/John Howes --Feminism and moral reasoning/Susan Parsons --On the nature of sexual harassment/Jan Crosthwaite and Christine Swanton --Against the sexuality of reason/Robert Pargetter and Elizabeth W. Prior.
Subjects: Feminist theory. Woman (Philosophy) Sexism -- Philosophy.
Other titles: Australasian journal of philosophy. Supplement.
Source: LAS LAS OCL AMH

[A] Women and social action [videorecording] / Board of Governors Universities in cooperation with Governors State University ; a production of Communications Services.
[1994]
12 videocassettes : sd., col. ; 1/2 in.

Local Call No: HQ1426 .W65 1994
VHS format.
Taped off-air by license.
Producer/director, Cheryl Lambert. [1] pt. 1. Social action and social change -- pt. 2.
Perspectives on women -- [2] pt. 3. Leadership and social action -- pt. 4. Commonalities
and differences -- [3] pt. 5. Gender socialization -- pt. 6. Transforming knowledge -- [4]
pt. 7. Families -- pt. 8. Child care -- [5] pt. 9. Women and health -- pt. 10. Women, weight
and food -- [6] pt. 11. Pregnancy and childbirth -- pt. 12. Motherhood -- [7] pt. 13.
Abortion and reproductive issues -- pt. 14. Religion [8] pt. 15 Work -- pt. 16 Sexual
harassment -- [9] pt. 17. Low-income resistance -- pt. 18. Homelessness -- [10] pt. 19.
Connecting the issues -- pt. 20. Violence against women -- [11] pt. 21. On the streets and
in the jails -- pt. 22. Rape and self defense -- [12] pt. 23. Perspectives on social change --
pt. 24. New directions. Martha Thompson, Ph. D., Northeastern Illinois University.
Subjects: Women -- United States -- Social conditions. Women -- History. Social action.
Social change. Sex discrimination against women. Women -- Family relationships. Women
-- Health and hygiene. Motherhood. Childbirth. Women -- Religious life. Sexual
harassment. Women -- Employment. Homeless women. Women -- Crimes against. Rape.
Other authors: Thompson, Martha and Lambert, Cheryl.
Other authors: Governors State University. Board of Governors Universities.
Communications Services (Firm) PBS Adult Learning Service.
Source: ZRS ZRS OCL SNN

[A] Women, violence, and social control / edited by Jalna Hanmer and Mary Maynard.
Atlantic Highlands, NJ : Humanities Press International, 1987.
xi, 213 p. ; 23 cm.
LC Call No.: HV6250.4.W65 W66 1987
ISBN: 0391035142
0391035150 (pbk.)
Includes index and bibliography: p. 193-209.
Subjects: Women -- Crimes against. Violence. Sexual harassment of women. Sex role.
Source: DLC DLC SNN

[A] Women's voices and experiences of the Hill-Thomas hearings
Trix, Frances; Sankar, Andrea
American Anthropologist.v. 100 no1 Mar. 1998 p. 32-40.
Women's experiences and opinions of the Hill-Thomas hearings were studied. Within 3
weeks of the end of the Senate Judiciary Committee hearings on Anita Hill's charges of
sexual harassment against Supreme Court nominee Clarence Thomas, in-depth, face-to-
face interviews on the hearings were conducted with 100 women aged 19-76, more than a
third of whom were African-Americans, from the Detroit area of Michigan. Contrary to
the results of polls conducted at the time, the survey's findings revealed that most women
strongly supported Hill, that there was a default category of support for Thomas, that age
rather than race was a predictor of strong support for Hill or Thomas, and that women

across the board felt anger and pain. The results also emphasized the strengths and challenges of activist research.

[A] Women's health : complexities and differences / edited by Sheryl Burt Ruzek, Virginia L. Olesen, Adele E. Clarke.
Columbus : Ohio State University Press, c1997.
xix, 689 p. : ill. ; 23 cm.
Series: Women and health series.
LC Call No.: RA564.85 W66686 1997
ISBN: 0814207049 (cloth : alk. paper)
0814207057 (paper : alk. paper)
Includes bibliographical references and index.
I. What is women's health? Social, biomedical, and feminist models of women's health / Sheryl Burt Ruzek, Adele E. Clarke, and Virginia L. Olesen -- Pattern and puzzles : the distribution of health and illness among women in the United States / Deborah L. Wingard. II. What we share and how we differ. What are the dynamics of differences? / Sheryl Burt Ruzek, Adele E. Clarke, and Virginia L. Olesen -- The last sisters : health issues of women with disabilities / Carol J. Gill. III. Creating women's health : health practices, working and living conditions, and medical care. Women, personal health behavior, and health promotion / Sheryl Burt Ruzek -- The ergonomics of women's work / Julia Faucett -- "Less than animals?" : the health of women workers in garment manufacture, agriculture, and electronics assembly / Virginia L. Olesen -- Access, cost, and quality of medical care : where are we heading? / Sheryl Burt Ruzek -- A note from Louise : understanding women's health in Appalachia / Judy M. Perry. IV. Culture and complexities. Beauty myths and realities and their impact on women's health / Jane Sprague Zones -- Old woes, old ways, new dawn : Native American women's health issues / Ann Metcalf -- Asian/Pacific American women and cultural diversity : studies of the traumas of cancer and war / Karen J. Ito, Rita Chi-Ying Chung, and Marjorie Kagawa-Singer -- Issues in Latino women's health : myths and challenges / Susan C.M. Scrimshaw, Ruth E. Zambrana, and Christine Dunkel-Schetter. V. Intersections of race, class, and culture. African American women's health : the effects of disease and chronic life stressors / Nikki V. Franke -- Women, power, and mental health / Lynn Weber, Tina Hancock, and Elizabeth Higginbotham -- Who cares? : women as informal and formal caregivers / Virginia L. Olesen -- Older women : income, retirement, and health / Vida Yvonne Jones and Carroll L. Estes. VI. Power and social control. Responses to stigma and marginality : the health of lesbians, imprisoned women, and women with HIV / Nancy E. Stoller -- "You can be safer, but--" : different women, many violences. Women's lived experiences of abuse / Lora Bex Lempert -- The battered women's movement ; Rape / Brandy M. Britton -- A survivor speaks about the Victim Input Program / Sally Pickels -- Anti-lesbian violence / Beatrice von Schulthess -- Sexual harassment / Brandy M. Britton. The ongoing politics of contraception : Norplant and other emerging technologies / Cheri A. Pies. VII. Challenges and choices for the twenty-first century. Research to improve women's health : an agenda for equity / Deborah Narrigan ... [et al.] -- Strengths and strongholds in women's health research / Virginia L. Olesen ... [et al.] -- Conversing with diversity : implications for social research

/ Sheryl Burt Ruzek, Virginia L. Olesen, and Adele E. Clarke.
Subjects: Women -- Health and hygiene. Women's Health Services. Women's Health.
Women's Health Services.
Series Entry: Women & health (Columbus, Ohio)
Source: DLC DLC C#P MMU NLM CUM OCL

[A]African American women speak out on Anita Hill-Clarence Thomas / edited by Geneva
Smitherman.
Detroit : Wayne State University Press, c1995.
276 p. : ill. ; 23 cm.
Series: African American life series.
LC Call No.: E185.86 .A3344 1995
ISBN: 0814325300 (pbk. : alk. paper)
Includes bibliographical references and index.
Subjects: Hill, Anita. Thomas, Clarence, 1948-. Afro-American women. Sexual
harassment of women -- United States. Sex role -- United States.
Other authors: Smitherman-Donaldson, Geneva, 1940-
Source: DLC DLC MTH

[A} Clarence Thomas and Anita Hill [videorecording] : public hearing, private pain /
produced and written by Ofra Bikel.
Alexandria, Va. : PBS Video, c1992.
1 videocassette (58 min.) : sd., col. ; 1/2 in.
Local Call No: KF8745.T48 C52 1992
Originally broadcast as a segment of the television program: Frontline.
Associate producer, Rachel Dretzin ; editor, Jay Freund ; narrator, Ofra Bikel.
Discusses the Thomas confirmation hearings and the charges of sexual harrassment by
Anita Hill from the perspective of Afro-Americans.
VHS format.
Subjects: Thomas, Clarence, 1948-. Hill, Anita. United States. Supreme Court -- Officials
and employees -- Selection and appointment. Afro-Americans -- Race identity.
Sexual harassment of women -- United States. Judges -- United States -- Selection and
appointment. United States -- Race relations.
Other authors: PBS Video.
Other titles: Frontline (Television program)
Other titles: Public hearing, private pain.
Source: ZIH ZIH MTH

[A} Spender, Dale.
Nattering on the net : women, power, and cyberspace / Dale Spender.
North Melbourne, Vic. : Spinifex Press, 1995.
xxvi, 278 p. ; 24 cm.
LC Call No.: HQ1233 .S68 1995
ISBN: 1875559094

Includes bibliographical references (p. 261-269) and index.
Subjects: Women's computer network resources. Information society. Computer networks
-- Social aspects. Books and reading. Sexual harassment of women. Women in technology.
Source: InU DLC AMH

2) SEXUAL HARASSMENT IN THE WORKPLACE

[B] A platform for gender tensions: women working and riding on Canadian urban public transit in the 1940s
Davis, Donald F; Lorenzkowski, Barbara
Canadian Historical Review.v. 79 no3 Sept. 1998 p. 431-65.
In 1940s Canada, urban transit provided a platform for negotiating gender relations in the context of "sexual harassment"; the rights of smokers and shoppers; and the employment of women drivers, conductors, and passenger guides. Unprecedented crowding resulted in men and women being obliged to invade each other's space, producing unwanted physical contact and the questioning of male "chivalry." However, the introduction of women "platform workers" in 1943 proved very uncontroversial with passengers.

[B] A woman's work is never done
Sexton, Sarah
The Ecologist.v. 26 July/Aug. 1996 p. 138-9.
Globalization and trade liberalization have resulted in the expansion of industrial sectors where women constitute the majority of the workforce. This new opportunity for employment, particularly in nonindustrialized countries, has brought many economic and social gains to women, helping them to overcome society's taboos and restrictions on women's behavior. However, declining economic and social conditions worldwide have forced women to work in low-paid jobs with little security, benefits, or future. This type of industrial setting can often replicate the patriarchal control that women work to escape from, often being exposed to sexual harassment, poor conditions, and little health care or education opportunities. In addition, women are expected to maintain their household and child-rearing duties.

[B] AAOHN J 1996 Feb;44(2):73-7
Violence and sexual harassment: impact on registered nurses in the workplace.
Williams MF
This study sought to determine the prevalence and impact of violence and sexual harassment experienced by registered nurses (RNs) in their workplaces in Illinois. About one third of those who indicated they had been sexually harassed also had been physically assaulted. Patients/clients were the most frequent perpetrators of sexual harassment and physical assault, while physicians committed over half of the sexual assaults. Results demonstrate that nurses need to take and active role in fostering a work environment free from violence and sexual harassment. They should be knowledgeable about institutional policies and, where none exist, they should work with administrators to develop them.

Prevention and intervention programs should be developed for both student and registered nurses.

[B] Addressing problems in the workplace
Helmlinger, Connie
American Journal of Nursing.v. 97 Jan. 1997 p. 73.
The Workplace Information Series is profiled. This American Nursing Association publication provides a comprehensive approach to coping with the hazards that nurses face on the job. The series deals with physical risks to nurses at work and behaviors that threaten nurses' job security, such as sexual harassment and the disregard of some employers for the Americans with Disabilities Act.

[B] Aggarwal, Arjun P.
Sexual harassment in the workplace 2nd ed
Toronto: Butterworths, c1992
xxx,385p; 24cm
Subjects: Sexual harassment—Canada. Sexual harassment of women--Law and legislation—Canada. Industrial law--Canada—1992. Canada--Industrial law--1992

[B] Ala Med 1994 Dec;64(6):4-6
Professional sexual misconduct: the current realty, current concepts, ignorance is not excuse.
Summer GL, McCrory E

[B] Aust Health Rev 1997;20(2):102-15
Australian registered nurses describe the health care workplace and its responsiveness to sexual harassment: an empirical study.
Madison J
Department of Health Studies, University of New England.
This report is a summary of findings from a 1995 study of Australian registered nurses and their perceptions of their health care workplaces, especially as it relates to sexual harassment. As the major employer of registered nurses, hospitals and health care facilities need to be concerned about employees' perceptions of the workplace.

[B] Berger, Gilda.
Women, work, and wages / Gilda Berger.
New York : F. Watts, 1986.
122 p. : ill. ; 24 cm.
LC Call No.: HD6095 .B47 1986
ISBN: 053110074X
Includes index and bibliography: p. [115]-116.
Examines women in the work force in the United States, with an emphasis on sex discrimination and related problems.
Subjects: Women -- Employment -- United States. Equal pay for equal work -- United

States. Sex discrimination in education -- United States. Sexual harassment of women --
United States.
Source: DLC DLC SNN

[B] Can Vet J 1995 Sep;36(9):531-2
Harassment in the workplace.
Gumley N
Publication Types: Comment Letter
Comments: Comment on: Can Vet J 1995 Jun;36(6):353

[B] Collier, Rohan, 1945-
Combating sexual harassment in the workplace/ Rohan Collier
Buckingham: Open University Press, 1995
vii,167p; 22cm
Series Managing work and organizations series
Subjects: Sexual harassment--Great Britain. Sex discrimination in employment--Great
Britain. Sexual harassment--Law and legislation--European Union countries. Sex
discrimination in employment--Law and legislation-- European Union countries

[B] Confronting sexual harassment
Nursing 94.v. 24 Oct. 1994 p. 48-50.
Sexual harassment of nurses in the workplace is discussed. In 1986 the U.S. Supreme
Court recognized sexual harassment as a form of discrimination. Although the number of
respondents to a survey on sexual harassment commissioned by the journal was small (75),
some patterns did emerge. Half of the 66 respondents experiencing harassment claimed
that they had been harassed by physicians. The majority of those who reported harassment
were ignored, whereas those who confronted offenders directly tended to get results. Some
stories of individual cases are related. Advice is offered on how to combat this problem.

[B] Creative labors: the lives and careers of women artists
Brooks, Geraldine S; Daniluk, Judith C
The Career Development Quarterly.v. 46 no3 (Mar. 1998) p. 246-61.
A study investigated the lived experience and meaning of career for women artists. The
participants were eight women artists between the ages of 40 and 65 years whose main
career pursuits were in the visual, performing, or literary arts. Analysis of the data
uncovered nine themes that applied to all participants: the sense of being an outsider, the
sense of validation through external recognition, the sense of being obstructed, the sense of
being torn between the needs of self and others, the sense of connection and belonging
through art, the sense of struggle to assume the identity of artist, the sense of self-
determination, the sense of being a pioneer, and the sense of harmony between self, art,
and career. A particularly salient factor in the career development of the women artists
was that of sex discrimination. Participants described overt and covert sexual harassment
and discrimination that had prevented them from receiving support and recognition for

their work and perceived the art world to be very much a "man's world." Discussion of the results and recommendations for counselors and for future research are provided.

[B] Dealing with sexual harassment
Nursing 96.v. 26 July 1996 p. 62.
Advice is given on dealing with sexual harassment. Sexual harassment should be recognized for what it is, and the victim should challenge the harasser. The victim should keep documentation for the duration of the harassment, and she should write the harasser a letter before alerting his supervisor about the situation, keeping a copy of the letter in a safe place. She should expect some results but not a reply. The harassed person should start to report the harassment formally through the chain of command in her workplace. Criminal charges should be filed with the police if rape or assault is threatened or occurs. Action may take several months.

[B] Deans Notes 1996 Nov;18(2):1-3
Raising awareness regarding the phenomenon of professional sexual misconduct.
Sheets VR

[B] Democracy, Inc.: the Hill-Thomas hearings
Hooks, Bell
Artforum.v. 30 Jan. 1992 p. 13-16.

[B] Don't tolerate sexual harassment at work
Horsley, Jack E., 1915
RN.v. 53 Jan. 1990 p. 69+.

[B] Employee Relat Law J 1991 Autumn;17(2):191-206
Effective sexual harassment policies: unexpected lessons from Jacksonville Shipyards.
Connell DS
Although many employers recognize the need for an effective sexual harassment policy, they have received only limited guidance from the EEOC and the courts on how to draft and implement one. This article examines a recent decision, Robinson v. Jacksonville Shipyards, in which the court imposed a comprehensive sexual harassment policy. This article suggests that employers should consider adopting similar policies to better protect themselves from liability for sexual harassment.

[B] Employee Relat Law J 1993 Spring;18(4):617-23
Reinstatement of the sexual harasser: the conflict between federal labor law and Title VII.
Piskorski TJ
Greater numbers of employers are adopting and vigorously enforcing policies prohibiting sexual harassment in the workplace. Discipline, including possible termination of employment, often is prescribed for the violation of such policies. When employees are represented by a union and covered by a collective bargaining agreement, final decisions relating to discipline often are made by arbitrators pursuant to the agreement's grievance

and arbitration procedure. For a variety of reasons, arbitrators may decide that a lesser form of discipline than that imposed by the employer is warranted for acts of sexual harassment. Such arbitration awards present a substantial conflict between two compelling public policies--the public policy favoring the private resolution of workplace disputes and the public policy against sexual harassment. This article will address the several federal courts of appeals' decisions that have attempted to resolve this conflict.

[B] Farley, Lin.
Sexual shakedown : the sexual harassment of women on the job / Lin Farley.
New York : McGraw-Hill, c1978.
xvii, 228 p. ; 24 cm.
LC Call No.: HD6095 .F37
ISBN: 0070199574 : $9.95
Includes bibliographical references and index.
Subjects: Sex discrimination against women -- United States. Sex discrimination in employment -- United States. Indecent assault -- United States. Sex discrimination against women -- Law and legislation -- United States.
Source: DLC DLC MTH m.c

[B] Fredrick, Candice, 1949-
Women, ethics and the workplace / Candice Fredrick and Camille Atkinson.
Westport, Conn. : Praeger, 1997.
xvi, 179 p. ; 25 cm.
LC Call No.: HD6060 .F73 1997
ISBN: 0275956431 (alk. paper)
0275960919 (pbk.)
Includes bibliographical references and index.
Subjects: Discrimination in employment. Sex discrimination against women. Sexual harassment of women. Business ethics.
Source: DLC DLC C#P AMH

[B] Gender discrimination in Jessica's career
Cook, Ellen Piel, 1952
The Career Development Quarterly.v. 46 (Dec. 1997) p. 148-54.
Gender discrimination in a case study of a hypothetical, Asian-American woman, Jessica Chang, is discussed. Jessica, a highly educated, well-paid technical professional, experienced gender discrimination throughout her career, which manifested itself in sexual harassment, external restrictions on her career advancement, and isolation.

[B] Gender segregation at work/ edited by S. Walby
Milton Keynes: Open U.P., 1988
x,190p; 23cm
Subjects: Sexual harassment of women--Great Britain, Women--Employment--Great Britain

[B] Gutek, Barbara A.
Sex and the workplace / Barbara A. Gutek. 1st ed.
San Francisco, Calif. : Jossey-Bass, 1985.
xix, 216 p. ; 24 cm.
Series: Jossey-Bass management series.
The Jossey-Bass social and behavioral science series.
LC Call No.: HD6060.3 .G88 1985
ISBN: 0875896561
Includes index and bibliography: p. 203-210.
Subjects: Sexual harassment of women. Sex discrimination in employment.
Organizational behavior.
Source: DLC DLC AUM

[B] Harassment blues
Munson, Naomi
Commentary.v. 93 Feb. 1992 p. 49-51.
The American public's dismissal of Anita Hill's allegations against Clarence Thomas
reveals how absurd the feminist definition of sexual harassment really is. Sexual
harassment, as properly understood, should involve something sexual--for example, a
boss's demand for sexual favors in exchange for raises or promotions. What Hill and her
supporters were talking about, on the other hand, was innuendo, ogling, obscenity, and
other allegedly insensitive behaviors that contribute to an "unpleasant atmosphere in the
workplace." Ordinary Americans know that they may well have to put up with an
unpleasant atmosphere in the workplace, whether it is caused by male "insensitivity" or
something else. Moreover, most people know that women can stand up for themselves.
Feminists, however, are fueled by rage against life's imperfections and against men. As a
result, they always want the rules changed to suit them.

[B] Healthc Exec 1996 Nov-Dec;11(6):43
American College of Healthcare Executives. Public policy statement. Preventing
and addressing sexual harassment in the workplace.
Publication Types: Guideline

[B] Herbert, Carrie M. H.
Eliminating sexual harassment at work/ Carrie M. H. Herbert
London: David Fulton, 1994
[6],148p; 23cm
Includes bibliographical references (p.143-145) and index
Subjects: 658.386, Sexual harassment, Work environment

[B] Hosp Health Netw 1995 Jan 20;69(2):54-7
Sexually harassed.
Sherer JL

When neurosurgeon Frances Conley resigned her Stanford University Medical School professorship over sexual harassment, her case received widespread notoriety. But Conley is far from alone in health care.

[B] How I was sexually harassed (and why you don't have to be)
Augmented title: with a reader poll
Brady, Barbara
Nursing 94.v. 24 May 1994 p. 52-6.
The issue of sexual harassment at work is addressed. Sexual harassment can be divided into physical, verbal, nonverbal, and quid-pro-quo harassment. A sexual harassment survey form is provided, and a sidebar discusses the implications of the U.S. Supreme Court's latest ruling on the issue. The writer, a nurse, describes how she was sexually harassed at work.

[B] If you're sexually harassed
Wolfe, Suzanne
RN.v. 59 Feb. 1996 p. 61-4.
The problem of sexual harassment in the workplace, particularly in a hospital setting, is discussed. Sexual harassment is a violation of the Civil Rights Act. The Equal Employment Opportunity Commission (EEOC), which is responsible for enforcing the relevant law, defines sexual harassment as unwanted sexual advances, requests for sexual favors, and other verbal or physical conduct of a sexual nature. The majority of claims (90 percent) filed with the EEOC are from women. As sexual harassment is typically perpetrated by people with power over their victims, nurses may be particularly vulnerable. The law is firmly behind the victims of such harassment.

[B] J Adv Nurs 1997 Jan;25(1):163-9
Sexual harassment in nursing.
Robbins I, Bender MP, Finnis SJ
North Devon District Hospital, Barnstaple, England.
Sexual harassment is a problem faced by women in the workplace which can lead to adverse psychological consequences as well as impaired work performance. Interventions need to be aimed at both individual and organizational levels if there is to be a prospect of reducing a major occupational stressor for nurses.

[B] J Am Vet Med Assoc 1996 May 15;208(10):1664-6
Avoiding sexual harassment liability in veterinary practices.
Lacroix CA, Wilson JF
University of Pennsylvania Law School, Whitehouse, NJ 08888, USA.
Harassment based on gender violates the rule of workplace equality established by Title VII of the Civil Rights Act and enforced by the EEOC. There have been few sexual harassment cases involving veterinary professionals, and it is our goal to help keep the number of filed actions to a minimum. The most effective way to avoid hostile environment sexual harassment.):1149-50

[B] J Appl Psychol 1997 Jun;82(3):401-15
Job-related and psychological effects of sexual harassment in the workplace: empirical
evidence from two organizations.
Schneider KT, Swan S, Fitzgerald LF
Department of Psychology, University of Texas at El Paso 79968, USA.
kschneid@mail.utep.edu
Previous evidence regarding the outcomes of sexual harassment in the workplace has come
mainly from self-selected samples or analogue studies or those using inadequate measures.
Results suggest that relatively low-level but frequent types of sexual harassment can have
significant negative consequences for working women.

[B] J Calif Dent Assoc 1996 Jul;24(7):42-8
Published erratum appears in J Calif Dent Assoc 1996 Aug;24(8):10
Controlling liability for sexual harassment complaints.
Gates MM
This article focuses on how an employer can control liability for sexual harassment
complaints. Sexual harassment and the employer's corresponding liabilities and duties are
defined. The proper response to a sexual harassment complaint--conducting a prompt
investigation reasonably calculated to end the harassment--is also detailed. It is through
such an investigation that the employer can restrict or avoid liability for sexual
harassment.

[B] J Gt Houst Dent Soc 1998 Sep;70(2):39-40
What employers should know about sexual harassment grievances.
Shepherd BW

[B] J Healthc Prot Manage 1998-99 Winter;15(1):118-22
Sexual harassment: what every security manager needs to know.
Costello R
SUNY Albany, NY, USA.
Security directors are responsible for protecting against sexual harassment and ultimately
may be civilly liable for any violations, says the author. His goals here are to highlight an
often-overlooked topic, provide the reader with a basic understanding of sexual
harassment, give a background of its growth since 1991, help security managers identify
and prevent sexual harassment, and provide resources for further investigation.

[B] J Healthc Risk Manag 1995 Summer;15(3):18-23
Sexual harassment: what employers and risk managers need to know.
Hovland DL
Smith Bakke & Hovland, Bismarck, ND, USA.

[B] J Healthc Risk Manag 1996 Winter;16(1):10-8
Sexual exploitation by health care professionals: guidelines for risk managers.

Schneider JP, Irons RR
El Dorado Medical Associates, Tucson, AZ, USA.

[B] J Occup Health Psychol 1996 Apr;1(2):224-35
Gender and ethnic differences in social constraints among a sample of New York
City police officers.
Morris A
School of Public Health, Health Policy and Administration, University of
California, Berkeley 94720-7360, USA.
Gender and ethnic differences in social constraints on and off the job among a sample of
372 police officers was examined.

[B] J Occup Health Psychol 1998 Jan;3(1):19-32
Stressors and adverse outcomes for female construction workers.
Goldenhar LM, Swanson NG, Hurrell JJ Jr, Ruder A, Deddens J
National Institute for Occupational Safety and Health, Cincinnati, Ohio 45226, USA.
The authors examined the impact of a number of job stressors, including sexual
harassment and gender-based discrimination, on female construction workers' level of job
satisfaction and psychological and physical health. Perceptions of overcompensation at
work and job uncertainty were positively associated with self-reports of insomnia. Finally,
sexual harassment and gender discrimination were positively related to reports of increased
nausea and headaches.

[B] J Occup Health Psychol 1998 Jan;3(1):33-43
Gender harassment, job satisfaction, and distress among employed white and
minority women.
Piotrkowski CS
Graduate School of Social Service, Fordham University, New York, NY 10023, USA.
This study tested the hypotheses that gender harassment is related to decreased job
satisfaction and increased distress, and that White and minority women differ in their
responses to it, in a sample of 385 women office workers. Findings indicate that gender
harassment is a commonplace workplace stressor that warrants serious attention.

[B] J Occup Health Psychol 1998 Jan;3(1):3-6
Sexual harassment at work. Introduction.
Quick JC
University of Texas at Arlington 76019-0313, USA. jquick@uta.edu
This article introduces the special section on sexual harassment at work. It discusses the
importance of sexual harassment as a continuing, chronic occupational health psychology
problem to which the public health and preventive medicine notions of prevention may be
applied. The article discusses the dilemmas in conducting and reviewing research on
harassment, briefly examining some alternative methods of inquiry. The preventive
management of sexual harassment is suggested.

[B] J Occup Health Psychol 1998 Jan;3(1):7-18
Personal and organizational predictors of workplace sexual harassment of women by men.
Dekker I, Barling J
School of Business, Queen's University, Kingston, Ontario, Canada.
The authors investigated the predictors of workplace sexual harassment in 278 male
university faculty and staff (M age = 45 years). Findings are discussed as they relate to
organizational efforts to reduce or prevent sexual harassment.

[B] J Psychol 1996 Nov;130(6):627-33
The relationship between age and gender in workers' attitudes toward sexual harassment.
Ford CA, Donis FJ
Dept. of Psychology, Central Connecticut State University, New Britain, CT 06050, USA.
The relationship between gender, age, and workers' attitudes toward sexual harassment as
measured by the Sexual Harassment Attitudes Scale was examined. Participants were full-
time workers employed at a local hardware-manufacturing company or a local utility
company in New England. Results indicated that the women younger than 40 years old
were significantly less tolerant of sexual harassment than older women were. In contrast,
male workers' tolerance of sexual harassment decreased with age up until the age of 50
years, after which their tolerance level of sexual harassment increased significantly.

[B] Lindemann, Barbara, 1935-
Sexual harassment in employment law / Barbara Lindemann, David D. Kadue.
Washington, D.C. : Bureau of National Affairs, c1992.
lvi, 824 p. ; 26 cm.
LC Call No.: KF3467 .L56 1992
ISBN: 0871797046
Includes bibliographical references and index.
Subjects: Sexual harassment of women -- Law and legislation -- United States.
Sex discrimination in employment -- Law and legislation -- United States.
Other authors: Kadue, David D.
Source: DLC DLC SNN

[B] MacKinnon, Catharine A.
Sexual harassment of working women: a case of sex discrimination/ Catharine A.
MacKinnon; foreword by Thomas I. Emerson
New Haven; London: Yale University Press, 1979
xiv,312p; 22cm
Includes index
ISBN 0-300-02299-9 Pbk: £3.75
Subjects: Women--Employment--United States
Sexual harassment of women--United States

[B] Massachusetts. Governor's Office on Women's Issues.

Sexual harassment at the workplace : it's no laughing matter / prepared by Governor's Office on Women's Issues.
[Boston, Mass.] : The Office, [1988]
i, 31 p. ; 28 cm.
Local Call No: HD6060.3 .M38 1988
"November 1988."
Title on cover: Sexual harassment in the workplace.
Bibliography: p. 30-31.
Subjects: Sexual harassment -- Massachusetts. Sex role in the work environment -- Massachusetts.
Other titles: Sexual harassment in the workplace.
Source: MAS MAS

[B] Mich Med 1995 Feb;94(2):30-2
Sexual harassment in the medical workplace.
Werbinski J

[B] Mich Med 1997 Jan;96(1):8, 43
Sexual harassment. Work environment policies demand attention.
Weber RD

[B] Mo Dent J 1996 Jan-Feb;76(1):35-7
Sexual harassment in the dental work place ... a student's experience.
Gilbert JA
School of Dentistry, University of Missouri-Kansas City, USA.

[B] N C Med J 1996 Jul-Aug;57(4):208-12
A case of professional sexual misconduct.

[B] NiCarthy, Ginny.
You don't have to take it! : a woman's guide to confronting emotional abuse at work / Ginny NiCarthy, Naomi Gottlieb, Sandra Coffman.
Seattle, WA : Seal Press, 1993.
xv, 377 p. ; 23 cm.
LC Call No.: HD6060.3 .N53 1993
ISBN: 1878067354
Includes bibliographical references (p. 357-370) and index.
Subjects: Sexual harassment of women. Sex role in the work environment.
Source: DLC DLC JTE MTH

[B] No easy path for women in non-traditional careers
Spain, Valerie
Techniques.v. 72 (Apr. 1997) p. 17-21.
The sexual discrimination faced by women who want to break into male-dominated careers

is discussed. Examples of the efforts being made by private consultants and federally funded education groups around the country to counsel employers and employees on tolerance, diversity, respect, and responsibility are outlined.

[B] Okla Nurse 1996 Apr-Jun;41(2):5
Sexual harassment: eliminating it from the workplace.
Monarch K

[B] Other women
O'Sullivan, Gerry
The Humanist.v. 52 May/June 1992 p. 47.
If the testimony of Rose Jordain and Angela Wright had been heard during Clarence Thomas's confirmation hearings before the Senate Judiciary Committee, says Lynda Edwards in the March issue of Spy, Thomas might not have been confirmed as a Supreme Court justice. Wright is the "other woman" Thomas supposedly harassed, and Jordain is alleged to have heard from Wright some details of the harassment at the time that Wright claims it occurred. Both women were willing to testify, but Sen. Joseph Biden, bullied by a Republican stampede, offered to have their testimony entered into the public record without rebuttal to save time. Neither woman's story was circulated, and the Federal News Service has apparently expunged Jordain's testimony from official hearing transcripts.

[B] Peters, Cara.
How to stop sexual harassment : strategies for women on the job / Cara Peters and Erin Van Bronkhorst. 2nd ed.
Seattle, Wash. : Facts for Women, 1982.
32 p. : ill. ; 18 cm.
Local Call No: HD6060 .P37 1982
Subjects: Sexual harassment. Women -- Employment.
Other authors: Van Bronkhorst, Erin.
Source: OSU OSU SNN

[B] Pflege Aktuell 1995 Feb;49(2):90-1
[Sexual molestation in the work place].
[Article in German]
Mrkwicka L

[B] Plast Surg Nurs 1998 Summer;18(2):99-102
Sexual harassment: establishing a workplace policy and procedure.
Cericola SA
Southern California Surgery Center, Huntington Park, USA.

[B] Prevalence and correlates of harassment among US women physicians
Frank, Erica; Brogan, Donna; Schiffman, Melissa
Archives of Internal Medicine.v. 158 no4 Feb. 23 1998 p. 352-8.

A study investigated the prevalence and correlates of harassment experiences among U.S. women physicians. The study group consisted of the 4,501 respondents to the Women Physicians' Health Study. Nearly half the women reported being harassed on the basis of gender, and more than one third reported some form of sexual harassment. Differences occur among individuals in terms of experiences of and sensitivity to harassment, and harassment may produce significant professional and personal consequences. Younger physicians reported higher rates of sexual harassment, suggesting that the situation is not improving.

[B] Prevention of sexual harrassment in the work place : a practical guide for employees, supervisors, and managers / prepared by the Office of Equal Opportunity, Federal Women's Program, Western Area Power Administration.
[Washington, D.C.?] : The Administration, [1985]
iv, 67 p.
Added t.p.: Prevention of sexual harassment in the work place.
"Regional Depository D-487. June 1985."
Includes index and bibliography: p. 57-58.
Photocopy. Oklahoma : Oklahoma Dept. of Libraries, 1997.
s 1997 oku n r.
Subjects: Sexual harassment -- United States. Sex discrimination in employment -- United States.
Other authors: United States. Western Area Power Administration.
Office of Equal Opportunity. Federal Women's Program.
Source: SNN SNN

[B] Pringle, Rosemary
Secretaries talk: sexuality, power and work/ Rosemary Pringle
Sydney; London: Allen & Unwin, 1988
xiv,283p; 23cm
Includes bibliographical references and index
Subjects: Secretaries, Sex discrimination against women, Sexual harassment of women, Feminism

[B] Pringle, Rosemary.
Secretaries talk : sexuality, power, and work / Rosemary Pringle.
London ; New York : Verso, 1989.
xiv, 283 p. : ill. ; 23 cm.
LC Call No.: HD8039.S58 P75 1989
ISBN: 0860912345
0860919501 (pbk.)
Includes bibliographical references (p. 272-278) and index.
Subjects: Secretaries. Sex discrimination against women. Sexual harassment of women. Feminism.
Source: DLC DLC MTH

[B] Protesting sexual harassment: was this a hostile work environment?
Nursing 98.v. 28 no9 Sept. 1998 p. 82.
The sexual harassment case brought by nurse Dolores Farpella-Crosby against the
Horizon Health Care Corporation is discussed. Farpella-Crosby testified that the director
of nursing at her work facility had made sexually offensive comments 2 or 3 times a week.
She also testified that she informed the human resources director about the situation and
that Horizon knew, or should have known, about her work environment. The judge
overturned a punitive damage award by the jury, due to poor evidence that Horizon knew
of the offensive comments, but upheld $7,500 in compensatory damages.

[B] Psychol Rep 1996 Feb;78(1):329-30
Sexual harassment: the "reasonable person" vs "reasonable woman" standards have
not been resolved.
Woody WD, Viney W, Bell PA, Bensko NL
Department of Psychology, Colorado State University, Fort Collins 80523, USA.
Previous research suggests that women are more likely than men to perceive a hostile
environment of sexual harassment in job-related scenarios. Such findings raise questions
about whether a "reasonable woman" standard might be preferable to a "reasonable
person" standard for adjudication of some sexual harassment cases. There are sound
arguments for both positions, and there is no basis at the present time for unequivocal and
categorical support for one position over the other.

[B] Russell, Diana E. H.
Sexual exploitation : rape, child sexual abuse, and workplace harassment / Diana E.H.
Russell.
Beverly Hills, California: Sage Publications, c1984.
319 p. ; 23 cm.
Series: Sage library of social research ; v. 155.
LC Call No.: HV6565.C2 R87 1984
ISBN: 0803923546
0803923554 (pbk.)
Includes indexes and bibliography: p. 291-303.
Subjects: Rape -- California. Child sexual abuse -- California. Sexual harassment --
California.
Source: DLC DLC AUM

[B] Segrave, Kerry, 1944-
The sexual harassment of women in the workplace, 1600 to 1993 / by Kerry Segrave.
Jefferson, N.C. : McFarland, c1994.
vi, 273 p. ; 24 cm.
LC Call No.: HD6060.3 .S43 1994
ISBN: 0786400072 (lib. bdg. : alk. paper)
Includes bibliographical references (p. 225-263) and index.

Subjects: Sexual harassment of women -- History.
Sex discrimination in employment -- History.
Source: DLC DLC UKM AMH
Control No.: 29796939

[B] Sex, lies, and the public sphere: some reflections on the confirmation of Clarence Thomas
Fraser, Nancy
Critical Inquiry.v. 18 Spring 1992 p. 595-612.

[B] Sexual harassment
Augmented title: Joseph Oncale v. Sundowner Offshore Services, Inc.
Pitman, Andrew
Journal of Physical Education, Recreation and Dance.v. 70 no1 (Jan. 1999) p. 9-10.
In Joseph Oncale v. Sundowner Offshore Services, Inc., Oncale lodged a complaint against Sundowner, maintaining that he was discriminated against because of his sex. The crux of the case was whether workplace harassment can violate Title VII's prohibition against discrimination because of sex when the harasser and the harassed employee are of the same sex. In its decision, the U.S. Supreme Court determined that sex discrimination consisting of same-sex sexual harassment is actionable under Title VII. Risk management advice about sexual harassment in the workplace is presented.

[B] Sexual harassment and generalized workplace abuse among university employees: prevalence and mental health correlates.
Richman JA, Rospenda KM, Nawyn SJ, Flaherty JA, Fendrich M, Drum ML, Johnson TP
Department of Psychiatry, University of Illinois at Chicago 60612, USA.
jrichman@uic.edu
This study hypothesized that interpersonal workplace stressors involving sexual harassment and generalized workplace abuse are highly prevalent and significantly linked with mental health outcomes including symptomatic distress, the use and abuse of alcohol, and other drug use. Interpersonally abusive workplace dynamics constitute a significant public health problem that merits increased intervention and prevention strategies.

[B] Sexual harassment and generalized workplace abuse among university employees: prevalence and mental health correlates
Richman, Judith A; Rospenda, Kathleen M; Nawyn, Stephanie J
American Journal of Public Health.v. 89 no3 Mar. 1999 p. 358-63.
This study hypothesized that interpersonal workplace stressors involving sexual harassment and generalized workplace abuse are highly prevalent and significantly linked with mental health outcomes including symptomatic distress, the use and abuse of alcohol, and other drug use. The data show high rates of harassment and abuse. Among faculty, females were subjected to higher rates; among clerical and service workers, males were subjected to higher rates. Male and female clerical and service workers experienced higher levels of particularly severe mistreatment. Generalized abuse was more prevalent than

harassment for all groups. Both harassment and abuse were significantly linked to most mental health outcomes for men and women.

[B] Sexual harassment at work
London, 1982

[B] *Sexual Harassment* in the Federal Workplace: Is It a Problem? A Report of the U.S. Merit Systems Protection Board Office of Merit Systems Review and Studies.
Mathis, Patricia A.; Prokop, Ruth T.
This report represents the culmination of a year-long evaluation of the nature and extent of *sexual harassment* in the federal government. The appendices contain the methodology, definitions, survey questionnaire, additional statistical analyses, official policy documents, agency actions, a literature review, and an annotated bibliography. (Author/NRB)

[B] *Sexual Harassment* in the Law Enforcement Workplace.
Irons, Nicholas H.
Considerable confusion exists over male/female relationships in the work place, especially in such male-dominated professions as law enforcement. The laws governing *sexual harassment* offer unclear guidelines regarding the definition of harm that results from such *harassment*. This paper addresses the special problems of *sexual harassment* in the police officer's world.

[B] Sexual harassment in the workplace : perspectives, frontiers, and response strategies / edited by Margaret S. Stockdale.
Thousand Oaks, Calif. : Sage, c1996.
xiv, 303 p. : ill. ; 23 cm.
Series: Women and work: a research policy series, 0882-0910 ; v. 5.
Local Call No: HD6050 .W65
ISBN: 0803957939
0803957947 (paper)
Includes bibliographical references and index. What we know and what we need to learn about sexual harassment / Margaret S. Stockdale. -- Sexual harassment in the academy: the case of women professors / Elizabeth Grauerholz. -- Sexual harassment and women of color: issues, challenges, and future directions / Audrey J. Murrell. -- Men's misperceptions of women's interpersonal behaviors and sexual harassment / Frank E. Saal. -- The implications of U.S. Supreme Court and Circuit Court decisions for hostile environment sexual harassment cases / Ramona L. Paetzold and Anne M. O'Leary-Kelly. -- Organizational influences on sexual harassment / Charles L. Hulin, Louise F. Fitzgerald, and Fritz Drasgow. -- Sexual harassment types and severity: linking research and policy / James E. Gruber, Michael Smith, and Kaisa Kauppinen-Toropainen. -- An integrated framework for studying the outcomes of sexual harassment: consequences for individuals and organizations / Kathy A. Hanisch. -- The real "disclosure": sexual harassment and the bottom line / Deborah Erdos Knapp and Gary A. Kustis. -- Understanding sexual harassment: contributions from research on domestic violence and organizational change /

Jeanette N. Cleveland and Kathleen McNamara. -- Dealing with harassment: a systems approach / Mary P. Rowe. -- Sexual harassment at work: when an organization fails to respond / Barbara A. Gutek.
Subjects: Sexual harassment -- United States. Sex discrimination -- United States.
Series Entry: Women and work (Beverly Hills, Calif.) ; v. 5.
Source: AJB AJB SNN

[B] Sexual harassment of women journalists
Walsh Childers, Kim; Chance, Jean; Herzog, Kristin, 1929
Journalism and Mass Communication Quarterly.v. 73 Autumn 1996 p. 559-81.
A survey of 227 women newspaper journalists revealed that more than 60 percent believe sexual harassment is at least somewhat a problem for women journalists; more than one-third said harassment has been at least somewhat a problem for them personally. Two-thirds experience nonphysical sexual harassment at least sometimes, and about 17 percent experience physical sexual harassment at least sometimes. News sources were the most frequent harassers, and harassment ranged from degrading comments to sexual assault.

[B] Sexual harassment of working women: a case of sex discrimination
New Haven, 1979
Mackinnon, C.A.

[B] Sexual harassment, work, and education: a resource manual for prevention
Paludi, Michele Antoinette; Barickman, Richard
State Univ. of N.Y. Press, 1998. 194 p.

[B] Sexual harassment/ producer Chris Oxley; director Cathy Elliott
[London]: Laurel Productions for Channel Four, 1996
1 videocassette (60min)
Series Cutting edge
Subjects: 658.386
Sexual harassment – videocassette, Work environment - videocassette

[B] Sexual Harassment: A Common Sample for the University and the Workplace.
Beauregard, Terri Kinion
The sexual harassment experienced by a sample of women (N=154) in a university setting was compared with the sexual harassment experienced by them in a workplace setting.

[B] *Sexual Harassment*: What It Is, Where It Is, and What to Do About It.
Weston, Ralph
Community & Junior College Libraries; v8 n1 p37-61 1995
Reviews issues and relevant court decisions related to *sexual harassment* in the workplace. Focuses on definitions and types of *sexual harassment*, circumstances and institutional settings under which it occurs, its effects on an organization, and steps an organization might take to keep *sexual harassment* out of the workplace. (35 citations) (MAB)

[B] Siegel, Deborah L.
Sexual harassment : research & resources : a report / prepared by the National Council for Research on Women ; [written by Deborah L. Siegel ; revised by Marina Budhos]. 3rd ed.
New York, NY : National Council for Research on Women, c1995.
iv, 90 p. ; 28 cm.
LC Call No.: HD6060.5.U5 S56 1995
ISBN: 1880547201 (pbk.)
Includes bibliographical references (p. 53-66)
Subjects: Sexual harassment of women -- United States. Sex discrimination in employment -- United States. Sexual harassment of women -- United States -- Information services. Sex discrimination in employment -- United States -- Information services.
Other authors: Budhos, Marina Tamar.
Other authors: National Council for Research on Women (U.S.)
Source: ISL ISL SNN

[B] Surviving sexual harassment
Howard, Melanie
American Health (New York, N.Y.).v. 18 no7 July/Aug. 1999 p. 24+.
The writer discusses the health impact, including post-traumatic stress disorder, of sexual harassment undergone by three women--Judy Jarvela, Lois Jenson, and Mavie Maki--at Eveleth Mines in northern Minnesota. Twenty-three women members of the workforce made history in 1988 when they launched the nation's first class-action sexual harassment suit against the company. After five years, the women were vindicated in federal court, when the mine was found liable for sexual harassment, but the 17 plaintiffs who remained at the end of the legal fight received a mere $182,000. The award decision was then overturned on appeal, and the case was finally settled out of court for an undisclosed figure. A sidebar offers advice on protecting yourself against sexual harassment at work.

[B] The Clarence Thomas hearings
Boot, William
Columbia Journalism Review.v. 30 Jan./Feb. 1992 p. 25-9.
The media's coverage of the Clarence Thomas-Anita Hill sexual harassment dispute drew protests from people all along the political spectrum. The writer evaluates complaints that reporters were out to block Thomas by exploiting a news leak, that there was a pervasive liberal bias in coverage, that the story was sensationalized, that too much graphic detail was provided, and that the media were manipulated by Republicans and used as tools to demolish Hill. He notes that the media provided critical commentary but that it had little effect on the public, probably because people watched the hearings and drew their own conclusions.

[B] The inappropriate patient
Sfikas, Peter M
Journal of the American Dental Association.v. 129 no9 Sept. 1998 p. 1312-15.

The sexual harassment of dental practice employees by nonemployees or patients is discussed. In the U.S., several federal courts of appeal and federal district courts have held that an employee has a "cause of action" against his employer when harassed by a nonemployee in the workplace. The Equal Employment Opportunity Commission's Guidelines Based on Sex also holds this opinion. Employers can be found liable if they know, or should know, that harassment is taking place and fail to take immediate remedial action.

[B] Tidsskr Sykepl 1997 Sep 2;85(14):8-13
[A working day with harassment, threats and violence].
[Article in Norwegian]
Aase KA

[B] Todays Surg Nurse 1996 Mar-Apr;18(2):50-1
Sexual harassment in the workplace (part I).
Rosen LF

[B] Trying times at Oak Ridge and beyond
Augmented title: for Ellen Cleminshaw Weaver
Horning, Beth
Technology Review.v. 96 Nov./Dec. 1993 p. 38-9.
Ellen Cleminshaw Weaver, who participated in the Manhattan Project as a chemist at Oak Ridge National Laboratory, has encountered gender-based discrimination throughout her career. At Oak Ridge, she and other women were paid a low hourly wage and required to punch a time clock, while men with the same qualifications were paid a salary that gave them twice as much take-home pay. Later, as a graduate student in biochemistry at the University of California at Berkeley, she received little encouragement. She eventually earned her Ph.D. and became well respected in her field, but she continued to experience discrimination and sexual harassment. She asserts that scientific institutions have made little progress toward rectifying this situation and that there are few women at the highest levels of academic administration.

[B] U.S. Supreme Court decision clarifies sexual harassment issues of employers, colleges
Kaplan, Rochelle K
Journal of Career Planning and Employment.v. 59 no1 (Fall 1998) p. 10-13+.

[B] United States. Merit Systems Protection Board.
Sexual harassment in the federal workplace : trends, progress, continuing challenges : a report to the President and the Congress of the United States / by the U.S. Merit Systems Protection Board.
Washington, DC (1120 Vermont Ave., NW, Washington
20419) : The Board : For sale by the U.S. G.P.O.,
Supt. of Docs., [1995]
xii, 73 p. : ill., forms ; 28 cm.

Local Call No: HD6060.5.U5 A35 1995
MS 1.2 SE 9/3
ISBN: 0160483700 : $6.00
Shipping list no.: 96-0046-P.
"October 1995"--1st prelim. p.
Includes bibliographical references.
Availability: 062-000-00041-4 GPO
Subjects: Sexual harassment -- United States. United States -- Officials and employees --
Discipline. Sex discrimination in employment -- United States.
Source: GPO GPO GAO SLU GPO SNN

[B] United States. Office of Merit Systems Review and Studies.
Sexual harassment in the federal workplace : is it a problem?: a report of the U.S. Merit
Systems Protection Board, Office of Merit Systems Review and Studies.
[Washington, D.C.] : The Board : For sale by the Supt. of Docs., U.S. G.P.O., 1981.
ca. 200 p. : charts, forms ; 27 cm.
Local Call No: JK721 .A74
JK721 .U5
MS 1.2 Se9. $6.00
"March 1981."
Bibliography: p. [H1-H14]
Availability: 062-000-00005-8 GPO
Subjects: Sexual harassment of women -- United States. Sexual harassment. United States
-- Officials and employees -- Attitudes.
Other authors: United States. Merit Systems Protection Board.
Source: HEW HEW GPO SNN

[B] United States. Small Business Administration. Office of Equal Employment
Opportunity.
Reference manual for the prevention of sexual harassment / prepared by Special Emphasis
Program Manager, U.S. Small Business Administration, Office of Equal Employment
Opportunity.
[Washington, D.C.?] : U.S. Small Business Administration, Office of Equal Employment
Opportunity, [1993]
1 v. (various pagings) : ill. ; 28 cm.
Local Call No: HD6060.3 .U5 1993
Shipping list no.: 93-0512-S.
"July 1993."
Includes bibliographical references.
Subjects: United States. Small Business Administration. Office of Equal Employment
Opportunity -- Handbooks, manuals, etc. Sexual harassment -- United States --
Handbooks, manuals, etc. Civil service -- United States -- Personnel management --
Handbooks, manuals, etc.
Other authors: United States. Small Business Administration. Office of Equal Employment

Opportunity. Special Emphasis Program Manager.
Source: GPO GPO AMH

[B] Violence Vict 1997 Fall;12(3):247-63
Harassment in the workplace and the victimization of men.
Einarsen S, Raknes BI
University of Bergen, Norway.
Harassment and victimization among male workers were studied in a sample of 460
industrial workers, supervisors and managers within a Norwegian marine engineering
industry. The results indicated that aggression and harassment are significant problems in
this organizational setting. Significant correlations were found between exposure to
harassment and both job satisfaction and psychological health and well-being. Strong
correlations were found between exposure to harassment and dissatisfaction with coworker interaction.

[B] WMJ 1998 Dec;97(11):62-3
Minimizing an employer's risk of liability for sexual harassment.
Cohen M

[B] Your rights in the workplace
Drake, Larry; Moskowitz, Rachel
Occupational Outlook Quarterly.v. 41 (Summer 1997) p. 14-21.
Over the last 100 years, a collection of laws, rules, and regulations has evolved to protect
workers' rights. These regulations cover many aspects of work. An overview of major
laws is presented that focuses on some of the most important issues for workers: wages
and required work hours, unemployment, safety, compensation for work-related injuries
and illnesses, protection from discrimination and sexual harassment, the right to join a
union, and employer administration of drug or polygraph tests.

3) Sexual Harassment in the Military

[C] 102d Congress, 2d session. Committee print. No. 12.
Distributed to some depository libraries in microfiche.
Shipping list no.: 92-0702-P.
"September 14, 1992."
Subjects: United States. Navy -- Women. Tailhook Symposium. Sexual harassment of women -- United States. Sex discrimination in employment -- United States. United States -- Armed Forces -- Women.

[C] Aviat Space Environ Med 1997 Oct;68(10):879-85
Interpersonal relationship and prisoner of war concerns of rated military male and female aircrew.
Voge VM, King RE
Naval School of Health Sciences, San Diego Detachment, Ft. Sam Houston, TX, USA.
The issue of women flying military aircraft in a combat role has been very controversial. To succeed, female military aircrew are very similar to their male peers. Although responding in a similar manner to most questions, male and female military aircrew differ in the perception of their ability to function in mixed squadrons because of their gender. Some of these perceptions can be modified through training, others may need to be resolved through high level orders/policy; while in others, the military may have to accept women are different from men in some aspects.

[C] DOD Service Academies. Update on Extent of *Sexual Harassment*. Report to Congressional Requesters.
This report provides an update on the nature and extent of *sexual harassment* at the three Department of Defense (DOD) service academies. Three appendixes provide survey response data on *sexual harassment* at U.S. service academies, the DOD definition of *sexual harassment*, and a description of the questionnaire methodology. (MDM)

[C] Honor Systems and *Sexual Harassment* at the Service Academies. Hearing before the Committee on Armed Services. United States Senate, One Hundred Third Congress, Second Session.
The U.S. Senate held a hearing to address two issues facing the nation's armed service academies--honor systems and *sexual harassment*. This was the first of several oversight hearings to be held regarding the service academies. Two events prompted the Senate to hold these hearings: (1) a cheating scandal at the U.S. Naval Academy that began in 1992; and (2) the publication of a U.S. General Accounting Office (GAO) report in 1994 entitled

"DOD Service Academies: More Action Needed to Eliminate *Sexual Harassment*." The hearing document includes the presentations of all three panels as well as text from the GAO report and the "Report of the Honor Review Committee to the Secretary of the Navy On Honor at the United States Naval Academy." (CK)

[C] J Psychosoc Nurs Ment Health Serv 1998 Aug;36(8):19-25
Wartime stressors and health outcomes: women in the Persian Gulf War.
Bell EA, Roth MA, Weed G
Veterans Administration Outpatient Clinic, Savannah, Georgia, USA.
This descriptive correlational study of war time stressors and stress responses of women from the Persian Gulf War examined numerous stressors both physical and psychological. The psychological stressors more directly impacted postwar physical and psychological symptoms than did physical stressors. These findings add to our understanding of women's reactions to wartime stress and the types of stressors affecting women. The study provides more data to support the contention that sexual harassment is widely prevalent in the military.

[C] Mil Med 1998 Feb;163(2):63-7
Psychological effects of sexual harassment, appraisal of harassment, and organizational climate among U.S. Army soldiers.
Rosen LN, Martin L
Walter Reed Army Institute of Research, Department of Military Psychiatry, Washington, DC 20307-5100, USA.
This study examines the effects of three types of unwanted sexual experiences in the workplace on the psychological well-being of male and female U.S. Army soldiers, and the mediating or moderating roles of appraisal of sexual harassment, organizational climate, and the sociodemographic profile of victims. Unwanted sexual experiences were found to be significant predictors of psychological symptoms for male and female soldiers.

[C] Posttraumatic stress disorder among female Vietnam veterans: a causal model of etiology
Fontana, Alan; Schwartz, Linda Spoonster; Rosenheck, Robert
American Journal of Public Health.v. 87 Feb. 1997 p. 169-75.
The Vietnam and Persian Gulf wars have awakened people to the realization that military service can be traumatizing for women as well as men. This study investigated the etiological roles of both war and sexual trauma in the development of chronic posttraumatic stress disorder among female Vietnam veterans. Within the constraints and assumptions of causal modeling, there is evidence that both war trauma and sexual trauma are powerful contributors to the development of posttraumatic stress disorder among female Vietnam veterans.

[C] Sexual assault on men in war
Carlson, Eric Stener
Lancet (North American edition).v. 349 Jan. 11 1997 p. 129.

Male sexual assault during war has received little recognition and is still a poorly understood, underinvestigated offense. However, measures can be taken to help male victims of sexual assault and to better understand the issues involved. Legislative changes are necessary, and medical personnel and police investigators should be trained and educated so that they can deal more sensitively and effectively with victims of male sexual assault.

[C] Tailhook 91.
[Washington, DC] : Dept. of Defense, Office of Inspector General, Assistant Inspector General for Investigations : Assistant Inspector General for Departmental Inquiries : For sale by the U.S. G.P.O., Supt. of Docs., [1992-1993]
2 v. : ill. (some col.) ; 29 cm.
Local Call No: VB223 .T34 1992
ISBN: 0160416639 (pt.2) : $18.00
Shipping list no.: 93-0243-P (pt. 2)
"September 1992."
"February 1993"--Pt. 2, cover.
Pt. 1. Review of the Navy investigations -- pt. 2. Events at the 35th Annual Tailhook Symposium.
Availability: 008-000-00623-7 (pt.2) GPO
Subjects: United States. Naval Investigation Service. United States. Navy -- Inspection. Tailhook Symposium. Sexual harassment of women -- Nevada -- Las Vegas. United States -- Armed Forces -- Women.
Other authors: United States. Dept. of Defense. Assistant Inspector General for Investigations. United States. Dept. of Defense. Assistant Inspector General for Departmental Inquiries.
Source: ARL ARL GPO MTH

[C] United States. Congress. House. Committee on Armed Services.
Sexual harassment of military women and improving the military complaint system : hearing before the Committee on Armed Services, House of Representatives, One Hundred Third Congress, second session, hearing held March 9, 1994.
Washington : U.S. G.P.O. : For sale by the U.S. G.P.O., Supt. of Docs., Congressional Sales Office, 1994.
iii, 276 p. : ill. ; 23 cm.
LC Call No.: KF27 .A7 1994b
Local Call No: UB418.W65 U45 1994
ISBN: 0160462207
Distributed to some depository libraries in microfiche.
Shipping list no.: 94-0413-P.
"H.A.S.C. no. 103-44."
Subjects: Sexual harassment of women -- United States. United States -- Armed Forces -- Women – Crimes against. Complaints (Military law) -- United States.
Source: DGPO/DLC GPO DLC MTH

[C] United States. Congress. Senate. Committee on Armed Services.
Army sexual harassment incidents at Aberdeen Proving Ground and sexual harassment
policies within the Department of Defense : hearing before the Committee on Armed
Services, United States Senate, One Hundred Fifth Congress, 1st session, Feb. 4, 1997.
Washington : U.S. G.P.O. : For sale by the U.S. G.P.O., Supt. of Docs., Congressional
Sales Office, 1997.
iii, 92 p. : ill. ; 24 cm.
Series: S. hrg. ; 105-76.
LC Call No.: KF26 .A7 1997
ISBN: 0160552753
Distributed to some depository libraries in microfiche.
Shipping list no.: 97-0332-P.
Subjects: United States. Dept. of Defense. United States -- Armed Forces -- Women –
Crimes against. Sexual harassment of women -- Maryland – Aberdeen Proving Ground.
Sexual harassment -- Government policy – United States.
Series Entry: United States. Congress. Senate. S. hrg. ; 105-76.
Source: DGPO/DLC GPO DLC

[C] Violence Vict 1998 Fall;13(3):269-86
Childhood maltreatment history as a risk factor for sexual harassment among U.S.
Army soldiers.
Rosen LN, Martin L
Department of Military Psychiatry, Walter Reed Army Institute of Research,
Washington, DC 20307-5100, USA.
Four different types of childhood maltreatment were examined as predictors of unwanted
sexual experiences and acknowledged sexual harassment among male and female active
duty soldiers in the United States Army. A greater variety of types of childhood
maltreatment predicted sexual harassment outcomes for male soldiers. Childhood
maltreatment and adult sexual harassment were predictors of psychological well-being for
soldiers of both genders.

[C] VMI sets rules for first female class
Black Issues in Higher Education.v. 14 (June 12 1997) p. 11.
Virginia Military Institute has set the rules and policies for its first female cadets. A report
filed in the U.S. District Court outlines the institute's sexual harassment and fraternization
policies, along with rules that include close-cropped haircuts, no makeup, and sleeping in
unlocked barracks.

[C] Wives and warriors : women and the military in the United States and Canada / edited
by Laurie Weinstein and Christie C. White ; foreword by Cynthia Enloe.
Westport, Conn. : Bergin & Garvey, 1997.
xix, 252 p. ; 24 cm.
LC Call No.: U21.75 .W58 1997

ISBN: 0897895266 (pbk.)
089789491X (alk. paper)
Includes bibliographical references and index. Blue navy blues: submarine officers and the two-person career / Laurie Weinstein and Helen Mederer -- The social networks of naval officers' wives: their composition and function / Barbara Marriott -- Gender, the military, and military family support / Deborah Harrison and Lucie Laliberté -- The "military academy": metaphors of family for pedagogy and public life / Abigail E. Adams -- Women in combat: the U.S. military and the impact of the Persian Gulf War/Georgia Clark Sadler --Behind the front lines: feminist battles over women in combat/Lucinda Joy Peach -- Sexual harassment in the Army/Lynn Meola --Conduct unbecoming: second annual report on "Don't ask, don't tell, don't pursue"/C. Dixon Osburn and Michelle M. Benecke -- Understanding women's exit from the Canadian forces: implications for integration?/Karen D. Davis --Policing the U.S. military's race and gender lines/Francine D'Amico --Tailhook: deinstitutionalizing the military's "woman problem"/Francine D'Amico.
Subjects: Women and the military -- United States. Women and the military -- Canada.
Source: DLC DLC C#P VVC NLC

[C] Women in the military : the Tailhook affair and the problem of sexual harassment : report of the Military Personnel and Compensation Subcommittee and Defense Policy Panel of the Committee on Armed Services, House of Representatives, One Hundred Second Congress, second session.
Washington : U.S. G.P.O. : For sale by the U.S.
G.P.O., Supt. of Docs., Congressional Sales Office, 1992.
v, 121 p. : ill. ; 24 cm.
Local Call No: UB418.W65 W6534 1992
ISBN: 0160392624

[C] Women in the *Military*. Hearings before the *Military* Personnel and Compensation Subcommitee of the Committee on Armed Services, House of Representatives. One Hundredth Congress, First and Second Sessions (October 1, November 19, 1987 and February 4, 1988).
Within this document is the testimony delivered by 15 individuals at congressional hearings. Among the issues spoken to are: the combat exclusion law and its effect on the careers of women in the *military*; the kinds of jobs open to female armed services personnel; special problems that women in the *military* face; their promotion and retention rates; *sexual harassment* of *military* women and the wives of male personnel; and the dissatisfaction of *military* spouses.

[C] Zimmerman, Jean.
Tailspin : women at war in the wake of Tailhook / Jean Zimmerman. 1st ed.
New York : Doubleday, c1995.
336 p. : ill., [16] p. of plates ; 25 cm.
LC Call No.: VB324.W65 Z55 1995
ISBN: 0385477899 : $24.95

Includes bibliographical references (p. [321]-328) and index.
Subjects: United States. Navy -- Women. Tailhook Scandal, 1991-1993. Women in combat -- United States. Sexual harassment of women -- United States. United States -- Armed Forces -- Women.
Source: DLC DLC IJC MTH

4) LAWS AND LEGISLATION ON SEXUAL HARASSMENT

[D] A new harassment ruling: implications for colleges
Augmented title: Davis v. Monroe County Board of Education
Williams, Verna L
The Chronicle of Higher Education.v. 45 no41 (June 18 1999) p. A56.

[D] A year in the life of the Supreme Court / by Paul Barrett ... [et al.] ; edited by Rodney
A. Smolla.
Durham, N.C. : Duke University Press, 1995.
300 p. ; 23 cm.
Series: Constitutional conflicts.
LC Call No.: KF8742 .Y43 1995
ISBN: 0822316536 (cloth)
082231665X (pbk.)
Includes index.
A case of old age / Paul Barrett -- The defining moments of Jayne Bray...and Justice
Blackmun / Lyle Denniston -- A search on the street / Richard Carelli -- The interpreter
and the establishment clause / Aaron Epstein -- A question of innocence / Marcia Coyle --
Hate speech, hate crimes, and the First Amendment / David Savage -- Civil rights and
higher education / Kay Kindred -- A claim of sexual harassment / Stephen Wermiel -- The
supremem court and the cult of secrecy / Tony Mauro.
Subjects: United States. Supreme Court. United States -- Constitutional law. Justice,
Administration of -- United States.
Source: DLC DLC ZYF

[D] Appeals court upholds U. of Hawaii's handling of a sexual-harassment complaint
Schneider, Alison
The Chronicle of Higher Education.v. 44 no41 (June 19 1998) p. A12.
A professor's free-speech rights were not violated by the University of Hawaii at Manoa
when it investigated a sexual-harassment claim against him, according to a ruling by a
federal appeals court. The professor's claim that his classroom speech was necessarily
protected by the First Amendment was also rejected by the court.

[D] Balance 1999 May-Jun;3(3):14-5
The Supreme Court opens the door wide for harassment claims.
Lasater NE, McEvoy TJ

[D] Caring 1998 Oct;17(10):48-50
Sexual harassment liability & disability discrimination: new rules apply.
Siegel PJ, Kaplan RS
Jackson, Lewis, Schnitzler and Krupman, Long Island, NY, USA.
Recent decisions by the Supreme Court give some indication of how a court would rule in a sexual harassment or disability discrimination suit. Home care providers need to understand the effect of these rulings and ensure that their own policies are clear and clearly disseminated to employees.

[D] Chan, Anja Angelica.
Women and sexual harassment : a practical guide to the legal protections of Title VII and the hostile environment claim / Anja Angelica Chan.
New York : Haworth Press, c1994.
xiv, 110 p. ; 22 cm.
LC Call No.: KF3467 .C47 1994
ISBN: 1560244089 (acid-free paper)
1560230401 (pbk. : acid-free paper)
Includes bibliographical references and index.
Subjects: Sexual harassment of women -- Law and legislation -- United States.
Discrimination in employment -- Law and legislation -- United States.
Source: DLC DLC MTH

[D] Competing interests
Kirtley, Jane
The Quill (Chicago, Ill.).v. 86 no7 Sept. 1998 p. 24-5.
Part of the 1998 special report on freedom of information. A discussion of access rights to court documents in the United States. The writer considers recent cases where motions were filed to deny access to court documents, including President Clinton's motion to reconsider an order unsealing most of the records in the Paula Jones sexual harassment case. In the judicial as in the executive branch, she argues, the question of public access to computerized records continues to percolate. She notes that the chief judge of Maryland's district courts blocked computerized access to unserved arrest warrants, which are public records, after an entrepreneur began making them available to attorneys to use for solicitation.

[D] Cornell, Drucilla.
The imaginary domain : abortion, pornography & sexual harassment / Drucilla Cornell.
New York : Routledge, 1995.
xii, 292 p. ; 24 cm.
LC Call No.: K644 .C67 1995
ISBN: 0415906008 (cl)
0415911605 (pb)
Includes bibliographical references (p. [275]-283) and index.

SC: Errors slip inserted.
Subjects: Women -- Legal status, laws, etc. Equality before the law. Sex differences.
Abortion. Pornography. Sexual harassment.
Source: DLC DLC MTH

[D] Court weighs harassment by students
Augmented title: Davis v. Monroe County Board of Education
Walsh, Mark
Education Week.v. 18 no19 (Jan. 20 1999) p. 1+.
A lawyer for a Georgia school district has said that the Supreme Court should not entertain
lawsuits seeking to make school districts liable for student-on-student sexual harassment.
The argument presented by the district received a sympathetic reaction from some justices,
who were concerned that ordinary children's behavior could result in a barrage of lawsuits
under Title IX of the Education Amendments of 1972. The argument was presented in the
case of Davis v. Monroe County Board of Education..

[D] Courts split on student harassment
Walsh, Mark
Teacher Magazine.v. 9 (Oct. 1997) p. 16.
The federal courts are continuing to struggle with the issue of whether school districts and
administrators can be held liable when students are sexually harassed by other students. In
August 1997, a federal appeals court in Georgia held that, under most circumstances,
school officials cannot be held liable for incidents of so-called peer sexual harassment.
However, a week before the ruling in Georgia, a federal appeals court in San Francisco
held that school officials have a "clearly established" duty to take "reasonable steps" to
prevent sexual harassment of students by other students.

[D] Danforth, John C.
Resurrection : the confirmation of Clarence Thomas / John C. Danforth. 1st trade ed.
New York : Viking, 1994.
viii, 225 p. ; 24 cm.
LC Call No.: KF8745.T48 D36 1994
ISBN: 0670860220 : $19.95
0453033245
Includes bibliographical references (p. 209-217) and index.
Subjects: Thomas, Clarence, 1948- United States. Supreme Court -- Officials and
employees -- Selection and appointment. Hill, Anita. Sexual harassment of women -- Law
and legislation -- United States.
Source: DLC DLC IAY MTH

[D] DC public library, Franklin in sexual harassment suit
Rogers, Michael, 1960
Library Journal.v. 122 (Oct. 1 1997) p. 14.
Two female managers at the District of Columbia Public Library have filed a sexual

harassment lawsuit implicating its former director Hardy Franklin. The plaintiffs claim that Franklin sexually harassed them for almost 20 years, that their careers were hampered, and that they had to seek psychiatric help as a result of the harassment.

[D] Education Dept. issues guidelines on anti-harassment policies
Lederman, Douglas
The Chronicle of Higher Education.v. 43 (Mar. 21 1997) p. A39.
The education department's guidelines to help colleges deal with the sexual harassment of students by their peers or professors have been welcomed by college officials. The guidelines, which were prepared by the agency's Office for Civil Rights, define sexual harassment and advise school and college officials about their obligations to respond when it occurs.

[D] Education related
Downing, Paul R
The Yearbook of Education Law.v. 1997 (1997) p. 355-78.
A review of decisions from the federal courts on topics that are relevant to and may influence education is presented. These cases pertain to the First Amendment and freedom of speech and religion, the Fourteenth Amendment and equal protection and due process, the Fourth Amendment, the Religious Freedom Restoration Act, collective bargaining, the Employee Retirement Income Security Act, and discrimination in the workplace involving the Age Discrimination in Employment Act, sexual harassment, the Pregnancy Discrimination Act, Section 504 and the Americans with Disabilities Act, and religious discrimination.

[D] Employee Relat Law J 1991 Autumn;17(2):191-206
Effective sexual harassment policies: unexpected lessons from Jacksonville Shipyards.
Connell DS
Although many employers recognize the need for an effective sexual harassment policy, they have received only limited guidance from the EEOC and the courts on how to draft and implement one. This article examines a recent decision, Robinson v. Jacksonville Shipyards, in which the court imposed a comprehensive sexual harassment policy.

[D] Erickson, Rosemary J.
The use of social science data in Supreme Court decisions / Rosemary J. Erickson and Rita J. Simon.
Urbana : University of Illinois Press, c1998.
190 p. ; 24 cm.
LC Call No.: KF8742 .E75 1998
ISBN: 0252066618 (pbk. : acid-free paper)
0252023552 (cloth : acid-free paper)
Includes bibliographical references (p. [167]-175) and index.
Social science and the law -- Expert witness testimony and amicus curiae -- Abortion -- Sex discrimination-- Sexual harassment.

Subjects: United States. Supreme Court. Judicial process -- United States. Social sciences -- United States. Sex and law -- United States.
Source: DLC DLC

[D] Goldstein, Leslie Friedman, 1945-
Contemporary cases in women's rights / Leslie Friedman Goldstein.
Madison, Wis. : University of Wisconsin Press, c1994.
xii, 339 p. ; 24 cm.
LC Call No.: KF478.A4 G65 1994
ISBN: 029914030X
0299140342 (pbk.)
Includes bibliographical references.
Historical evolution of the right of privacy : early judicial invocation of unwritten rights. Marital and procreative freedom : Skinner v. Oklahoma (1942) and its predecessors, discussion ; Contraceptive freedom and marital privacy : Poe v. Ullman (1961) and its predecessor, discussion ; Victory for marital privacy and contraception : Griswold v. Connecticut (1965), discussion ; From marital to extramarital privacy and an abortion forecast : Eisenstadt v. Baird (1972), discussion ; The right to abortion : Roe v. Wade and Doe v. Bolton (1973), discussion ; Post-Roe abortion restrictions, discussion of Planned Parenthood v. Danforth (1976) ; Roe v. Wade under siege : discussion of Akron I (1983), Simopoulos v. Virginia (1983), Planned Parenthood v. Ashcroft (1983), Thornburgh v. ACOG (1986) ; Public funds for abortion : discussion of Beal v. Doe (1977), Maher v. Roe (1977), Poelker v. Doe (1977), Harris v. McRae (1980) -- Current trends in abortion. Death knell for Roe v. Wade? : Webster v. Reproductive Health Services (1989); Parental notice for minors : discussion of Hodgson v. Minnesota (1990) and Ohio v. Akron Center for Reproductive Health (Akron II) (1990) ; Freedom of speech vs. limits on abortion : Rust v. Sullivan (1991) ; Reaction to Rust v. Sullivan ; Reprieve for Roe v. Wade : Planned Parenthood v. Casey (1992) ; Follow-up to Casey -- Parenthood and privacy : contemporary applications. Coerced caesareans : in re A.C. (1990) ; Child custody ; Surrogate mothers : The Baby M. case (1988) ; Adulterous fathers : Michael H. v. Gerald D. (1989) ; Native Americans and familial privacy : Mississippi Choctaw Indians v. Holyfield (1989) -- Sex discrimination. Historical background ; Employment opportunity ; Gender stereotyping and the workplace : Price Waterhouse v. Hopkins (1988) ; The Civil Rights Act of 1991, discussion ; Protection of the fetus vs. opportunity for women : UAW v. Johnson Controls (1991) ; Sexual harassment as sex discrimination ; Supreme Court guidelines : Meritor Savings Bank v. Vinson (1986), discussion ; Lower court innovation : Ellison v. Brady (1991) ; Educational opportunity : Franklin v. Gwinnett County Schools (1992), discussion -- Sexual violence and pornography. Rape ; Statutory rape and sexual violence : Michael M. v. Sonoma County (1981) ; Nonviolent, coerced intercourse : State v. Rusk (1981) ; Wife abuse and husband homicide : State v. Stewart (1988) ; Pornography, obscenity, and hate speech ; Obscenity doctrine ; Anti-pornography ordinances : American Booksellers Association v. Hudnut (1985) ; Hate speech and the future of pornography laws : R.A.V. v. St. Paul (1992), discussion. Subjects: Women -- Legal status, laws, etc. -- United States -- Cases. Women's rights -- United States -- Cases.

Abortion -- Law and legislation -- United States -- Cases. Sex discrimination against women -- Law and legislation -- United States -- Cases.
Source: DLC DLC PSM UKM MTH

[D] Haley v. Virginia Commonwealth University (948 F.Supp. 573)
West's Education Law Reporter.v. 115 (Apr. 3 1997) p. 728-38.
The text of the 1996 decision rendered in Haley v. Virginia Commonwealth University, which was heard in the United States District Court, E.D. Virginia, Richmond Division. Stephen Haley, a student, sued Virginia Commonwealth University alleging violations of Title IX, equal protection, due process, and state law in the handling of a sexual harassment complaint against him.

[D] Harassment ruling poses challenges
Augmented title: Gebser v. Lago Vista Independent School District
Walsh, Mark
Education Week.v. 18 no38 (June 2 1999) p. 1+.
In Davis v. Monroe County Board of Education, the Supreme Court held that schools can be sued for damages if they fail to respond to student sexual harassment of other students. School administrators reacted with surprising acceptance to the ruling, and many of them said they were comforted by what they viewed as a high legal threshold for holding schools responsible for such peer harassment.

[D] High Court addresses harassment
Augmented title: Doe v. Lago Vista Independent School District
Walsh, Mark
Education Week.v. 17 no29 (Apr. 1 1998) p. 1+.
The U.S. Supreme Court has been considering the circumstances under which school districts can be held liable under federal antidiscrimination law for a teacher's sexual harassment of a student. In Gebser v. Lago Vista Independent School District, Alida Gebser is seeking monetary damages for the sexual relationship she had with a teacher when she was a student.

[D] High Court to hear sexual-harassment case
Augmented title: Faragher v. City of Boca Raton
Walsh, Mark
Education Week.v. 17 (Nov. 26 1997) p. 17.
The U.S. Supreme Court has agreed to hear the case of Faragher v. City of Boca Raton. In the case, Faragher, a former beach lifeguard for the Florida city, alleges that she was subjected to offensive comments and unwanted touching by two supervisory lifeguards over a five-year period. In 1995, a federal district court ruled that the supervisors' conduct was severe and pervasive enough to create a hostile work environment for Faragher. However, the full U.S. Court of Appeals for the 11th Circuit reversed this decision in 1997.

[D] Higher education
Hendrickson, Robert M
The Yearbook of Education Law.v. 1997 (1997) p. 245-336.
A review of litigation in higher education is presented. Higher education suits and claims
concerned with intergovernmental relations, discrimination in employment, faculty
employment, all employees, administration and staff, sexual harassment, students,
discipline, and liability are discussed.

[D] Hill, Anita
Speaking truth to power / Anita Hill. 1st ed.
New York : Doubleday, c1997.
374 p. ; 24 cm.
LC Call No.: KF373.H46 A3 1997
ISBN: 0385476256
Includes index.
Subjects: Hill, Anita. Women lawyers -- United States -- Biography.
Sexual harassment of women -- Law and legislation -- United States.
Source: DLC DLC

[D] Houghton-James, Hazel
Sexual harassment
London: Cavendish Publishing, c1995
xviii,228p; 22cm (pbk)
Subjects: Sexual harassment of women--Great Britain Sexual harassment of women--Law
and legislation--Great Britain Sex discrimination in employment--Law and legislation--
Great Britain. Equal rights--England—1995. England--Equal rights--1995

[D] Incident at Ziman Brothers: the politics of gender and race in a Pretoria factory, 1934
Hyslop, Jonathan
The International Journal of African Historical Studies.v. 28 no3 1995 p. 509-25.
An examination of the 1934 Ziman affair in which a black man, Frans Tomane, was
accused of sexually harassing a female Afrikaner factory worker. Exploring what the
incident tells us about the construction of a racial order in South African industry, the
writer finds that racial hierarchy at Ziman's was not as clearly defined as one might
expect. He notes that there was clearly a great deal of racist sentiment among the white
Afrikaner workforce but suggests that this had not yet produced an effective, bureaucratic
regulation of racial boundaries in the factory. He argues that the affair may throw some
light on working-class attitudes to sexuality and how these intermeshed with race.

[D] Judge allows lawsuit by transsexual student against New York U. to proceed
Selingo, Jeffrey
The Chronicle of Higher Education.v. 44 (Oct. 24 1997) p. A12.
A federal judge has ruled that a lawsuit by a transsexual student against New York

University can proceed. The plaintiff alleges that she was the subject of "unwelcome sexual advances" by her musicology professor. The university had urged the judge to throw out the $28 million suit because the plaintiff was not technically a woman at the time of the alleged harassment and because the university was not responsible for the professor's actions.

[D] Justices decline to hear peer-sex-harassment case
Augmented title: J.W. v. Bryan Independent School District
Walsh, Mark
Education Week.v. 16 (May 21 1997) p. 20.
The U.S. Supreme Court has declined to review a case involving peer sexual harassment in schools. The justices refused to hear J.W. v. Bryan Independent School District, an appeal by a mother who alleged that school district officials failed to curtail a pattern of sexual harassment of her daughter by middle school boys in 1992 and 1993.

[D] Labor laws: working to protect you
Calfee, Barbara E
Nursing 96.v. 26 Feb. 1996 p. 34-40.
Nurses should become familiar with the labor laws that protect them before they become involved in problems related to job termination, discrimination, sexual harassment, or wages. Job termination can be one of the most painful work-related experiences for both employers and employees. The ability of employers to terminate employment at will is restricted by federal statutes that cover civil rights, age, pregnancy, and disabilities. State statutes also provide protection for employees on the basis of marital status, sexual orientation, personal appearance, and other factors. Labor laws also prohibit discrimination against employees or job applicants on the grounds that they belong to a protected class, although a certain degree of discrimination in the workplace is legal, provided it is based on legitimate business needs. Sexual harassment and wages and working hours are also addressed by labor laws.

[D] Lindemann, Barbara, 1935-
Primer on sexual harassment / Barbara Lindemann, David D. Kadue.
Washington, D.C. : Bureau of National Affairs, c1992.
xvii, 302 p. ; 23 cm.
LC Call No.: KF3467 .L55 1992
ISBN: 087179764X (pbk.)
Includes bibliographical references and index. Theories of liability under employment discrimination statutes : Characteristics of sexual harassment in the workplace -- Quid pro quo harassment -- Hostile environment harassment -- Claims by third parties -- Constructive discharge -- Retaliation -- State fair employment practices statutes -- Other sources of legal protection : Federal constitutional, statutory, and civil rights law -- Unemployment compensation statutes -- Workers' compensation statutes -- The common law -- Criminal law -- Collective bargaining agreements, union obligations, and arbitration -- Preventive, investigative, and corrective action : Developing preventive policies --

Conducting the internal investigation -- Taking prompt corrective action -- The agency investigation -- Special litigation issues : The defense litigation strategy -- Insurance coverage -- Evidence and discovery -- Remedies -- Settlement -- Appendices.
Subjects: Sexual harassment of women -- Law and legislation -- United States.
Sex discrimination in employment -- Law and legislation -- United States.
Other authors: Kadue, David D.
Source: DLC DLC IOP SNN

[D] Love, lust, and the law: sexual harassment in the academy
Alger, Jonathan R
Academe.v. 84 no5 (Sept./Oct. 1998) p. 34-9.
The writer discusses the current state of the law on sexual harassment and how it applies to higher education. He discusses sexual harassment in relation to Title VII and Title IX; the principles set forth by the Supreme Court concerning sexual harassment, who is protected from sexual harassment under Title VII and Title IX, and the establishment of liability; and the decisions that the Supreme Court has yet to make about the nature and extent of academic freedom.

[D] Making sense of sexual harassment law
Altman, Andrew, 1950
Philosophy and Public Affairs.v. 25 Winter 1996 p. 36-64.
The writer undertakes an explication, refinement, and defense of the existing U.S. law on sexual harassment. To this end, he seeks to explain why sexual harassment should be conceived of as a form of sex discrimination under Title VII of the Civil Rights Act of 1964. He examines the answer supplied by the most famous theorist in the field, Catharine MacKinnon, and suggests an alternative one. He then gives an account of why sexual harassment may reasonably be regarded as a form of discrimination and discusses the doctrinal categories of quid-pro-quo harassment and hostile environment harassment. Finally, he considers two issues where the current law is unsettled: sexual favoritism and the choice between a gendered or a gender-neutral standard.

[D] Minister set to tackle inequality and violence
MacGregor, Karen
The Times Educational Supplement.no4248 (Nov. 28 1997) p. 19.
In South Africa, government advisers are outlining proposals for new laws against sexual harassment and violence in schools. Their report, Gender Equity in Education, which calls for an extensive study of the problem, is to be handed in to Professor Sibusiso Bengu, the education minister.

[D] New sexual harassment rules under Title VII of the Civil Rights Act of 1964.
Williams KG
MedManagement, Inc., Moses Ludington Hospital, Ticonderoga, NY 12883, USA.
williamk@medmanagement.com

[D] Nurs Manage 1998 Feb;29(2):40-3; quiz 44
Sexual harassment. Where to draw the line.
Davidhizar R, Erdel S, Dowd S
Bethel College, Mishawaka, Indiana, USA.
Research reveals a widespread and frequently mismanaged problem--sexual harassment.
Federal and state rulings, workplace guidelines and the Equal Opportunity Commission's
definition of sexual harassment can help determine where to draw the line.

[D] Petrocelli, William.
Sexual harassment on the job/by William Petrocelli and Barbara Kate Repa.
1st ed., National ed.
Berkeley : Nolo Press, c1992.
1 v. (various pagings) ; 23 cm.
LC Call No.: KF3467.Z9 P47 1992
ISBN: 0873371771 : $14.95
Includes index.
Background, causes and effects -- The legal view -- First steps to stopping harassment –
Workplace policies and programs -- A look at the legal remedies -- The EEOC and the
U.S. Civil Rights Act -- State fair employment practices laws – Common law tort actions -
- Lawyers and legal research.
Subjects: Sexual harassment of women--Law & legislation--United States--Popular works.
Sex discrimination in employment--Law & legislation--United States--Popular works.
Other authors: Repa, Barbara Kate.
Source: DLC DLC ZZC AMH

[D] Posner on legal texts: law, literature, <economics>, and "welcome harassment"
Ranney, Frances
College Literature.v. 25 Winter 1998 p. 163-83.
Part of a special issue on law, literature, and interdisciplinarity. The writer offers a literary
analysis of Judge Posner's judicial opinion in the case of Carr v. General Motor's Allison
Gas Turbine Division. Questioning the establishment of the judicial voice of authority in
Carr, it can be seen that the meaning created is an individual exercise, one from which
Posner specifically excludes the reader through the effective use of rhetoric as he
understands it. Rather than expose the grounds on which he may legitimately refuse to
consider "welcome sexual harassment," he dismisses the concept as an oxymoron--a
rhetorical, hence literary, hence fictive device.

[D] Psychiatr Clin North Am 1999 Mar;22(1):129-45
Forensic aspects of sexual harassment.
Rosman JP, McDonald JJ Jr
Law Firm of Fisher & Phillips LLP, Newport Beach, California, USA. Sexual harassment
law presents a complex set of issues not only for lawyers but also for psychiatrists in their
roles both as evaluators and clinicians. The US Supreme Court has stressed the need for

common sense in evaluating cases of sexual harassment. Perhaps psychiatrists can play a sobering role in developing answers to these questions.

[D] Race, gender, and power in America: the legacy of the Hill-Thomas hearings/ edited by Anita Faye Hill, Emma Coleman Jordan
New York; Oxford: Oxford University Press, 1995
xxxii, 302p; 25cm
Subjects: "Thomas, Clarence, 1948- Hill, Anita
United States. Supreme Court--Officials and employees-- Selection and appointment--History--20th century
Sexual harassment of women--Law and legislation--United States

[D] Race-ing justice, en-gendering power: essays on Anita Hill, Clarence Thomas and the construction of social reality/ edited by Toni Morrison
London: Chatto Windus, 1993
xxx, 475p; 23cm
Subjects: Women's rights--United States Sexual harassment of women--Law and legislation--United States United States--Law and legislation

[D] Recent trends and current Title IX developments involving peer based student sexual harassment
Stevenson, David S
Journal of Law and Education.v. 26 (July 1997) p. 133-9.
The writer discusses current developments in peer-based student sexual harassment and recent litigation trends under Title IX of the Education Amendments of 1972. Recent cases of peer-based student sexual harassment illustrate that school officials are abandoning commonsense notions of right and wrong in an effort to make schools safe from inappropriate sexual behavior. Until the Supreme Court elects to tackle the issue, the proper standard of liability for school districts will remain uncertain. However, school officials should know the difference between episodes of serious sexual harassment and simple incidents of child's play and should act accordingly.

[D] Regan Rep Nurs Law 1996 Oct;37(5):2
"Same-sex" sexual harassment violates Civil Rights Act. Case in point: Johnson v. Community Nursing Services 932 F. Supp. 269--UT (1996).
Tamelleo AD

[D] Reinhold v. Commonwealth of Virginia (947 F.Supp. 919)
West's Education Law Reporter.v. 115 (Apr. 3 1997) p. 666-71.
The text of the 1996 decision rendered in Reinhold v. Commonwealth of Virginia, which was heard in the United States District Court, E.D. Virginia, Richmond Division. Kathryn Reinhold, a female employee of a state school, brought an action against the Commonwealth of Virginia alleging hostile work environment sexual harassment, quid pro quo sexual harassment, and retaliation.

[D] Revolution 1998 Spring;8(1):23-8
Fighting the good fight--legal issues and legislative update for nurses.
Stearley H

[D] School district liability for peer sexual harassment: a review of current theories
Michaelis, Karen L
Catalyst for Change.v. 25 (Winter 1997) p. 8-13.
The current theories for peer to peer hostile environment sexual harassment have failed to be effective in imposing school district liability. The Substantive Due Process Clause of the Fourteenth Amendment fails, as it has been declared that injuries caused by private, third parties are not the responsibility of state institutions. Therefore, it is clear that the solution to peer to peer sexual harassment lies not in the judicial arena but in the prejudicial arena when a formal complaint of abuse has been made but a lawsuit has not yet been filed.

[D] Schulhofer, Stephen J.
Unwanted sex : the culture of intimidation and the failure of law / Stephen J. Schulhofer.
Cambridge, Mass. : Harvard University Press, 1998.
xii, 318 p. ; 25 cm.
LC Call No.: KF9325 .S38 1998
ISBN: 0674576489 (alk. paper)
Includes bibliographical references (p. 285-314) and index.
Subjects: Sex crimes -- United States. Sexual harassment -- Law and legislation – United States. Sex and law -- United States. Law reform -- United States.
Source: DLC DLC C#P

[D] Sexual harassment: let the punishment fit the crime
Williams, Verna; Brake, Deborah L
The Chronicle of Higher Education.v. 43 (Apr. 18 1997) p. A56.
The Department of Education has produced new guidelines on the prevention and elimination of sexual harassment at educational institutions. The guidelines draw on the expertise of the department's Office for Civil Rights in investigating harassment complaints. While acknowledging the complexity of the problem, the guidelines urge institutions to use their judgment and common sense to avoid violating Title IX of the Education Amendments of 1972.

[D] Sexual harassment: speaking up
Nursing 98.v. 28 no7 July 1998 p. 22.
Some of the legal issues involved in dealing with cases of sexual harassment are briefly discussed. If a nurse-manager learns that a nurse is being sexually harassed, then she must report what has happened and take action, even if the victim is unwilling to report the problem herself. The nurse-manager might also help the victim to avoid situations where she is vulnerable to the harasser.

[D] *Sexual Harassment*: Understand It, Talk about It, Post a Policy against It.
Monograph, Volume 7, Number 2.
Fear-Fenn, Marcia
This four-page monograph discusses the legal background of *sexual harassment*, provides
explanations for *sexual harassment*, and lists the effects of *sexual harassment*. It then
moves to actions that individuals, educators, and administrators can take to combat *sexual
harassment*. Also included arc six annotated resources for educators to use in preparing
students for *sexual harassment* situations and nine references. (KC)

[D] Stetson, Dorothy M.
Women's rights in the U.S.A. : policy debates and gender roles / Dorothy McBride Stetson.
Edition: 2nd ed.
New York : Garland Pub., 1997.
xxii, 383 p.; 24 cm.
LC Call No.: HQ1236.5.U6 S74 1997
ISBN: 0815320752 (alk. paper)
0815320752 (pbk)
0815320760 (hardcover : alk. paper)
Includes bibliographies and index.
Introduction -- Sex, gender, feminism, and women's rights -- The U.S. Constitution -- The
Equal Rights Amendment -- Political resources -- The vote -- Reproduction --
Contraception -- Abortion – The battle over abortion rights -- Education – Family --
Marriage -- Divorce -- Work and pay -- Work and family -- Pregnancy and childbirth--
Child care -- Sexuality -- Prostitution -- Pornography --Rape--Sexual harassment--Lesbian
issues–Economic status--Single mothers and welfare–Battered women and dependency.
Subjects: Women's rights -- United States. Sex role -- United States. Women -- Legal
status, laws, etc. -- United States.
Source: DLC DLC C#P MLX SNN

[D] Supreme Court addresses two more harassment cases
Augmented title: Bruneau v. South Kortright Central School District and Board of
Trustees of the University of Illinois v. Doe
Walsh, Mark
Education Week.v. 18 no39 (June 9 1999) p. 19.
In Bruneau v. South Kortright Central School District, the Supreme Court let stand
without comment a federal appeals court ruling upholding a jury verdict against a New
York state student who alleged she was subjected to sexual harassment by other students
when she was in sixth grade. In Board of Trustees of the University of Illinois v. Doe, the
court told another federal appellate court to reexamine the case in light of the Supreme
Court's recent ruling in Davis v. Monroe County Board of Education..

[D] Supreme Court limits school district liability in sexual harassment
The American School Board Journal.v. 185 no8 (Aug. 1998) p. 6.

In a 5-4 vote, the U.S. Supreme Court has given school systems some protection against sexual abuse and harassment suits. The court ruled that the Lago Vista Independent School District in Texas was not liable for damages because it had no knowledge of a teacher's affair with a high school student.

[D] The lynching of language: gender, politics, and power in the Hill-Thomas hearings/ edited by Sandra L. Ragan ... [et al.] ; foreword by Julia T. Wood.
Urbana : University of Illinois Press, c1996.
xxiii, 293 p. ; 23 cm.
LC Call No.: KF8745.T48 L96 1996
ISBN: 0252021266
0252065174 (pbk.)
Includes bibliographical references and index.
Subjects: Thomas, Clarence, -- 1948-. United States. Supreme Court -- Officials and employees -- Selection and appointment. Hill, Anita. Sexual harassment of women -- Law and legislation -- United States. Law and politics. Truthfulness and falsehood.

[D] The message from the Supreme Court: clarify sexual-harassment policies
Franke, Ann H
The Chronicle of Higher Education.v. 44 no45 (July 17 1998) p. B6-B7.
In the light of recent U.S. Supreme Court decisions, colleges and universities should initiate or sustain strong internal procedures to address sexual harassment. The Supreme Court in its rulings distinguished between protection for students and for employees, but colleges would be foolish to mirror those distinctions in their internal policies. The legal landscape of harassment is discussed in relation to the two major federal laws that define the responsibilities of colleges and universities with regard to harassment.

[D] The press and the law; Olson suit invites regulation of press
Denniston, Lyle
WJR.v. 13 July/Aug. 1991 p. 40-1+.

[D] The Supreme Court 1998
McConnell, Michael W
First Things.no87 Nov. 1998 p. 37-9.
A discussion of some of the cases brought to the U.S. Supreme Court during the 1997/1998 term. The most significant cases of the term were the sexual harassment decisions, Burlington Industries v. Ellerth and Faragher v. City of Boca Raton. The constitutional case of the term with the greatest potential effect on the tone and quality of American public culture was National Endowment for the Arts (NEA) v. Finley. In this case the Court ducked the significant question that was raised, namely what limits, if any, apply to the government's decision to grant or withhold subsidies for speech or artistic expression.

[D] The Supreme Court opens the door wide for harassment claims.
Lasater NE, McEvoy TJ

[D] The United States Supreme Court and sexual harassment: clarification of issues
Carpenter, Linda Jean, 1943
Strategies.v. 12 no2 (Nov./Dec. 1998) p. 8-10+.
Using a question and answer format, the writer clarifies the U.S. Supreme Court's sexual harassment decisions.

[D] Title IX and student-to-student sexual harassment: past, present, and future
Thompson, David P., 1959
Catalyst for Change.v. 25 (Winter 1997) p. 14-19.
The writer explores recent federal case law dealing with students' claims of peer sexual harassment. The writer discusses Title IX and its relevance to student-to-student sexual harassment, the Franklin decision, post-Franklin decisions, and future directions for litigation.

[D] Turning to the feds for guidance
Augmented title: student-to-student sexual harassment
Jacobs, Jennifer W
School Administrator.v. 54 (Nov. 1997) p. 20-2.
Superintendents confronting student-to-student sexual harassment should follow the new federal guidelines. The guidelines, from the Department of Education's Office for Civil Rights, suggest that school districts have a student code of conduct prohibiting sexual harassment. They also state that a school district's student code of conduct may be used to respond to student conduct determined to be sexual harassment. Under the guidelines, public school districts are expected to have a grievance procedure in place so that students who have been harassed may appeal the discipline meted out to the student accused of sexual harassment. Immediate steps that can be taken to implement the guidelines are presented, and practical responses to sexual harassment cases are suggested.

[D] United States. National Institute of Justice Civil rights and criminal justice: primer on sexual harassment/ by Paula N. Rubin
Washington: National Institute of Justice, 1995
10p; 28cm
Series Research in Action
Subjects: QWUHb (QWUH)

[D] Wolfson, Nicholas.
Hate speech, sex speech, free speech / Nicholas Wolfson.
Westport, Conn. : Praeger, 1997.
169 p. ; 22 cm.
LC Call No.: KF4772 .W65 1997

ISBN: 0275957705 (alk. paper)
Includes bibliographical references (p. [151]-159) and index.
Subjects: Freedom of speech--United States. Hate speech--United States. Pornography --
United States. Sexual harassment--Law and legislation–United States. Racism in language.
Source: DLC DLC

5) SEXUAL HARASSMENT IN EDUCATION

[E] "Consensual" relations in the academy: gender, power, and sexuality
Lane, Ann J., 1931
Academe.v. 84 no5 (Sept./Oct. 1998) p. 24-31.
Although everyone is opposed to sexual harassment in principle, "consensual" relations
between students and teachers are more contentious. Such relationships, which most often
involve male professors and female students, highlight issues of professional responsibility,
privacy, sexual freedom, and the meaning of consent. Regulations regarding consensual
sex are opposed by certain groups and involve complex issues, but their passage would
make many students more comfortable with faculty. It must confront directly and firmly
the challenge of ensuring that the university is a place that is safe from sexual exploitation.

[E] A communication perspective on sexual harassment: affiliative nonverbal behaviors in
asynchronous relationships
Hickson, Mark; Grierson, R. D; Linder, Barbara C
Communication Quarterly.v. 39 Spring 1991 p. 111-18.

[E] A culture of disrespect
Augmented title: sexism in high school
Smith, Kelly J
Mercury (San Francisco, Calif.).v. 26 Mar./Apr. 1997 p. 16-17.
Part of a special issue on astronomy and young people. High school students are being
taught to accept the rules of sexual discrimination. High school students must deal with
sexism in the science classroom on a daily basis. Many female students will not report
sexual discrimination by teachers because they are afraid of grade sabotage; they
rationalize their inaction by regarding their grades as more important than their self-
esteem. Indeed, for some women, sexual discrimination in high school provides a valuable
lesson in dealing with adult life. However, if sexism is tolerated and accepted in high
schools, it will be hard to convince people later in life that it is unacceptable to ridicule
someone because of their gender.

[E] A history department implodes over sex-bias charges and a suicide
Leatherman, Courtney
The Chronicle of Higher Education.v. 45 no35 (May 7 1999) p. A16-A18.
Academic culture, gender, and productivity issues are at the center of a dispute in the
history department of the University of California, Riverside. Sexual discrimination,
harassment, and assault allegations have resulted in a campus investigation of the

department, charges against five male professors by the university, and the suicide of one of them. Defenders of the accused men have started a counterinvestigation.

[E] A professor's personal teaching style wins him praise and costs him his job
Wilson, Robin
The Chronicle of Higher Education.v. 44 (Nov. 14 1997) p. A12-A13.
Adam M. Weisberger, a former assistant professor of sociology at Colby College, has filed a lawsuit charging the institution with defamation and infliction of emotional distress. Dr. Weisberger was denied tenure over charges that he created a sexually threatening classroom environment. His defenders claim that his teaching style of connecting theoretical material to students' lives is not unusual.

[E] A scandalous sexual harassment case
Augmented title: at Simon Fraser University
McConaghy, Tom
Phi Delta Kappan.v. 79 (Oct. 1997) p. 167-8.
The writer discusses a sexual harassment case at Simon Fraser University, Canada, involving student Rachel Marsden and swimming coach Liam Donnelly. Marsden made a complaint to the university's sexual harassment committee, alleging she was forced to have sex with Donnelly in the course of an 18-month relationship in 1994-1995. Donnelly was fired but has since been awarded back pay and as much as $35,000 for legal costs, and a board of governors' decision has exonerated him. The case was one of the nation's more notorious sexual harassment fiascoes, and it sent powerful signals about the numerous inequities in the handling of sexual harassment cases by Canadian universities.

[E] A sexual-harassment case tarnishes the image of Canada's Simon Fraser U
Augmented title: fired coach is reinstated as questions emerge about the fairness of panel that reviewed him
Monaghan, Peter
The Chronicle of Higher Education.v. 44 (Dec. 19 1997) p. A43-A44.
A coach fired over an allegation of sexual harassment has been reinstated at Simon Fraser University in Canada after an independent arbitrator overturned the university's decision. A major breach of the university's procedures for selecting members of panels that hear harassment complaints has also been uncovered by officials. The university's poor handling of the case has tarnished its image considerably.

[E] A sexual-harassment lawsuit shakes up the tight-knit world of women's soccer
Haworth, Karla
The Chronicle of Higher Education.v. 45 no11 (Nov. 6 1998) p. A63-A64.
Two female soccer players, Debbie Keller, a member of the U.S. Women's National Team, and Melissa Jennings, a walk-on goalkeeper, have filed a $12 million lawsuit against Anson Dorrance, the head coach at the University of North Carolina at Chapel Hill, for alleged sexual harassment and emotional abuse. Dorrance, a legend in the world of women's athletics, denies the charges.

[E] A Study Concerning Sexual Harassment among School Personnel.
Peach, Larry; Reddick, Thomas L.
This paper describes a study conducted in 22 counties in Middle Tennessee to determine the extent to which teachers have experienced sexual harassment. The paper also provides an overview of two recent Supreme Court rulings: "Burlington Industries v. Ellerth"; and "Faragher v. Boca Raton." Also mentioned are the inclusion of sexual harassment in Title VII of the Civil Rights Act and Title IX of the Education Amendments. (RIB)

[E] A war on sexual predators or a war against dissent?
Selingo, Jeffrey
The Chronicle of Higher Education.v. 44 no30 (Apr. 3 1998) p. A12-A14.
President Angelo Armenti's aggressive approach to eradicating sexual harassment on the campus of California University of Pennsylvania has divided faculty. Although Armenti has claimed he is trying to create a workplace "free of the terrors of sexual harassment," his opponents claim that the campaign is a ruse for getting rid of his detractors and long-term employees.

[E] Absolute zero
Augmented title: zero-tolerance policies
Jones, Rebecca
The American School Board Journal.v. 184 (Oct. 1997) p. 29-31.
Zero tolerance has become the battle cry of and an embarrassment to those who are trying to alleviate weapons, drugs, sexual harassment, and other misconduct in schools. Policy experts say that school boards introducing such policies should ask the community, decide what they want, allow some slack, make sure students can appeal decisions, explain the policy, and be ready for unfair criticism.

[E] Acad Med 1995 May;70(5):434-5
A sexual harassment workshop for medical students.
Jacobs C, Bergen M
Stanford University School of Medicine, USA.

[E] Acad Med 1996 Jan;71(1 Suppl):S113-8
Sexual harassment in medical education: a review of the literature with comments from the law.
Nora LM
University of Kentucky College of Medicine, Lexington 40536, USA.

[E] Acad Med 1996 Oct;71(10 Suppl):S22-4
Does exposure to gender discrimination and sexual harassment impact medical students' specialty choices and residency program selections?
Nora LM, McLaughlin MA, Fosson SE, Jacob SK, Schmidt JL, Witzke D

Office of Academic Affairs, University of Kentucky College of Medicine,
Lexington 40536-0084, USA.

[E] Acad Med 1996 Oct;71(10 Suppl):S25-7
Residents' and medical students' reports of sexual harassment and discrimination.
Baldwin DC Jr, Daugherty SR, Rowley BD
Rush Primary Care Institute, Chicago, IL 60612, USA.

[E] Acad Med 1998 Feb;73(2):180-6
Relationships of gender and career motivation to medical faculty members' production of
academic publications.
Barnett RC, Carr P, Boisnier AD, Ash A, Friedman RH, Moskowitz MA, Szalacha L
Women's Studies Program, Brandeis University, Waltham, Massachusetts, USA.
r_barnett@harvard.edu
PURPOSE: To evaluate the relationships between both internal and external career-
motivating factors and academic productivity (as measured by the total numbers of
publications) among full-time medical faculty, and whether these relationships differ for
men and women.

[E] Against zero tolerance
Fekete, John
Journal of Canadian Studies.v. 29 Spring 1994 p. 144-8.
A discussion of the Ontario Ministry of Education's 1993 zero-tolerance initiative in
Canadian universities, "Framework Regarding Prevention of Harassment and
Discrimination in Ontario Universities." It should be emphasized that the debate about
academic freedom and freedom of speech sparked by this initiative is a policy debate--it is
concerned with what constitutes discriminatory or sexual harassment and how it can be
addressed, not whether such harassment is acceptable. This debate is also concerned with
the extent to which cultural and political process should be translated into, supplemented
with, or decided by legislative or regulative power. The zero-tolerance model makes it
impossible to deal with "the ways in which academic freedom, non-discrimination and
pluralism intersect.".

[E] Ala Med 1995 Jun;64(12):5
Education in preventing sexual misconduct in Alabama.
Summer GL

[E] Anderson v. Boston School Committee (105 F.3d 762)
West's Education Law Reporter.v. 115 (Apr. 3 1997) p. 629-37.
The text of the 1997 decision rendered in Anderson v. Boston School Committee, which
was heard in the United States Court of Appeals, First Circuit. Eugene Anderson, a black
former public school teacher, brought an action against the principal and the Boston
School Committee, alleging racial discrimination and various tort claims.

[E] Arbitrator orders California U. of Pennsylvania to reinstate former professor
Selingo, Jeffrey
The Chronicle of Higher Education.v. 44 (Feb. 13 1998) p. A16.
For the second time in nine months, California University of Pennsylvania has been
ordered to reinstate a former professor. William Parnell, a professor of education, was
dismissed in 1996 after being accused of failing a graduate student because the student had
filed sexual harassment complaints against another professor. The cases have raised
questions about the conduct of the university's president, according to the president of the
faculty union.

[E] Arch Sex Behav 1996 Apr;25(2):201-15
Sexual harassment of Chinese college students.
Tang CS, Yik MS, Cheung FM, Choi PK, Au KC
Psychology Department, Chinese University of Hong Kong, Shatin New Territories, Hong
Kong.
Sexual harassment of Chinese college students with a focus on their awareness,
experiences, responses, and expectations of institutional intervention to the problem was
examined. Comparisons with U.S. studies suggested that Chinese college students had a
lower awareness and experience level in sexual harassment than U.S. students.

[E] Besieged, bothered, and bewildered
Green, Jason
Black Issues in Higher Education.v. 15 no13 (Aug. 20 1998) p. 20+.
Clea Patrick Hollis, affirmative action director at the University of Pittsburgh at
Johnstown, has filed a lawsuit against the university and its president Dr. Albert L.
Etheridge. The lawsuit charges Etheridge and the university with sexual harassment and
retaliation, sex discrimination in hiring, race discrimination in employment, retaliatory
harassment, and deprivation of civil rights and sex discrimination in employment.

[E] Brown U. cleared in suit brought by student who accused professor of assault
Gose, Ben
The Chronicle of Higher Education.v. 44 no31 (Apr. 10 1998) p. A54.
A federal jury in Providence, Rhode Island, has found that Brown University was not
negligent in failing to fire an assistant professor of chemistry before he assaulted a student.
The student had argued that the university knew that the professor had a history of
harassing students and should have taken action to stop him before he assaulted her in his
office. However, the jury cleared the university of the charges of negligent supervision and
of fostering a hostile environment because of sexual harassment.

[E] Brown University faces new accusations that it mishandles sex-offense charges
Gose, Ben
The Chronicle of Higher Education.v. 43 (May 9 1997) p. A43-A44.
Information about the way in which Brown University has handled certain cases of date

rape and sexual harassment has led many people on campus to wonder if the university favors the alleged perpetrator if hc has influence or is black.

[E] Campus culture wars [videorecording] : five stories about PC / presented by Manifold Productions, Inc. in association with South Carolina ETV ; produced and directed by Michael Pack ; co-producer and writer, John Prizer.
Santa Monica, CA : Direct Cinema Ltd., c1993.
1 videocassette (86 min.) : sd., col. ; 1/2 in.
Local Call No: BD175.5.P65 C34 1993
ISBN: 1559744901
Narrator, Lindsay Crouse.
Examines five controversial incidents at universities around the country involving conflicts of values and "political correctness". Cases involve the use of racially insensitive language, gay rights and religious expression, pursuit of multicultural ideals, sexual harassment in the classroom, and radical feminism.
VHS format.
Subjects: Political correctness -- United States. Freedom of speech -- United States. Academic freedom -- United States.
Other authors: Pack, Michael and Crouse, Lindsay.
Other authors: Manifold Productions. South Carolina Educational Television Network. Direct Cinema Ltd.
Source: WCL WCL PMD MTH

[E] Campus wars : multiculturalism and the politics of difference / edited by John Arthur, Amy Shapiro.
Boulder [Colo.] : Westview Press, 1995.
vii, 279 p. ; 24 cm.
LC Call No.: LC196.5.U6 C36 1995
ISBN: 0813324807 (alk. paper)
0813324815 (pbk.)
Includes bibliographical references.
Multiculturalism and the college curriculum. The closing of the American mind / Allan Bloom -- What's all the fuss about this postmodernist stuff? / Barry W. Sarchett -- Postmodernism and the western rationalist tradition / John R. Searle -- Is there a text in this class? / Stanley Fish -- Relativism, deconstruction, and the curriculum / Amy Gutmann -- Sex on campus : sexual harassment and date rape. Sexuality / Catharine A. MacKinnon -- Date rape : a feminist analysis / Lois Pineau -- An interview about sex and date rape / Camille Paglia – Free speech, hate speech, and campus speech codes. Good speech, bad speech-- no / Gerald Gunther – Campus speech codes : Doe v. University of Michigan -- Liberalism and campus hate speech / Andrew Altman -- Race and affirmative action on campus. Affirmative action in universities : Regents of the University of California v. Bakke -- Affirmative discrimination / Lino A. Graglia. A cultural pluralist case for affirmative action / Duncan Kennedy -- The recoloring of campus life : student racism, academic pluralism, and the end of a dream / Shelby Steele -- Identity,

assimilation, and politics. Age, race, class, and sex : women redefining difference / Audre Lorde – Social movements and the politics of difference / Iris Marion Young -- The disuniting of America : reflections on a multicultural society / Arthur M. Schlesinger, Jr. -- Separation or assimilation? / Bernard R. Boxill -- The politics of recognition / Charles Taylor -- Pragmatism, relativism, and the justification of democracy / Hilary Putnam. Subjects: Critical pedagogy -- United States. Multiculturalism -- United States. Education, Higher -- Political aspects – United States. Social conflict -- United States. Source: DLC DLC LRW WEA MTH

[E] Can a child say yes? How the unwelcomeness requirement has thwarted the purpose of Title IX
Augmented title: Mary M. v. North Lawrence Community School
Duffy, Angela
Journal of Law and Education.v. 27 no3 (July 1998) p. 505-10.
The writer examines the case of Mary M. v. North Lawrence Community School Corporation to explore the unwelcomeness requirement in cases under Title IX of the Education Amendments of 1972. An examination of the case indicates that if a student first has to prove that he/she did not welcome the perceived harassment, then the purpose of Title IX has been defeated. Moreover, the current legal situation creates the illogical possibility, which occurred in the Mary M. case, that an individual can be convicted of child molestation and not be responsible for sexual advances under Title IX.

[E] Child Welfare 1999 Jul-Aug;78(4):435-60
School-based peer sexual harassment.
Kopels S, Dupper DR
School of Social Work, University of Illinois at Urbana-Champaign, USA.
Peer sexual harassment in schools is an often overlooked problem that contributes to a hostile school environment: one major study found that 85% of girls and 76% of boys reported experiencing some form of sexual harassment in school. This article describes the extent and impact of peer sexual harassment in schools and the responses of the victims, school personnel, and perpetrators to peer sexual harassment. It discusses and analyzes the evolution of peer sexual harassment lawsuits and the recent U.S. Supreme Court decision concerning such actions. It concludes steps that social workers and other school personnel should take to prevent or alleviate such problems.

[E] Cleaning up the library
Augmented title: rowdy teenagers; with discussion
Anderson, A. J
Library Journal.v. 123 (Mar. 1 1998) p. 66+.
A case study in which a family threatens to bring a sexual harassment lawsuit against a library and its custodian based on what the custodian had said to an adolescent female member of the family is presented.

[E] Clinton administration requests High Court ruling on harassment

Augmented title: Davis v. Monroe County Board of Education
Walsh, Mark
Education Week.v. 18 no1 (Sept. 9 1998) p. 35.
The U.S. Supreme Court has been asked by the Clinton administration to rule on whether school districts can be held liable, under federal law, for sexual harassment of students by other students. Justices have been asked to review a Georgia case in which an appeals court held that districts could not be held responsible for student-student sexual harassment under Title IX of the Education Amendments of 1972.

[E] CMAJ 1996 Jun 1;154(11):1657-65
Residents' experiences of abuse, discrimination and sexual harassment during residency training. McMaster University Residency Training Programs.
Cook DJ, Liutkus JF, Risdon CL, Griffith LE, Guyatt GH, Walter SD
Department of Medicine, McMaster University Faculty of Health Sciences, Hamilton, Ont.
Objective: To assess the prevalence of psychological abuse, physical assault, and discrimination on the basis of gender and sexual orientation, and to examine the prevalence and impact of sexual harassment in residency training programs. Psychological abuse, discrimination on the basis of gender and sexual harassment are commonly experienced by residents in training programs. A direct, progressive, multidisciplinary approach is needed to label and address these problems.
Comments: Comment in: Can Med Assoc J 1996 Jun 1;154(11):1705-8 and in Can Med Assoc J 1996 Oct 15;155(8):1042; discussion 1042-3

[E] Community building: risks and rewards
Augmented title: symposium
Thrust for Educational Leadership.v. 28 no1 (Sept./Oct. 1998) p. 6-38.
Articles discuss community building in schools, a three-tiered teaching and learning program on ethics, citizenship education in the school playground, ten schools that have been recognized for exemplifying the Character Education Partnership's 11 principles of effective education, seven steps to building a sense of community in schools, and how to create schools that are free from sexual harassment.

[E] Confronting sexual harassment (book review)
Brandenburg, Judith Berman; Heimann, Sue, reviewer
American Secondary Education.v. 26 no3 (Mar. 1998) p. 26-7.

[E] Confronting sexual harassment: what schools and colleges do
Brandenburg, Judith Berman
Teachers College Press, 1997. 174 p.

[E] Court accepts case on peer harassment
Augmented title: Davis v. Monroe County Board of Education
Walsh, Mark
Education Week.v. 18 no6 (Oct. 7 1998) p. 1+.

The U.S. Supreme Court has agreed to hear Davis v. Monroe County Board of Education. In this case, the Court will decide whether Title IX can be used to recover money damages from school districts when they fail to address sexual harassment of a student by other students.

[E] Creating harassment free schools
Kulisch, W. Anthony; Whittenbury, Elizabeth R. Koller
Thrust for Educational Leadership.v. 28 no1 (Sept./Oct. 1998) p. 36-8.
Part of a special issue on citizenship education in California. Administrators must take steps to create schools that are free from sexual harassment. Information on federal law regulations on school sexual harassment and the requirements of the California Education Code with regard to sexual harassment is provided.

[E] Curcio, Joan L.
Sexuality and the schools: handling the critical issues/ Joan L. Curcio, Lois F. Berlin, Patricia F. First
Thousand Oaks, Calif.: Corwin Press; London: Sage, c1996
ix,58p; 22cm
Series Roadmaps to success
Includes bibliography: pp.55-58
Subjects: Students--United States--Sexual behavior, Sexual ethics--Study and teaching--United States, Hygiene, Sexual--Study and teaching--United States, Sexual harassment in education--United States—Prevention, Sex instruction--United States, 371.7, Sexuality, Sex education

[E] Doe by and through Doe v. Petaluma City School District (949 F.Supp. 1415)
West's Education Law Reporter.v. 115 (Apr. 3 1997) p. 854-66.
The text of the 1996 decision rendered in Doe by and through Doe v. Petaluma City School District, which was heard in the United States District Court, N.D. California. Doe, a junior high school student, brought an action against the Petaluma City School District and its counselor and principal, alleging that the defendants failed to stop sexual harassment inflicted on Doe by her peers.

[E] Doe v. Claiborne County, Tennessee, by and through the Claiborne County Board of Education (103 F.3d 495)
West's Education Law Reporter.v. 115 (Mar. 20 1997) p. 265-86.
The text of the 1996 decision rendered in Doe v. Claiborne County, Tennessee, by and through the Claiborne County Board of Education, which was heard in the United States Court of Appeals, Sixth Circuit. Jane Doe, a high school student who had been sexually abused by a teacher at school, brought an action against the Claiborne County Board of Education, members of the board, past and present school superintendents, and the school principal, in which she asserted federal civil rights and Title IX claims.

[E] Dziech, Billie Wright, 1941-

The lecherous professor : sexual harassment on campus / Billie Wright Dziech, Linda
Weiner. 2nd ed.
Urbana : University of Illinois Press, 1990.
xxxi, 251 p. ; 23 cm.
LC Call No.: LC212.862 .D95 1990
ISBN: 0252061187 (pbk. : alk. paper)
"Illini Books edition"--Verso t.p.
"An Illini book from the University of Illinois
Press"--P. [4] of cover.
Includes bibliographical references (p. 239-246) and index.
Subjects: Sexual harassment in universities and colleges -- United States. Women college
students -- United States. Sexual harassment of women -- Law and legislation -- United
States. College teachers -- United States.
Source: DLC DLC AMH

[E] Dziech, Billie Wright, 1941-
The lecherous professor : sexual harassment on campus / Billie Wright Dziech, Linda
Weiner.
Boston : Beacon Press, c1984.
vii, 219 p. ; 22 cm.
LC Call No.: LC1756 .D97 1984
ISBN: 0807031003 : $16.95
Includes index and bibliography: p. 210-214.
Subjects: Women college students--United States. Sexual harassment of women--United
States. College teachers--United States. Sexual harassment--Law & legislation–United
States.
Other authors: Weiner, Linda.
Source: DLC DLC AUM

[E] Education's right and left
Augmented title: symposium
Contemporary Education.v. 68 (Summer 1997) p. 213-64.
Articles discuss why education is the nation's main worry, the teacher's role and attitude
toward multicultural education, the Religious Right's view of public schools, affirmative
action programs, the inclusion of disabled children in mainstream classrooms, federal
educational policy, religious studies in community colleges, school reform, identity
formation, sexual harassment, the need to teach the concept of public interest in social
studies classes, and why vouchers are the wrong solution to the ills of public education.

[E] Erickson, J. Bianca.
Peer sexual harassment in schools : reaction, attributional style, and self-esteem / J. Bianca
Erickson.
1996.
v, 66 leaves ; 28 cm.

Typescript.

Honors Paper - Mount Holyoke College, 1996. Dept. of Psychology and Education.

Includes bibliographical references (leaves 37-40)

Subjects: Sexual harassment in education -- United States.

Sexual harassment -- Psychological aspects.

Source: MTH MTH

[E] Ethiop Med J 1998 Jul;36(3):167-74

Prevalence and outcomes of sexual violence among high school students.

Mulugeta E, Kassaye M, Berhane Y

Department of Community Health, Faculty of Medicine, Addis Ababa University. A cross sectional, school-based survey using self administered anonymous questionnaire was conducted in Addis Ababa and Western Shoa among high school students to determine the prevalence, and reported outcomes of sexual violence. It is concluded that the prevalence of sexual violence among high school students is a serious problem and concern. Awareness creation to adolescents and the family need to be introduced and schools should also devise appropriate sex education regarding damaging effect of rape and educate youth on sexuality and responsible sexual decision making.

[E] Faculty-student sexual involvement: issues and interventions

Stamler, Virginia Lee; Stone, Gerald L., 1941

Sage Publs., 1998. 109 p.

[E] Fekete, John.

Moral panic : biopolitics rising / John Fekete.

Montréal : R. Davies Publishing, 1994.

383 p. ; 21 cm.

Series: Food for thought.

Local Call No: JA79 .F45 1994

ISBN: 1895854091 : $14.99

Includes bibliographical references (p. 357-376) and index.

Subjects: Biopolitics. Political correctness. Women -- Crimes against. Sexual harassment in universities and colleges -- Canada.

Series Entry: Food for thought (Montréal, Quebec)

Source: CaQMBN eng NLC CLU MTH

[E] Francis, Leslie P.

Sexual harassment in academe: the ethical issues.

N.Y.: Rowman & Littlefield,1998.

ISBN: 0847681718

[E] Gallop, Jane, 1952-

Feminist accused of sexual harassment / Jane Gallop.

Durham : Duke University Press, 1997.

101 p. ; 22 cm.
Series: Public planet books.
LC Call No.: LC212.862 .G35 1997
ISBN: 082231925X (cloth : alk. paper)
0822319187 (pbk. : alk. paper)
Subjects: Gallop, Jane, 1952-. Sexual harassment in universities and colleges -- United States. Feminism and education -- United States. Women college teachers -- United States -- Biography. Feminists -- United States -- Biography.
Source: DLC DLC YDX

[E] Garner, Helen, 1942-
The first stone: some questions about sex and power/ Helen Garner
Sydney: Pan Macmillan, 1995
[vii],222p; 20cm (pbk)
Subjects: Sexual harassment of women, Sexual harassment in universities and colleges, Women—Attitudes, Feminism—Australia, Women--Australia

[E] Ground zero
Lozada, Marlene
Techniques.v. 73 (Mar. 1998) p. 36-41.
There is disagreement over the adoption by many school districts of a policy of "zero tolerance" toward drug use, weapon possession, and sexual harassment on school grounds. Proponents of the policy say that it is a disciplinary equalizer that leaves no flexibility for administrators or for students accused of wrongdoing and therefore allows no room for misinterpretation or favoritism. However, it is this inflexibility that opponents dislike. A sizeable camp argues in favor of administrators being given more discretion in dealing with rule violations, saying that the policy hurts otherwise good children. Advice on managing zero tolerance and a list of resources for information on zero-tolerance policies are provided.

[E] Guidebook on harassment prevention due out
Hoff, David J
Education Week.v. 18 no19 (Jan. 20 1999) p. 20.
A guidebook recommending procedures that school districts should embrace to prevent sexual, physical, and emotional abuse and to punish students and teachers who violate those codes is to be released by the National Association of Attorneys General and the Department of Education. The book provides model policies adopted by state agencies and local districts and offers checklists of what school officials should consider doing as they write their own policies.

[E] Hands off consensual sex
Alston, Kal
Academe.v. 84 no5 (Sept./Oct. 1998) p. 32-3.
The writer, an associate professor of education policy studies and women's studies at the

University of Illinois at Urbana-Champaign, responds to proposals to prohibit personal relationships put forward by the university's Sexual Harassment Task Force. She opposes the policy on the basis of her belief that the state should have very limited power over state employees' and adult students' lives, arguing that the state and its institutions have failed to adequately protect those most vulnerable to its powers. She argues that teachers must make decisions about engaging in consensual relationships with students in the context of their understanding of professional and personal ethics rather than abdicating such decisions to the state, a task force, or the faculty handbook.

[E] Harassment and discrimination: news stories show litigation on the rise
Cantu Weber, Josie
Change.v. 31 no3 (May/June 1999) p. 38-45.
As colleges and universities increasingly become the targets of lawsuits, they may well have two budget options: retain more lawyers and/or allocate more funds into educating the academic community and setting up more informal mechanisms for resolving disputes. Based on a study of reports that appeared in The Chronicle of Higher Education throughout 1997, the writer discusses the types and increasing regularity of lawsuits against academic institutions.

[E] Harassment policies: structural limitations and hidden connections
Reed, Carole Ann
Initiatives (Washington, D.C.).v. 58 no1 (1996) p. 21-6.
The limitations of harassment policies used in public educational institutions in North America are explored. Sexual harassment is defined, an overview of the development of sexual harassment law is presented, how harassment policies and procedures chiefly benefit male respondents is discussed, and the experiences of a harassment prevention adviser in a higher learning institution are described.

[E] Help with harassment
The American School Board Journal.v. 184 (May 1997) p. 14.
The Department of Education has published new guidelines on sexual harassment that should help school leaders identify genuine acts of sexual harassment. The department urges school leaders to use common sense and judgment when determining what constitutes genuine and punishable sexual harassment and provides examples of what constitutes sexual harassment in its guidelines.

[E] Herbert, Carrie M. H.
A study of the sexual harassment of London schoolgirls/ by Caroline Mary Heaven Herbert
[n.pub.], 1990
272p; 30cm
Thesis (PhD) - University of Cambridge, 1990
Includes bibliography p257-72
Subjects: R362.7

Sexual harassment – thesis. Sex bias – thesis. Secondary school pupils – thesis. Girls – thesis.

[E] Herbert, Carrie M. H.
Talking of silence: the sexual harassment of schoolgirls/ Carrie M.H. Herbert
London [England]; Philadelphia: Falmer Press, 1989
200p; 25cm
Notes: Includes bibliographical references (p. 186-194)
Subjects: Child sexual abuse--Great Britain--Case studies. Sexual harassment--Great Britain--Case studies. Sex crimes--Great Britain--Case studies.

[E] High Court shows interest in peer-sexual-harassment case
Augmented title: Davis v. Monroe County Board of Education
Walsh, Mark
Education Week.v. 17 (Feb. 4 1998) p. 30.
The U.S. Supreme Court has asked the Clinton administration for its opinion on whether school districts can be held liable for student-on-student sexual harassment. The request was made in connection with Davis v. Monroe County Board of Education, a case involving the alleged harassment of a fifth-grade girl by one of her male classmates in 1992-93 at an elementary school in Monroe County, Georgia.

[E] High Court to weigh teacher-pupil sex harassment
Augmented title: Doe v. Lago Vista Independent School District
Walsh, Mark
Education Week.v. 17 (Dec. 10 1997) p. 20.
The U.S. Supreme Court is to consider the contentious issue of when school districts may be held liable for student sexual harassment. In Doe v. Lago Vista Independent School District, the Court accepted an appeal by a woman whose daughter allegedly was involved sexually with one of her teachers. The family is seeking to hold the school district liable for the girl's alleged sexual harassment.

[E] Higher education leadership: analyzing the gender gap
Chliwniak, Luba
ASHE ERIC Higher Education Reports.v. 25 no4 (1997) p. 1-97.
The writer discusses the gender gap in higher education leadership. Currently, 16 percent of college and university presidents are female, 13 percent of chief business officers are female, and 25 percent of chief academic officers are female. If the gender gap was closed in higher education leadership, many believe that institutions would become more centered on process and persons than on tasks and outcomes, that is, a shift toward concerns described as "feminine" from those described as "masculine." Small but effective changes can be instituted by attending to such traditional practices as exclusionary tenure criteria, sexual harassment, and wage gaps.

[E] Hostile environment?

Augmented title: Nicole K. v. Upper Perkiomen School District
Zirkel, Perry A
Phi Delta Kappan.v. 79 (Jan. 1998) p. 409-10.
The writer discusses the case of a student in a middle school in the Upper Perkiomen School District of Pennsylvania who was referred to as a neo-Nazi by a teacher because of her German parentage. The student's parents filed suit on her behalf in federal court but their claims were dismissed. Their attorney filed an appeal with the Third Circuit, which assigned a mediator to the case, and the parties eventually reached a confidential settlement. The decision illustrates the importance of choosing the correct forum for legal resolution of such cases, is a reminder of the legal difficulties associated with umbrella "hate speech" policies, and is evidence of the increasing education litigation concerning "hostile atmosphere" based on protected civil rights.
Teachers Verbal behavior Suits and claims; Teachers and students Difficulties Suits and claims; Sexual harassment Suits and claims.

[E] Hostile hallways : the AAUW survey on sexual harassment in America's schools / commissioned by the American Association of University Women Educational Foundation ; researched by Harris/Scholastic Research.
Washington, DC : The Foundation, 1993.
25 p. : ill. ; 28 cm.
LC Call No.: LC212.82 .H68 1993
ISBN: 1879922010 : $11.95 ($8.95 AAUW members)
SC: Second printing: June 1994.
Subjects: Sexual harassment in education -- United States.
Educational surveys -- United States.
Other authors: American Association of University Women. Educational Foundation.
Harris/Scholastic Research.
Source: DLC DLC SNN

[E] How not to get sued
Utley, Alison
The Times Higher Education Supplement.no1338 (June 26 1998) p. I-II.
Part of a special section on teaching. Advice for university teachers who are trying to keep their balance as students become more litigious is presented. Some of the steps that lecturers can take to avoid complaints involve being aware of the level of performance required by the institution, avoiding physical conflict and being aware of the potential for allegations of sexual harassment, adhering to faculty statements in references, and logging meetings to show that supervision has taken place.

[E] Integrating theory and practice: counselor educator-school counselor collaborative
Hayes, Richard L, 1946 ; Paisley, Pamela O; Phelps, Rosemary E
Professional School Counseling.v. 1 (Oct. 1997) p. 9-12.
Part of a special section on partnerships between school counselors and counselor educators. The writers describe the efforts of a team of university-based counselor

educators and teams of school-based counselors to integrate theory and practice by developing a deliberate program of practical research. The faculty of the School Counseling Program at the University of Georgia collaborates with local school counselors in the program. Graduate students are required to go into the schools and talk to students, faculty, counselors, administrators, and parents in order to identify problems. If a problem is raised by one or more groups in the school, the graduate students bring it back to class where they recommend ways of working collaboratively with others in the school to address the problem.

[E] Is nothing sacred? the betrayal of the ministerial or teaching relationship
Fortune, Marie M
Journal of Feminist Studies in Religion.v. 10 Spring 1994 p. 17-26.
A discussion of sexual harassment within the church and university. Professional ethics are violated if any person in a ministerial or teaching role engages in sexual conduct or sexualized behavior with a congregant, client, employee, or student within the professional relationship. The essential harm done by this violation is betrayal of trust. With continuing revelations of pedophilia by Roman Catholic priests in the United States and Canada and of ministerial misconduct involving sexual abuse of congregants, as well as an increasing number of complaints brought against faculty and numerous complaints in every denomination, there can be no question that religious and academic institutions are in crisis. Both institutions face the challenge to respond in ways that can restore the integrity of the ministerial or teaching relationship.

[E] Ivory power : sexual harassment on campus / edited by Michele A. Paludi.
Albany, N.Y. : State University of New York Press, c1990.
xxv, 309 p. ; 23 cm.
Series: SUNY series in the psychology of women.
LC Call No.: LC212.862 .I95 1991
Local Call No: LC212.826 .I95 1990
LC212.862 .I95 1990
ISBN: 0791404579 (alk. paper)
0791404587 (pbk. : alk. paper)
Includes bibliographical references and index.
Subjects: Sexual harassment in universities and colleges -- United States.
Source: DLC DLC HAM

[E] J Am Coll Health 1997 Jul;46(1):3-8
Weapon carrying and substance abuse among college students.
Presley CA, Meilman PW, Cashin JR
Core Institute, Southern Illinois University at Carbondale, USA.
Results from administering the Core Alcohol and Drug Survey on 61 US campuses during the 1994/95 academic year were analyzed to assess weapon carrying among college students. A comparison with a matched sample of nonweapon carriers revealed that a greater percentage of the armed than the unarmed students had experienced harassment,

violence, and threats of violence, and that they felt less safe on their campuses. The weapon-carrying men consumed significantly more alcohol than their unarmed counterparts, and a higher percentage reported binge drinking, use of other drugs, and adverse consequences from substance abuse.

[E] J Am Coll Health 1997 Nov;46(3):127-31
College women's perceptions regarding resistance to sexual assault.
Easton AN, Summers J, Tribble J, Wallace PB, Lock RS
Department of Health Promotion, University of Toledo, Ohio, USA.
College women's perceptions about resistance to sexual assault were examined. Twenty-one percent of the 334 women surveyed stated that they had been sexually assaulted. The findings indicate the need for an increase in the number of women taking self-defense classes and a revision in women's perceptions about resisting sexual assault.

[E] J Clin Ethics 1996 Winter;7(4):341-6; discussion 347-8
A model policy addressing mistreatment of medical students.
Strong C, Wall HP, Jameson V, Horn HR, Black PN, Scott S, Brown SC
Department of Human Values and Ethics, College of Medicine, University of Tennessee, Memphis, USA.

[E] J Sch Health 1998 Aug;68(6):237-42
Sexual harassment policies in Florida school districts.
Moore MJ, Rienzo BA
Dept. of Public Health, Western Kentucky University, Bowling Green 42101, USA. brienzo@hhp.ufl.edu
Until recently, little attention has focused on the sexual harassment that occurs in primary and secondary schools. Several school-related lawsuits and study results heightened awareness of the issue. This study investigated the extent to which Florida's school districts complied with the Florida Department of Education's (FDOE) recommendation and guidelines for addressing sexual harassment in schools. Results suggest problems with sexual harassment will continue due to lack of efforts in promoting awareness of the policy and education about the issue, which scholars insist are necessary for effectiveness.

[E] J Sch Health 1998 Nov;68(9):370-5
Sexual coercion content in 21 sexuality education curricula.
Beyer CE, Ogletree RJ
Dept. of Health Education, North Carolina Central University, Durham, NC 27707, USA. cbeyer@nccu.edu
Sexual coercion, a topic of relevance to school health personnel, may be as common in high school populations as in university populations. Twenty-one sexuality education curricula were examined for information on the topics of date rape, stranger rape, pressure, incest, sexual harassment, unwanted/inappropriate touch, and exploitation/victimization.

[E] J Sch Nurs 1997 Aug;13(3):24-8
Preventing verbal harassment and violence toward gay and lesbian students.
Adams RS
Kenmore Junior High School, Bothell, Washington, USA.
School nurses (as well as other school personnel) have a role and a responsibility to help prevent verbal harassment and violence toward gay and lesbian students. The literature about verbal harassment and violence toward students in schools is scant, and there is even less written about the school nurse's role in addressing such concerns. This article points out the potential role of school nurses in addressing this issue if they will put aside personal biases and get involved in, or initiate, homophobia awareness programs and advocate for gay and lesbian students.

[E] Japanese academic in sex scandal
Rich, Vera
The Times Higher Education Supplement.no1381 (Apr. 23 1999) p. 11.
An associate professor of agriculture from the University of the Ryukyus in Okinawa, Japan, is being dismissed after being found guilty of sexual harassment and falsifying research data. The charges were heard by a court, which ordered the academic to pay his victim 1.7 million yen in compensation.

[E] Junior high school students' perceptions regarding nonconsensual sexual behavior
Jordan, Timothy R; Price, James H; Telljohann, Susan Kay, 1958
The Journal of School Health.v. 68 no7 (Sept. 1998) p. 289-96.
A study investigated junior high school students' perceptions regarding nonconsensual sexual behavior. The participants were 371 students, 94 percent of whom were aged between 12 and 14 years, from three public junior high schools. It was found that 35 percent of the students reported having engaged in sexual intercourse, that 19 percent reported feeling pressurized by friends to have sexual intercourse, that 17 percent reported having been sexually coerced by an adolescent, that 7 percent reported having been sexually coerced by an adult, and that 6 percent reported having sexually coerced someone else. The results show that early adolescents require education and skill-based training to recognize, define, and respond properly to sexual behavior of a nonconsensual nature.

[E] Kiok, Jennifer.
Are the teachers watching? : sexual harassment in our schools / by Jen Kiok.
Amherst, Mass. : [s.n.], 1998.
110 leaves ; 29 cm.
Local Call No: Div III SS99 .K5
A Division III examination in the School of Social Science, Hampshire College, January 1999. Chairperson, Marlene Fried.
Includes bibliographical references.
Subjects: Sexual harassment in education -- United States -- Massachusetts.
Source: HAM HAM

[E] Lakartidningen 1998 Apr 15;95(16):1817-9
[Medical students about sexual perspective].
[Article in Swedish]
Westerstahl A
Avdelningen for allmanmedicin, Goteborgs universitet.

[E] Layman, Nancy S., 1942-
Sexual harassment in American secondary schools : a legal guide for administrators, teachers, and students / Nancy S. Layman.
Dallas : Contemporary Research Press, 1994.
207 p. ; 24 cm.
LC Call No.: KF4155 .L39 1993
ISBN: 0935061525
Includes bibliographical references and index.
Subjects: Sex discrimination in education -- Law and legislation -- United States.
Education, Secondary -- Law and legislation -- United States.
Source: DLC DLC UIU OCL

[E] Learning, satisfaction, and mistreatment during medical internship: a national survey of working conditions
Daugherty, Steven R; Baldwin, DeWitt C., Jr; Rowley, Beverley D
JAMA.v. 279 no15 Apr. 15 1998 p. 1194-9.
Concerns about the working and learning environment of residency training continue to surface. Previous surveys of residents have focused on work hours and income, but have shed little light on how residents view their training experience. To provide a description of the internship year as seen by a large cross section of second-year residents. Mail survey conducted in 1991 on residency programs in the United States. Participants are a random 10% sample (N = 1773) of all second-year residents listed in the American Medical Association's medical research and information database.

[E] Medical student abuse: an international phenomenon
Uhari, Matti; Kokkonen, Jorma; Nuutinen, Matti
JAMA.v. 271 Apr. 6 1994 p. 1049-51.
The prevalence of physical and psychological mistreatment of medical students at 2 medical schools in Finland was evaluated. A sample of students at both institutions was surveyed. In this self-report survey, 3 of every 4 students reported experiencing some kind of mistreatment during their medical education. The students most commonly reported sexual mistreatment, which usually took the form of slurs and sexual discrimination from classmates, preclinical teachers, clinical teachers, clinicians, nurses, and patients. All forms of mistreatment were reported as occurring less frequently within the Finnish system than in the U.S. medical education system.

[E] Meeting the needs of all students and staff members: the challenge of diversity

Howard Hamilton, Mary F; Phelps, Rosemary E; Torres, Vasti
New Directions for Student Services.no82 (Summer 1998) p. 49-64.
Promoting multiculturalism while maintaining individual rights and freedom often poses
difficulties for student affairs practitioners. These difficulties converge in the two broad
areas of laws and regulations and the promotion of diversity. Legislative actions that have
been significant in higher education are affirmative action, civil rights codes, the First
Amendment, the Americans with Disabilities Act, financial aid, and sexual harassment
regulations.

[E] Membership has its costs
Augmented title: mistreatment of medical students
Lee, Francis S
JAMA.v. 271 Apr. 6 1994 p. 1048-9.
This issue of Pulse, the medical student section of the journal, contains a study by Uhari
and colleagues of medical student abuse among Finnish medical students. In this self-
report survey, the majority of Finnish medical students reported episodes of mistreatment,
including a high rate of sexual harassment of female students. This study, and other
literature on the topic, raises the question of why an environment of acceptable hostility
and exploitation exists within the medical training system.

[E] Mixed messages: sexual harassment in the public schools
Marczely, Bernadette
The Clearing House.v. 72 no5 (May/June 1999) p. 315-18.
Four major U.S. Supreme Court decisions about liability for claims of sexual harassment
are discussed. These cases have codified the need to recognize discriminatory behavior
wherever it takes place and to provide effective procedures for reporting and dealing with
it. In their dual roles as federally funded agencies and employers, schools must develop and
enforce clear sexual harassment policies.

[E] Ms Behaved?
Cornwell, Tim
The Times Higher Education Supplement.no1280 (May 16 1997) p. 17.
Jane Gallop, a distinguished professor of literature at the University of Wisconsin, has
written about her experiences of being accused of sexual harassment by two female
students in her book Feminist Accused of Sexual Harassment. In the book, which has
resulted in a storm of criticism, Gallop says that harassment applies only to men and that
consensual teacher-student sex is, in her experience, not a bad thing.

[E] Nurse Educ 1996 Jul-Aug;21(4):3
Reporting sexual harassment in an undergraduate nursing program.
Barnett KH

[E] Paludi, Michele Antoinette.
Academic and workplace sexual harassment : a resource manual / Michele A. Paludi and

Richard B. Barickman.
Albany, N.Y. : State University of New York Press, c1991.
xix, 215 p. : ill. ; 24 cm.
Series: SUNY series, the psychology of women.
LC Call No.: LC212.862 .P35 1991
ISBN: 0791408299 (CH : alk. paper)
0791408302 (pbk. : alk. paper)
Includes bibliographical references and index.
Subjects: Sexual harassment in universities and colleges -- United States. Sex
discrimination in employment -- United States. Sexual harassment of women -- United
States.
Other authors: Barickman, Richard B.
Series Entry: SUNY series in the psychology of women.
Source: DLC DLC VFC MTH

[E] Patai, Daphne, 1943-
Heterophobia : sexual harrassment and the future of feminism / Daphne Patai.
Lanham, MD : Rowman & Littlefield, 1998.
xvi, 276 p. ; 24 cm.
Series: American intellectual culture.
LC Call No.: LC212.86 .P37 1998
ISBN: 0847689875 (cloth : alk. paper)
Includes bibliographical references and index.
Subjects: Sexual harassment in universities and colleges. Sexual harassment in the
workplace. Misandry. Men's studies. Feminist theory.
Source: DLC DLC

[E] Prevalence of harassment and discrimination among 1996 medical school graduates: a
survey of eight US schools
Mangus, R. S; Hawkins, C. E; Miller, M. J
JAMA.v. 280 no9 Sept. 2 1998 p. 851-3.
A study examined the prevalence and forms of harassment and discrimination experienced
by medical students. A survey was mailed 1,001 students graduating at 8 U.S. medical
schools in 1996; 548 surveys were returned. Forty-six percent of the students reported
experiencing some kind of harassment, and 41 percent reported some form of
discrimination from instructors or supervisors. Nonsexual verbal harassment was reported
by 41 percent of students, sexual verbal harassment by 10 percent. Twenty-nine percent of
students reported discrimination based on gender, and 12 percent reported discrimination
based on race.

[E] Pride and prejudice
Augmented title: gay students sue school district over harassment
Ruenzel, David
Education Week.v. 18 no31 (Apr. 14 1999) p. 34-9.

Six former and current students of Live Oak High School in California have filed a federal civil rights lawsuit against the school district. The students say that they were subjected to "pervasive, severe, and unwelcome" verbal and physical antihomosexual harassment almost every day. They maintain that school officials were aware of the abuse yet repeatedly failed to take action. This suit suggests that the culture of the large American high school is partly to blame for this kind of abuse.

[E] Professional ethics in university administration / Ronald H. Stein, M. Carlota Baca, guest editors.
San Francisco : Jossey-Bass, c1981.
ix, 100 p. ; 24 cm.
Series: New directions for higher education ; 0271-0560 ; no. 33.
LC Call No.: LB2341 .P77
ISBN: 0875898319 (pbk.)
Includes bibliographies and index.
Foundations of ethical responsibility in higher education administration / Charles M. Chambers -- The president as ethical leader of the campus / Donald E. Walker -- Sexual harassment of women students / Susan Margaret Vance -- Ethical issues in recruiting students / Edward B. Fiske --Moral and ethical obligations of colleges and universities to minority students / Paul B. Zuber -- Self-regulation / Elaine El-Khawas -- Academic chivalry and professional responsibility / John M. Farago -- Statement on professional ethics / American Association of University Professors –Professional standards for administrators / American Association of University Administors -- Conclusions and further readings / M. Carlota Baca, Ronald H. Stein.
Subjects: College administrators -- Professional ethics.
Source: DLC DLC SNN

[E] Professor cited for 'amorous' relationship with student accuses Appalachian State U. of violating his rights
Wilson, Robin
The Chronicle of Higher Education.v. 44 no28 (Mar. 20 1998) p. A13-A14.
Officials at Appalachian State University have charged Michael Siede, an assistant professor, with violating the university's policy forbidding "amorous" relationships between faculty members and their students and plan to punish him severely. However, Siede claims that he is the victim of a student seeking revenge for a poor grade and that his rights to due process and privacy have been violated by the university.

[E] Professor faces harassment charge for disclaimer about 'adult themes' in his class
Wilson, Robin
The Chronicle of Higher Education.v. 44 (Dec. 12 1997) p. A14.
Joel M. Cohen, a professor at Oakland Community College, is facing a harassment charge over a disclaimer he issued warning that "adult themes and topics" would be discussed in his introductory psychology course. The charge was filed by a female student who took offense at the disclaimer. Dr. Cohen says there have been increasing complaints about his

course content over the past ten years but that being forced to tone down his subject matter would violate his academic freedom.

[E] Pupil-class determinants of aggressive and victim behaviour in pupils
Mooij, Ton
The British Journal of Educational Psychology.v. 68 pt3 (Sept. 1998) p. 373-85.
Aggressive behaviour in pupils is expressed in, e.g., bullying, sexual harassment, and violence. A national survey was carried out to identify different kinds of aggressive and victim behaviour displayed by pupils and to assess other variables related to pupils, classes, and schools. A total of 1998 pupils from 100 third and fourth year classes attending 71 different secondary schools took part in the research.

[E] Questions raised on handling of harassment allegations at Western Kentucky U
Schneider, Alison
The Chronicle of Higher Education.v. 45 no36 (May 14 1999) p. A16.

[E] Rape case threat to colleges
Marcus, Jon
The Times Higher Education Supplement.no1279 (May 9 1997) p. 12.
Earlham College in Indiana is being sued by a female student who alleges she was raped by the father of a family she was staying with while studying in Japan. The lawsuit could dramatically increase the legal liability of all universities that send students abroad.

[E] Ready to learn : how schools can help kids be healthier and safer / edited by Edward Miller.
Cambridge, MA : Harvard Education Letter, c1995.
xii, 121 p. ; 23 cm.
Series: HEL reprint series ; no. 2.
LC Call No.: LB3409.U5 R35 1995
ISBN: 1883433010
Articles previously published in the Harvard education letter.
Includes bibliographical references. Introduction : not ready to learn / Edward Miller -- Most schools do a poor job of promoting students' health / Adria Steinberg -- What's for lunch? A menu for changing what schools teach children about food / Edward Miller -- Youth sports : when winning is the goal, kids are the losers / Adria Steinberg -- Teaching children about sex / Adria Steinberg and Lisa Birk -- Beyond the condom wars : a comprehensive approach to AIDS education / Susan Eaton -- Drug and alcohol education : what works / Adria Steinberg and Lisa Birk -- A culture obsessed with thinness pushes some adolescents into eating disorders / Susan Eaton -- Preventing adolescent suicide : beyond myths to a new understanding / Helen Featherstone and Lisa Birk -- The killing grounds : can schools help stem the violence? / Adria Steinberg -- Research raises troubling questions about violence prevention programs / Marc Posner -- Peer mediation catches on, but some adults don't / Edward Miller -- We need a national strategy for safe schools / Gus Frias -- The physically or sexually abused child : what teachers need to

know ; Courts hold coworkers liable for knowledge of sexual abuse / Richard Fossey --
Sexual harassment at an early age : new cases are changing the rules for schools / Susan
Eaton -- Guidelines for recognizing and dealing with sexual harassment -- Sexual
harassment : Lisa's complaint / Edward Miller -- Gay students find little support in most
schools / Susan Eaton.
Subjects: Students -- Health and hygiene -- United States. Education -- Social aspects --
United States. Risk-taking (Psychology) in adolescence – United States. School violence --
United States -- Prevention. Sexual harassment in education -- United States. Child sexual
abuse -- United States.
Source: MH-Ed DLC GGN MTH

[E] Reconstructing the academy : women's education and women's studies / edited by
Elizabeth Minnich, Jean O'Barr, and Rachel Rosenfeld.
Chicago : University of Chicago Press, 1988.
vii, 312 p. : ill. ; 24 cm.
LC Call No.: LC1756 .R43 1988
ISBN: 0226530132 (alk. paper) : $27.50 (est.)
0226530140 (pbk. : alk. paper) : $19.95 (est.)
Selection of essays originally appearing in Signs.
Includes bibliographies and index. The education of women as philosophers / Elisabeth
Young-Gruehl -- An analysis of university definitions of sexual harassment / Phyllis L.
Crocker -- Changing the curriculum in higher education / Margaret L. Andersen -- For and
about women : the theory and practice of women's studies in the United States / Marilyn J.
Boxer -- Trying transformations : curriculum integration and the problem of resistance /
Susan Hardy Aiken, et al. -- The costs of exclusionary practices in women's studies /
Maxine Baca Zinn, et al. -- Alliances between women : overcoming internalized oppression
and internalized domination / Gail Pheterson -- Educating women in America / Sally
Schwager -- Women's colleges and women achievers / Mary J. Oates, Susan Williamson --
Women's colleges and women ahcievers revisited / M. Elizabeth Tidball -- Women's
colleges and women achievers : an update / Joy K. Rice, Annette Hemmings -- Wandering
in the wilderness: the search for women role models / Berenice Fisher -- Cultural feminism
versus post-structuralism : the identity crisis in feminist theory / Linda Alcoff.
Subjects: Women -- Education (Higher) -- United States. Women's studies -- United
States. Women's colleges -- United States.
Other titles: Signs.
Source: DLC DLC IOP

[E] Reports about sexual assaults inflame students at Bates College
Haworth, Karla
The Chronicle of Higher Education.v. 44 no30 (Apr. 3 1998) p. A41.
Rumors that officials at Bates College had failed to investigate a series of sexual assaults
caused an outcry on campus, leading to a protest by 300 women outside the president's
house.

[E] Research opportunities
The Times Higher Education Supplement.no1280 (May 16 1997) p. I-XXXVI.
Topics discussed relate to job-hunting, the director of the Population and Household
Change Programme, media and science, standards for graduate work, the taught doctorate,
dress in higher education, dealing with badly behaved students, sexual harassment in one-
to-one research supervision meetings, the concerns of international postgraduates, and the
ethical aspects of research.

[E] Responding effectively to sexual harassment: victim advocacy, early intervention, and
problem-solving
Hippensteele, Susan; Pearson, Thomas C
Change.v. 31 no1 (Jan./Feb. 1999) p. 48-53.
Students, faculty, and staff are being sexually harassed on campus to an epidemic degree.
Information reflected in studies over the last decade consistently shows that between 25 to
30 percent of undergraduate students are sexually harassed in a given year. During this
time, there have been great steps forward in studies of the incidence and effect of this
harassment on college campuses. As academic communities come to better comprehend the
complexities of the issue, their strategies keep evolving.

[E] Riggs, Robert O.
Sexual harassment in higher education : from conflict to community / by Robert O. Riggs,
Patricia H. Murrell, and JoAnn C. Cutting.
Washington, D.C. : George Washington University,
School of Education and Human Development, [1993]
xvii, 96 p. : ill. ; 23 cm.
Series: ASHE-ERIC higher education report, 0884-0040 ; no. 2, 1993.
LC Call No.: LC212.86 .R54 1993
ISBN: 1878380230
"Prepared by ERIC Clearinghouse on Higher Education, the George Washington
University, in cooperation with ASHE, Association for the Study of Higher Education."
Includes bibliographical references (p. 75-84) and index. The legal context of sexual
harassment -- What is the nature and prevalence of sexual harassment on campus? --
Effective policy and practice for the elimination of sexual harassment -- Model sexual
harassment policy and procedure -- From conflict to community.
Subjects: Sexual harassment in universities and colleges.
Other authors: ERIC Clearinghouse on Higher Education.
Association for the Study of Higher Education.
Series Entry: ASHE-ERIC higher education report ; 1993, no. 2.
Source: CValA DLC

[E] Riley restates rules against harassment
Augmented title: Gebser v. Lago Vista Independent School District
Walsh, Mark

Education Week.v. 17 no42 (July 8 1998) p. 1+.
Richard W. Riley, the education secretary, has said that although district liability for
damages in harassment cases was limited by the high court's ruling in Gebser v. Lago
Vista Independent School District, some districts are still in violation of Title IX of the
Education Amendments of 1972, which bans discrimination based on sex in schools
receiving federal funds.

[E] Roiphe, Katherine.
The morning after : sex, fear, and feminism on campus / Katie Roiphe. 1st ed.
Boston, Mass. : Little, Brown and Co., c1993.
xii, 180 p. ; 22 cm.
LC Call No.: LC197 .R65 1993
ISBN: 0316754315 : $18.95
Includes bibliographical references.
Subjects: Feminism and education -- United States. Education, Higher -- Political aspects
-- United States. Feminism -- United States. Sexual harassment -- United States.
Source: DLC DLC MTH

[E] Ruling out sexual harassment
Fuertes, Monica
Techniques.v. 73 no8 (Nov./Dec. 1998) p. 42-3.
According to research, the most common form of sexual harassment in schools occurs
between students. Any teacher, administrator, or school official who is approached by a
student about a potential sexual harassment situation should listen to but not judge the
truth of the student's allegations, respond to the student's concerns, explain the complaints
procedure, and immediately report the facts to the Title IX coordinator.

[E] Saying the unsaid: girl killing and the curriculum
Perlstein, Daniel
Journal of Curriculum and Supervision.v. 14 no1 (Fall 1998) p. 88-104.
The media coverage of and the authorities' response to the killing of four schoolgirls and
one woman teacher in Jonesboro, Arkansas, obscured the gender conflicts at the heart of
the tragedy. Students repeatedly claimed that the killings were motivated by a young man's
desire to get revenge on a young woman who would not be his girlfriend. However,
reporters and authorities avoided the social and cultural roots of the Jonesboro killings by
dismissing this explanation, and news coverage embraced sentimental and superficial
notions of Southern culture. Unwilling to explore the place of Jonesboro's violence in
Southern culture or American society, the authorities and the media gave up efforts to find
a cause for the shootings. Police strategies, which did not deal with gender conflicts and
are poorly suited to preventing school violence, were the primary response to the killings.
The Jonesboro shootings and the response to them suggest that apart from curricula
focused specifically on sexual harassment, schools also need to integrate the question of
gender violence into the mainstream curriculum.

[E] Scandinavian universities respond to complaints of sexual harassment
Bollag, Burton
The Chronicle of Higher Education.v. 43 (Apr. 4 1997) p. A37-A38.
Academic institutions across Scandinavia are recognizing sexual harassment and taking action to combat it, with institutions in Sweden in the vanguard.

[E] School counselors' perceptions of nonconsensual sexual activity among high school students
King, Keith A; Tribble, Joanne L; Price, James H
Professional School Counseling.v. 2 no4 (Apr. 1999) p. 286-90.
A study investigated the perceptions of school counselors regarding nonconsensual sexual activity among high school students. Participants were 235 secondary school counselors. Results revealed that 97 percent of the participants felt that it was their responsibility to counsel students involved in nonconsensual sexual activity.

[E] School officials' liability limited in teacher-student harassment case
Augmented title: Gebser v. Lago Vista Independent School District
Essex, Nathan L
American Secondary Education.v. 27 no2 (Winter 1998) p. 23-7.
The recent landmark decision taken by the U.S. Supreme Court in Gebser v. Lago Vista Independent School District is discussed. The case concerns a student, Alida Star Gebser, who filed charges against her teacher, Frank Waldrop, for luring her into a sexual relationship. The ruling held that students who are sexually harassed by their teachers cannot recover monetary damages from school districts unless district officials were in a position to have taken corrective actions or knew of the abuse and did nothing about it. The various levels of sexual harassment that may affect school districts are described, and administrative guidelines for dealing with sexual harassment are presented.

[E] Schools called unfair to gay kids
The American School Board Journal.v. 185 no11 (Nov. 1998) p. 12+.
A study examined public school districts' efforts to protect the rights of gay and lesbian students and teachers. Participants were 42 of the country's largest public school districts. Researchers gave 16 districts a grade F and three districts a grade D for failing to protect gay and lesbian students and teachers from harassment and discrimination. They rewarded only eight districts with a Grade A or A-.

[E] Schools face blame over pupil assault
Marcus, Jon
The Times Educational Supplement.no4310 (Feb. 5 1999) p. 22.
The U.S. Supreme Court is considering whether crude remarks and taunts between children can constitute sexual harassment and whether schools can be deemed liable for it. The family of a girl who was teased and groped by a boy in her class at an elementary

school in Georgia contends that sexual discrimination in educational institutions that accept money from the federal government is forbidden under a 1972 federal law.

[E] Secrets in Public: *Sexual Harassment* in Public (and Private) Schools. Working Paper Series No. 256. Revised.
Stein, Nan D.
This document, part of the Wellesley College (Massachusetts) Center for Research on Women's working papers series, examines the issue of *sexual harassment* in education. The report explores a number of incidents in which female students have been the targets of unwanted *sexual* comments, advances, and assaults.

[E] Seeing Is Not Believing: *Sexual Harassment* in Public School and the Role of Adults.
Stein, Nan
Peer-to-peer *sexual harassment* is rampant in elementary and secondary schools. While sometimes identified and curtailed, it is usually tolerated and characterized as normal. Regardless of the ways school authorities regard *sexual harassment*, it interferes with a student's right to receive equal educational opportunities and violates Title IX. This paper describes the experiences of students who have experienced *sexual harassment* by their peers and discusses its ramifications.

[E] Sex equity and sexuality in education / edited by Susan Shurberg Klein.
Albany : State University of New York Press, c1992.
vi, 381 p. : ill. ; 24 cm.
LC Call No.: HQ57.5.A3 S48 1992
ISBN: 0791410331 (alk. paper)
079141034X (pbk. : alk. paper)
Includes bibliographical references. Sex equity and sexuality in education : breaking the barriers / Susan Shurberg Klein -- Sexism, sexuality, and education : feminist thought then and now / Selma Greenberg and Patricia B. Campbell -- Passions and power : sexuality, sex equity, and education in historical perspective / John Rury -- Global perspectives on sexuality and equity in education / Nelly P. Stromquist -- Goals for sex-equitable sexuality education / Mariamne H. Whatley -- The impact of puberty and sexual activity upon the health and education of adolescent girls and boys / Jeanne Brooks-Gunn -- Sexism and early parenting : cause and effect? / Theresa Cusick -- Sex equity and sexuality in college-level sex education / Marilyn Myerson -- Emerging equity issues related to homosexuality in education / Dolores A. Grayson -- Breaking the silence : sexual and gender-based harassment in elementary, secondary, and postsecondary education / Karen Bogart ... [et al.] Power, politics, and sexuality in mentor-protégée relationships : implications for women's achievement and career development / Marilyn Haring and Michele A. Paludi -- Sexuality and latchkey children / Thomas J. Long and Lynette Long -- The role of sexuality and sex equity in the education of minority adolescents / Saundra Murray Nettles and Diane Scott-Jones -- Disabled women : the myth of the asexual female / Corbett Joan O'Toole and Jennifer L. Bregante --Sex equity principles for evaluating sexuality education materials / Bonnie Trudell and Mariamne H. Whatley -- Using legal resources and

community action to resist sexual harassment in higher education / Richard Barickman --
Sexuality and sexism in school : how should educators be prepared? / Myra Sadker, David
Sadker, and Charol Shakeshaft.
Subjects: Sex instruction -- United States. Sex discrimination in education -- United
States. Sexism -- United States. Sex educators -- United States. Sexism in higher education
-- United States.
Source: DLC DLC PMC MTH

[E] Sex scandal has electoral impact
Augmented title: Universite Nationale, Guinea
Fatunde, Tunde
The Times Higher Education Supplement.no1362 (Dec. 11 1998) p. 12.
A major issue in the run-up to Guinea's presidential elections centers on claims that
academics have sexually harassed students at the Universite Nationale. Allegations leveled
at some professors and lecturers in the medicine and pharmacy faculties have motivated
30,000 students at the university to begin an indefinite strike. The protests are on behalf of
female students who maintain that some teachers have asked for sex in return for exam
passes.

[E] Sex scandal takes its toll
Augmented title: Simon Fraser University president resigns amidst controversy over
handling of sexual harassment case involving swimming coach
Fine, Philip
The Times Higher Education Supplement.no1314 (Jan. 9 1998) p. 11.
John Stubbs, president of Simon Fraser University, has resigned after a highly-publicized
sex harassment case involving a swimming coach and a student. Varsity swimming coach
Liam Donnelly was fired in May 1997 after a student alleged she had been date-raped by
him. However, Donnelly was subsequently rehired when it was discovered that the
investigative hearing procedure had been flawed. Stubbs resigned his post as president in
December 1997, following almost six months of leave for depression, which many believe
was due to the pressure of the sexual harassment case.

[E] Sexual abuse making women drop out
Kikotho, Wachira
The Times Higher Education Supplement.no1302 (Oct. 17 1997) p. 14.
Sexual harassment is a reality in many universities in sub-Saharan countries, according to
senior researchers with the World Bank. In Ghana, Nigeria, Kenya, Uganda, and
Zimbabwe the dropout rate for women is high compared to that for men, and aid agencies
say that there is high wastage among women students due to inefficiency, poverty, abuse,
and lack of female role models among lecturers. The efforts of Makerere University, the
University of Nairobi, Kenyatta University, and Egerton University to counteract the
problem are outlined.

[E] Sexual and gender harassment in the academy : a guide for faculty, students, and

administrators / Phyllis Franklin ... [et al.] ; Commission on the Status of Women in the Profession.
New York : Modern Language Association of America, 1981.
74 p. ; 21 cm.
LC Call No.: LB2332.3 .S49
Local Call No: LB2332.3 .S49 1981
ISBN: 0873523334 (pbk.) : $3.50
Bibliography: p. 45-52.
Subjects: Modern Language Association of America. Women college teachers -- United States. Sex discrimination in education -- United States.
Other authors: Modern Language Association of America. Commission on the Status of Women in the Profession.
Source: DLC DLC SNN

[E] Sexual harassment and the university
Holmes, Robert L
The Monist.v. 79 Oct. 1996 p. 499-518.
The writer discusses sexual harassment within the context of universities. He defines sexual harassment as "repeated unwanted sexual attention." He disputes the view that this activity is wrong for one reason only, such as that it represents sexual discrimination or is an expression of sexism (specifically, the domination of women by men), or both. He argues that such a view is an oversimplification and that various considerations contribute to its wrongness, depending on the context. Bearing that in mind, he considers what is distinctive in the university setting to understand fully why it is wrong there.

[E] Sexual harassment during medical training
JAMA.v. 262 Nov. 3 1989 p. 2390.

[E] Sexual harassment in academia: a hazard to women's health
Van Rossmalen, Erica; McDaniel, Susan A
Women and Health.v. 28 no2 1998 p. 33-54.
Universities and colleges have for a long time ignored sexual harassment, hoped it was non-existent or waited for it to disappear. Recently, however, students, professors and university administrators have begun to recognize the perniciousness and pervasiveness of the problem. Based on data collected by questionnaire from 455 women university undergraduate and graduate students and nine follow-up in-depth interviews, this study examines the dimensions and dynamics of sexual harassment as a health hazard for women. Sexual harassment is found to have both direct and indirect health effects. In contributing to the literature on women's culturally and socially determined health problems, this study sheds light on the ways in which women students' economic, political, social and personal well-being can be undermined by sexual harassment.

[E] Sexual harassment in academia: a hazard to women's health.
van Roosmalen E, McDaniel SA

Department of Sociology and Social Anthropology, Dalhousie University, Halifax, Nova Scotia, Canada.

Universities and colleges have for a long time ignored sexual harassment, hoped it was non-existent or waited for it to disappear. Recently, however, students, professors and university administrators have begun to recognize the perniciousness and pervasiveness of the problem but thus far with little attention to sexual harassment as a health hazard. In contributing to the literature on women's culturally and socially determined health problems, this study sheds light on the ways in which women students' economic, political, social and personal well-being can be undermined by sexual harassment.

[E] Sexual Harassment in Education. Second Edition.
Lewis, John F.; Hastings, Susan C.

[E] Sexual harassment in higher education: reflections and new perspectives
Dziech, Billie Wright; Hawkins, Michael W
Garland, 1998. 191 p.

[E] Sexual harassment in North Dakota public schools: a study of eight high schools
Stratton, Stanley D; Backes, John S
The High School Journal.v. 80 (Feb./Mar. 1997) p. 163-72.
A study examined the extent of student sexual harassment in North Dakota public schools. Both male and female students identified sexual comments, jokes, gestures, or looks as the most frequent type of sexual harassment experienced.

[E] Sexual harassment in schools
Flynn, Andrea Feltus
The Education Digest.v. 62 (Apr. 1997) p. 34-5.
An article condensed from the February 1997 issue of Tips for Principals. Strategies for dealing with sexual harassment and student peer harassment at school are presented.

[E] Sexual harassment in schools: a guide for teachers
London, 1992
Herbert, C.M.H.

[E] Sexual harassment in schools: they stray, you pay
Gehring, Donald D; Bailey, Joe
Rural Educator.v. 18 (Spring 1997) p. 1-6.
The writers discuss the way the courts have interpreted Title IX of the Education Amendments Act of 1972 to include the sexual harassment of students and the way the "deliberate indifference" standard may be applied in instances of sexual harassment.

[E] Sexual Harassment in the 90's.
Wasserman, Nora M. Fraser
This document discusses the developing law of sexual harassment. Sexual harassment is

discussed not only in the school environment, but also in the workplace. Two legally recognized forms of sexual harassment are described: (1) quid pro quo, or demanding sexual favors in exchange for grades, raises, promotions; and (2) the hostile environment claim, in which sexual harassment is so pervasive that even women not being directly subjected to sexual advances suffer because of the atmosphere.

[E] *Sexual Harassment* in the Schools: A Statewide Project for Secondary and Vocational Schools. Revised.
This report describes ways of eliminating *sexual harassment* from Washington State schools. Appendices include supplementary information on laws regarding *sexual harassment* and school responsibility, and on dealing with and documenting individual cases. (KH)

[E] *Sexual Harassment* of Women Graduate Students: The Impact of Institutional Factors. Fuehrer, Ann; Schilling, Karen Maitland
Sexual harassment is one concern of women graduate students in community psychology programs. When a *sexual* relationship exists between male faculty and female students, the distribution of power reflects the subordinate status of women and the dominant position of men. Walker, Erickson, and Woolsey (1985) suggest three sets of ethical issues raised by such contact: (1) unwanted *sexual* advances limit the victim's ability to choose when and with whom she will have a *sexual* relationship; (2) *sexualization* of a professional relationship interferes with mentoring; and (3) the mentor abuses his power to obtain personal gratification. *Sexual harassment* within academia may be understood within a framework which suggests that competing moralities are likely to perpetuate such behaviors.

[E] Sexual harassment on campus : a legal compendium / edited by Elsa Kircher Cole.
Edition: 2nd ed.
Washington, D.C. (1 Dupont Circle, Suite 620,
Washington 20036) : National Association of College and University Attorneys, 1990.
iv, 265 p. ; 28 cm.
Series: NACUA, the publication series.
Local Call No: KF3467 .S48 1990
Includes bibliographical references: (p. 263-265)
Subjects: Sexual harassment of women -- Law and legislation -- United States. Women college students -- Legal status, laws, etc. -- United States. Women teachers -- Legal status, laws, etc. – United States. Grievance procedures -- United States. College personnel management -- United States. Sex discrimination against women -- Law and legislation -- United States.
Other authors: National Association of College and University Attorneys (U.S.)
Source: HVC HVC ZRS AMH

[E] Sexual Harassment on Campus. A Guide for Administrators, Faculty, and Students.
Sandler, Bernice R., Ed.; Shoop, Robert J., Ed.

This book discusses many of the problems faced by higher education institutions in addressing sexual harassment on campus. It is an attempt to help institutions involved in the process of reexamining and revising their policies and procedures that deal with sexual harassment. The 19 chapters, each written by a nationally recognized scholar, provide sociological and psychological insights, cover current legal thought, and offer specific recommendations and guidelines for identifying and dealing with sexual harassment issues.

[E] Sexual Harassment on Campus: A Legal Compendium.
Van Tol, Joan E., Ed.
Law review and journal articles on sexual harassment in higher education are presented along with policies and procedures from selected universities and organizations, guidance on drafting policies, and a selected bibliography.

[E] Sexual harassment on college campuses : abusing the ivory power / edited by Michele A. Paludi.
Albany : State University of New York Press, c1996.
xxviii, 311 p. ; 24 cm.
Series: SUNY series, the psychology of women.
LC Call No.: LC212.862 .S49 1996
ISBN: 079142801X (alk. paper)
0791428028 (pbk. : alk. paper)
Rev. and expanded ed. of: Ivory power. c1990.
Includes bibliographical references and index.
Subjects: Sexual harassment in universities and colleges -- United States.
Other titles: Ivory power.
Series Entry: SUNY series in the psychology of women.
Source: DLC DLC MTH

[E] Sexual harassment on the job : a guide for employers, a guide / prepared by the New Hampshire Advisory Committee to the U.S. Commission on Civil Rights.
Washington, D.C. : U.S. Commission on Civil Rights ; USGPO, 1982.
22 p. ; 23 cm.
Local Call No: HD6060.5.U5 S4
"September 1982."
Bibliography: p. 19.
Subjects: Sexual harassment of women. Sex discrimination in employment -- United States.
Other authors: United States Commission on Civil Rights. New Hampshire Advisory Committee.
Source: STU STU GPO MTH

[E] Sexual harassment policies in Florida school districts
Moore, Michele Johnson; Rienzo, Barbara A
The Journal of School Health.v. 68 no6 (Aug. 1998) p. 237-42.

A study examined the extent to which Florida's school districts complied with Florida Department of Education (FDOE) recommendations on sexual harassment policies. Data were obtained from telephone surveys of equity coordinators for the school districts and analysis of districts' sexual harassment policies. Most school districts had either adopted policies or were developing one, and these policies closely conformed to the sample polices included in the FDOE's Guidelines for Policies Addressing Sexual Misconduct Toward Students in Public Schools. However, districts' policies rarely addressed suggestions included in the guidelines but not in the sample policies.

[E] Sexual Harassment Protocol.
This document spells out policy regarding sexual harassment in the Connecticut vocational-technical school system that was developed by the Connecticut State Department of Education, the Connecticut Division of Vocational, Technical, and Adult Education, and the Connecticut Women's Education and Legal Fund, Inc.

[E] Sexual Harassment: A Common Sample for the University and the Workplace.
Beauregard, Terri Kinion
The sexual harassment experienced by a sample of women (N=154) in a university setting was compared with the sexual harassment experienced by them in a workplace setting.

[E] *Sexual Harassment*: A Hidden Issue.
A discussion of *sexual harassment* on college and university campuses addresses a number of questions and issues: myths of *sexual harassment*; what is *sexual harassment*, how widespread is it, and why are women reluctant to talk about it?; *sexual harassment* and the law; is *harassment* a violation of Title VII of the Civil Rights Act (for employees) or of Title IX (for students)?; can an employer ignore complaints of *harassment*?; can damages be awarded to persons successfully claiming *harassment*?; Title IX and grievance procedures; and implications for institutions.

[E] *Sexual Harassment*: A Problem Shielded by Silence.
Hotelling, Kathy
Journal of Counseling and Development; v69 n6 p497-501 Jul-Aug 1991
Offers an overview of complex issue of *sexual harassment*. Outlines definitions, prevalence data, cultural context, barriers to reporting these experiences to appropriate resources, and effects of *sexual harassment* on victims. Concludes educators must seek out opportunities to raise awareness of *sexual harassment* and prevent its occurrence. (Author/ABL)

[E] Sexual harassment: the Supreme Court speaks
Augmented title: Gebser v. Lago Vista Independent School District
Mann, Richard L; Hughes, William
American Secondary Education.v. 27 no2 (Winter 1998) p. 28-31.
The U.S. Supreme Court ruling on school district liability for sexual harassment in Gebser v. Lago Vista Independent School District is discussed. Recommendations for school

officials are presented, and school policy, procedure, and notice requirements under Office of Civil Rights guidelines are described.

[E] Sexual harassment: what is happening in our dance schools?
Hamilton, Linda H
Dance Magazine.v. 69 Dec. 1995 p. 86-8.
Dance students need to be prepared to handle situations in which they could be sexually harassed. Education on sexual harassment gives a name to inappropriate behaviors that may already exist in the performing arts. A school policy should offer protection and help determine the truth while guarding against frivolous or malicious accusations brought against faculty members, employees, or students. Dance companies should likewise have specific guidelines to protect members, as well as any youths who perform in their productions. The writer defines sexual harassment and discusses the prevalence of harassment in schools, the implications for dance schools, and the steps students should take if they have been sexually harassed.

[E] Shifting legal ground on harassment has made it harder for victims to win
Hendrie, Caroline
Education Week.v. 18 no15 (Dec. 9 1998) p. 18.
In Gebser v. Lago Vista Independent School District, the U.S. Supreme Court ruled that districts are liable only if a school official with authority to stop the abuse both knew about it and displayed "deliberate indifference" by failing to act. Critics of the ruling claim that it would encourage school authorities not to become informed about sexual harassment in order to avoid being financially liable.

[E] Speaking up: what teachers must do about sexual harassment
Lengel, Gena
The Clearing House.v. 70 (May/June 1997) p. 246-9.
Teachers must speak out on the issue of sexual harassment. Individual teachers must recognize sexual harassment and be aware of its destructive effects, report it when it occurs, and teach and model proper conduct and behavior, mutual respect, and equality between the sexes. Examples of sexual harassment at the school and college level are provided.

[E] Stanford surgeon tells all
Holden, Constance
Science.v. 280 no5365 May 8 1998 p. 813.
Neurosurgeon Frances Conley's Walking Out on the Boys has been met with deafening silence at Stanford University. Conley's book is an autobiographical account of her clashes with aggressive male department chiefs at Stanford's Medical School during the 1980s and 1990s. She says there is an ingrained and traditional pattern of sexual harassment in medicine and cites flagrant instances at Stanford.

[E] Stein, Nan D., 1947-

Flirting or hurting? : a teacher's guide on student-to-student sexual harassment in schools (grades 6 through 12) / written by Nan Stein and Lisa Sjostrom.
Washington : National Education Association, c1994.
viii, 106 p. : ill. ; 28 cm.
LC Call No.: LC212.8 .S74 1994
ISBN: 0810618648
"A joint project of the NEA Women and Girls Center for Change and the Wellesley College Center for Research on Women."
"An NEA Professional Library publication."
Includes bibliographical references (p. 77-78)
Subjects: Sexual harassment in education -- United States -- Handbooks, manuals, etc.
Students -- United States -- Conduct of life -- Handbooks, manuals, etc.
Source: DLC DLC DAY PIT IAY MTH

[E] Stop it! Students speak out on sexual harassment (videotape review)
Davis, Sue, reviewer
School Library Journal.v. 43 (Apr. 1997) p. 70-1.
Stop It! Students Speak Out on Sexual Harassment ($89), from Films for the Humanities and Sciences, is a thought-provoking 17-minute video in which male and female students share their experiences of being sexually harassed at school.

[E] Students accuse drama professor of sex harassment and verbal abuse
Leatherman, Courtney
The Chronicle of Higher Education.v. 44 (Oct. 17 1997) p. A14.
David Hammond, a drama professor at the University of North Carolina at Chapel Hill, has been accused of the sexual harassment and verbal abuse of his students. As many as ten graduate students have made allegations against the professor, although others in his program have come to his defense, describing him as an "incredible teacher" and characterizing his accusers as thin-skinned. Hammond, who has protested his innocence in a statement, has been put on a paid leave of absence.

[E] Students as victims of sexual harassment: the evolving law
McCarthy, Martha M
Journal of Law and Education.v. 27 no3 (July 1998) p. 401-21.
Sexual harassment victims can seek damages from school districts under Title IX and from districts and individual state actors under Section 1983. Although the courts have recognized a Fourteenth Amendment liberty right to bodily security under the Due Process Clause and a right to be free from purposeful sex discrimination by state actors under the Equal Protection Clause, students carry a heavy burden of proof in establishing that these rights have been impaired by public school districts or authorities.

[E] Student-to-student sexual harassment (book review)
Brown, Lisa A; Jones, Rebecca, reviewer
The American School Board Journal.v. 185 no6 (June 1998) p. 42+.

[E] Supreme Court declines to hear appeal over college's harassment policy
Leatherman, Courtney
The Chronicle of Higher Education.v. 43 (Mar. 28 1997) p. A14.
The Supreme Court has denied a petition to hear a case involving San Bernardino Valley College and a tenured professor of English. The Supreme Court has let stand a unanimous ruling by the Court of Appeals that Dean Cohen's free speech rights were violated when the college decided that his explicit classroom discussions constituted sexual harassment.

[E] Supreme Court says colleges may be liable for student-on-student harassment
Augmented title: Davis v. Monroe County Board of Education
Hebel, Sara
The Chronicle of Higher Education.v. 45 no39 (June 4 1999) p. A40-A41.
The Supreme Court has ruled that schools and colleges may be held responsible for violating federal laws prohibiting gender bias if they are deliberately indifferent to a student's sexual harassment by a peer. The decision was made in Davis v. Monroe County Board of Education, a case that centered on the alleged abuse of a fifth-grader by a classmate and the school's failure to take disciplinary action.

[E] Systemic violence in education : promise broken / edited by Juanita Ross Epp and Ailsa M. Watkinson.
Albany : State University of New York Press, c1997.
xvii, 220 p. ; 24 cm.
Series: SUNY series, education and culture.
LC Call No.: LB3013.3 .S97 1997
ISBN: 0791432955 (hardcover : alk. paper)
0791432963 (pbk. : alk. paper)
Includes bibliographies and index.
I. Systemic violence in administrative practice. Administrative complicity and systemic violence in education / Ailsa M. Watkinson -- Authority, pedagogy, and violence / Juanita Ross Epp -- Who knows? who cares? : schools and coordinated action on child abuse / Rosonna Tite. II. Systemic violence in pedagogical practice. Opening spaces : examining the blocks / Pam Whitty -- Video games : playing on a violent background / Linda Wason-Ellam -- Discourses and silencing in classroom space / Mutindi Ndunda -- Lethal labels : miseducative discourse about educative experiences / Sandra Moneath and Karyn Cooper -- The other side of labeling / Linda Rossler. III. Systemic violence, women, and teachers. The family romance and the student-centered classroom / Lisa Jadwin -- Disrupting the code of silence : investigating elementary students sexually harassing their teachers / Elizabeth Richards -- Learning from the learning place : case studies of harassment in a post-secondary institution / Catharine E. Warren -- Systemic violence : linking women's stories, education, and abuse / Laura Ho, Kathie Webb, and Anne Hughson. IV. Keeping promise. Personal reconstruction : when systemic violence stops / Myrna Yuzicapi -- Addressing systemic violence in education / Ailsa M. Watkinson and Juanita Ross Epp.
Subjects: School violence -- Canada -- Case studies. School violence -- United States --

Case studies. School management and organization -- Case studies. Classroom management -- Social aspects – Case studies. Sexual harassment in education -- Case studies. Schools -- Sociological aspects -- Case studies.
Other authors: Epp, Juanita Ross and Watkinson, Ailsa M.
Source: DLC DLC CUM SNN

[E] Systemic violence in education: promise broken
Epp, Juanita Ross, ed; Watkinson, Ailsa M., ed
State Univ. of N.Y. Press, 1997. 220 p.

[E] Systemic violence in education: promise broken/ edited by Juanita Ross Epp and Ailsa M. Watkinson
Albany: State University of New York Press, c1997
xvii,220p; 23cm
Series SUNY Series, education and culture
Subjects: School violence--Canada--Case studies School violence--United States--Case studies School management and organization--Case studies Classroom management--Social aspects--Case studies Sexual harassment in education--Case studies Schools--Sociological aspects--Case studies

[E] Systemic violence: how schools hurt children/ edited by Juanita Ross Epp and Ailsa M. Watkinson
London: Falmer, 1996
xii,203p; 24cm (pbk)
Subjects: School violence, School management and organization, Classroom management--Social aspects, Sexual harassment in education, Schools--Sociological aspects, 371.5, Violence, Child abuse, Pupil welfare, Pupil school relationship, School safety

[E] Taking sexual harassment seriously
Augmented title: Oona R.-S. by Kate S. v. McCaffrey
Sendor, Benjamin
The American School Board Journal.v. 185 (Feb. 1998) p. 16-17.
The recent decision by the U.S. 9th Circuit Court of Appeals in Oona R.-S. by Kate S. v. McCaffrey follows the trend among federal courts to apply Title IX's prohibition against sexual harassment to peer sexual harassment and to sexual harassment of a student by a school employee. The decision supports the contention that there is a clear trend to interpret Title IX to require school officials to prevent sexual harassment of students by both school employees and students.

[E] Talking of silence: the sexual harassment of schoolgirls
London, 1989
Herbert, C.M.H.

[E] Teacher leadership

Augmented title: symposium
The Clearing House.v. 70 (May/June 1997) p. 233-56.
Topics discussed are the hierarchical chain of command in schools, encouraging teachers
to work with administrators as collegial leaders, collaboration between school and
university faculty, how teachers must speak out on the issue of sexual harassment, a letter
from a new teacher to experienced teachers, why teachers need to stop avoiding contact
with the community, and volunteering for school committees.

[E] The culture of sexual harassment
Augmented title: summary of research by V. Lee and others
Bracey, Gerald W
Phi Delta Kappan.v. 78 (May 1997) p. 725-6.
The writer discusses the findings of a study into sexual harassment in schools conducted
by Valerie Lee, Robert Croninger, Eleanor Linn, and Xianglei Chen of the University of
Michigan and reported in the summer 1996 issue of the American Educational Research
Journal.

[E] The Evolution of the Concept of *"Sexual Harassment"* in Higher Education.
Rice, Suzanne
Courts have tended to find that more and more behavior can be classified as *sexual
harassment,* and many academic feminists have also pressed for a more inclusive
conception of *sexual harassment.* Phyllis Crocker has argued that institutions of higher
education should remove distinctions between "more and less" serious forms of *sexual
harassment* and should adopt "victim-based" definitions. Her ideas have been extended
with the concept of "contrapower *sexual harassment.*" Educational institutions have
addressed the problem by implementing policies expansively proscribing certain conduct
procedures.

[E] The first stone (book review)
Garner, Helen, 1942 ; Sage, Lorna, reviewer
The Times Literary Supplement.no4931 Oct. 3 1997 p. 13.
This book is based on a real-life case in which the Master of Ormond College of the
University of Melbourne was accused of sexual harassment. It is compulsive reading
containing many culture clashes between generations, between metaphorical mothers and
daughters, between patriarchal institutions and their students and radical faculty, and
between institutional life itself and freelance mores.

[E] The lecherous professor: sexual harassment on campus
Boston, 1984

[E] The man who knew too much
Augmented title: professor's probing teaching methods put his career in jeopardy
Shalit, Ruth
Lingua Franca.v. 8 (Feb. 1998) p. 31-40.

The probing teaching methods of Adam M. Weisberger, a former sociology professor at Colby College in Maine, resulted in charges of impropriety and ended his career as a sociology professor. Weisberger has now filed a civil rights complaint accusing the college of gender discrimination and, ironically, of unlawful sexual harassment.

[E] 'The ones who just patronise seem genial by comparison': an enquiry into sexual harassment of women in Oxford University
Oxford, 1984
Oxford University Student Union. Women's Committee

[E] Theater and tragedy: sexual harassment in the academy
Nelson, Cary
Academe.v. 84 no5 (Sept./Oct. 1998) p. 14-23.
For decades, neither serious nor nonserious sexual harassment cases were pursued, and brutal sexual harassers operated with impunity. Gradually, the concept of sexual harassment was defined and popularized with the help of legislation and broad feminist theorizing about gender relations and politics. Influenced heavily by legal considerations, bureaucratic campus procedures have tended to aim mainly at protecting the institution rather than honoring academic principles or discovering the truth. At the same time, the concept of sexual harassment has been broadened, modified, and related to a range of larger social agendas with often troubling consequences. The real task for the academy is to discourage or punish acts of sexual harassment rather than to police the whole realm of human behavior.

[E] Tidsskr Nor Laegeforen 1994 Sep 10;114(21):2491-4
[Occurrence of sexual abuse among students in Trondheim].
[Article in Norwegian]
Schei B, Muus KM, Bendixen M
Institutt for samfunnsmedisinske fag, medisinke fakultet, Universitetet i Trondheim.
Few studies of the prevalence and incidence of sexual abuse have been conducted in the Nordic countries. The aim of the present study was to estimate the prevalence of accounts of sexual abuse and to calculate the incidence of rape and attempted rape among students. A questionnaire was handed out to a random sample of 1,322 students in Trondheim. Based on information on reported events during the year prior to the study, the yearly incidence of rape/attempted rape among women was 12 per 1,000. Only attempted rape was reported in the same time interval among men, giving a yearly incidence of two per 1,000. Applied to the total population of students in Trondheim, 87 female and 16 male students are exposed to rape/attempted rape every year.

[E] Till, Frank J.
Sexual harassment : a report on the sexual harassment of students / by Frank J. Till.
Washington, D.C. : National Advisory Council on
Women's Educational Programs, 1980.

51, 35 p. ; 28 cm.
Local Call No: HQ23 .T56x
ED 1.2 Se9
Bibliography: p. 29.
Subjects: Sexual harassment of women. Women college students.
Other authors: United States. National Advisory Council on Women's Educational
Programs.
Source: BGU BGU SNN

[E] Title VII Sexual Harassment Guidelines and Educational Employment [and] What Can
Students Do About Sex Discrimination?
Howard, Susan; And Others
Guidelines concerning sexual harassment of employees at educational institutions under
Title VII of the Civil Rights Act of 1964 are considered. The text of the guidelines, as
reprinted from the "Federal Register," is included. Guidelines for students, based on a
model developed at Utah State University, are also included in a separate attachment.
Actions to be taken are listed in priority order, beginning with personal talk with the staff
person, and concluding with filing a formal complaint. (SW)

[E] Transsexual student loses sex-harassment claim against New York U
Schneider, Alison
The Chronicle of Higher Education.v. 44 no33 (Apr. 24 1998) p. A14.
Although Jennifer Miles, a transsexual student at New York University, has proved in
court that she was sexually harassed by Cliff Eisen, an assistant professor of musicology,
Miles has failed to establish that the university was liable. The university is pleased with
the court verdict, however, Miles's lawyer says she will appeal the decision.

[E] Two single females and a slimy supervisor
Lee, Deborah
The Times Higher Education Supplement.no1280 (May 16 1997) p. V.
The writer discusses cases where two white, single, heterosexual, female students had
sexual harassment problems in one-to-one research supervision meetings with the same
white, married, male supervisor.

[E] Vermont agency faults Goddard for response to complaint of on-line harassment
Ma, Kenneth
The Chronicle of Higher Education.v. 45 no29 (Mar. 26 1999) p. A33.
The Vermont Human Rights Commission has concluded that Goddard College violated a
state discrimination law in the way it responded to a sexual harassment complaint. The
commission voted in favor of an alumna who had claimed that the college had not taken
prompt and appropriate action in relation to an employee who had sent her sexually
explicit e-mail messages.

[E] Violence Vict 1996 Summer;11(2):175-80

The prevalence of sexual harassment among female family practice residents in the United States.
Vukovich MC
Family Health Care of Wadsworth OH 44281, USA.
The purpose of this study was to determine the prevalence of sexual harassment as defined by the AMA among female family practice residents in the United States. Sexual harassment is a common occurrence among family practice residents during residency training. Further studies are needed to examine the effect of sexual harassment policies instituted by the American Graduate Council on Medical Education on the prevalence of sexual harassment in medical training since the time of this study.

[E] When no means no
Crisci, George S
The American School Board Journal.v. 186 no6 (June 1999) p. 25-9.
Advice for educators on recognizing and preventing sexual harassment in schools is provided. The advice relates to recent court rulings on school liability claims, school policy regarding sexual harassment and implementation of the policy, and when to investigate claims of sexual harassment.

[E] When teachers harass students
Augmented title: Gebser v. Lago Vista Independent School District
Sendor, Benjamin
The American School Board Journal.v. 185 no10 (Oct. 1998) p. 18-19+.
The writer discusses the U.S. Supreme Court's June 1998 decision in Gebser v. Lago Vista Independent School District. The sexual harassment suit was brought by Alida Star Gebser and her mother against the school district and Frank Waldrop, an English teacher, on the grounds that Waldrop and Alida had had a sexual relationship.

[E] Who's the Boss?
Augmented title: Boss v. Fillmore School District No. 19
Zirkel, Perry A
Phi Delta Kappan.v. 79 (Oct. 1997) p. 165-6.
The writer discusses the case of Rodney Boss, who was dismissed as superintendent of the Fillmore County School District No. 14, Nebraska. On July 30, 1993, the school board informed Boss that it was contemplating terminating his contract due to his incompetence in managing the financial affairs of the district; his mishandling of a number of special education complaints, which parents had then filed with the U.S. Office for Civil Rights; and his unprofessional conduct in relation to staff, students, parents, and a board member, which included violating the district's sexual harassment policy. The case eventually reached the supreme court of Nebraska, which voted 5 to 2 in Boss's favor on February 7, 1997. In retrospect, the school board may have done better with a written reprimand or even unpaid suspension.

[E] Women fight uphill battle for equity

Kinoshita, June
Science.v. 274 Oct. 4 1996 p. 50.
Part of a special section on science in Japan. Although growing numbers are working in
Japanese university labs and represent a immensely underutilized resource, women remain
invisible to Japan's policymakers. For example, virtually nothing is being done about such
issues as workplace discrimination, sexual harassment, and the need for satisfactory child
care. One of the reasons why women's issues do not receive much attention in Japan may
be that conditions in academia, although difficult, are better than in society as a whole.
Although academia may be more tolerant of women, that tolerance falls well short of equal
status. According to 1992 figures from the Ministry of Education, Science, Sports, and
Culture, only 6.7 percent of women on natural science faculties are full professors,
compared to 29.6 percent of male faculty. The experiences of some Japanese women
scientists are discussed.

[E] Women in academia: work-related stressors
Keim, Jeanmarie S; Erickson, Chris D
Equity and Excellence in Education.v. 31 no2 (Sept. 1998) p. 61-7.
Women in academia, especially those at junior rank, experience many common difficulties
and stressors in the areas of teaching, scholarship, and service. Barriers to academic
success that are related to teaching include time demands, evaluations, and harassment.
Another problems for female faculty is sexual harassment, which can come from male
colleagues, supervisors, and male students. The writers discuss strategies for female
faculty and strategies for institutions that can help female faculty overcome these barriers.

[E] Women in astronomy: inclusion in introductory textbooks
Larsen, Kristine M
American Journal of Physics.v. 63 Feb. 1995 p. 126-31.
The recognition given to the contributions of women astronomers in introductory textbooks
is examined. It is estimated that women comprise less than 5 percent of all physicists and 7
percent of all astronomers. Such statistics, in addition to research into sexual harassment,
clearly demonstrate the daunting climate facing young female scientists and students. The
rates of inclusion of 10 famous women astronomers in textbooks published in the 1960s,
1970s, 1980s, and 1990s were examined. It was found that the inclusion ratios of most
textbooks were abysmally low.

[E] Women professors' assertive-empathic and non-assertive communication in sexual
harassment situations
Augmented title: with appendices
Krolokke, Charlotte
Women's Studies in Communication.v. 21 no1 Spring 1998 p. 91-103.
A study of when, how, and why women professors use assertive-empathic and nonassertive
communication in sexual harassment situations with other faculty members. Assertive-
empathic communication is defined as a communication strategy that stands up for one's
rights in such a way that the rights of others are not violated; nonassertive communication

is defined as insecure statements, justifications for one's actions, profuse apologies, and permission-seeking statements. Thirty women professors were interviewed about their sexual harassment experiences and their actual responses to such experiences. It was found that only a few reported using assertive-empathic communication, while most relied on nonassertive communication. The women's reasons for employing either communication strategy were based primarily on instrumental, relational, or self-identity communication goals.

[E} 'The ones who just patronise seem genial by comparison': an enquiry into sexual harassment of women in Oxford University
Oxford, 1984
Oxford University Student Union. Women's Committee
Sexual harassment at work
London, 1982

6) PSYCHOLOGICAL ASPECTS OF SEXUAL HARASSMENT

[F] Beauregard, Audra Rae.
The effects of negative images of women in the mass media on adolescent males' acceptance of sexual harassment behavior : a project based upon an independent investigation / Audra R. Beauregard. 1994.
iv, 75 leaves ; 28 cm.
Local Call No: SSW 05 B3846 1994
Thesis (M.S.)--Smith College School for Social Work, 1994.
Includes bibliographical references (leaves 61-65)
Subjects: Teenage boys -- Attitudes. Teenage boys -- Psychology. Sexual harassment of women. Women in mass media.
Source: SNN SNN

[F] Carlson, Karen J.
The women's concise guide to emotional well-being / Karen J. Carlson, Stephanie A. Eisenstat, Terra Ziporyn.
Cambridge, Mass. : Harvard University Press, 1997.
248 p. ; 23 cm.
LC Call No.: RC451.4.W6 C37 1997
ISBN: 0674954904 (cloth)
0674954912 (paper)
Includes bibliographical references and index.
Depression in women -- Antidepressants – Seasonal affective disorder -- Manic-depressive disorder -- Anxiety in women -- Panic disorder -- Phobias -- Obsessive-compulsive disorder – Posttraumatic stress disorder -- Antianxiety drugs -- Anorexia and bulimia -- Personality disorders – Psychosomatic disorders -- Multiple personality disorder -- Postpartum psychiatric disorders -- Schizophrenia -- Alzheimer's disease -- Domestic abuse – Sexual harassment -- Rape -- Sexual abuse and incest -- Sexual response -- Sexual preference – Sexual dysfunction -- Stress -- Premenstrual syndrome -- Menopause -- Postpartum emotions -- Insomnia -- Alcohol addiction -- Substance abuse -- Body image -- Psychotherapy -- Alternative therapies.
Subjects: Women -- Mental health.
Source: DLC DLC CPA SNN

[F] Ex-chancellor found liable for harassment

Selingo, Jeffrey
The Chronicle of Higher Education.v. 45 no8 (Oct. 16 1998) p. A53.
A federal jury has agreed that the former chancellor of Indiana University at South Bend
was liable for sexually harassing a female employee. In the complaint, the plaintiff, Lynn
Fall, claimed that the then chancellor David Cohen groped and kissed her in his office. Ms.
Fall claimed the university failed to take action against Mr. Cohen despite previous claims
of sexual harassment. The woman was awarded $800,000 in punitive damages.

[F] Health Care Women Int 1998 May-Jun;19(3):181-92
A diminishing of self: women's experiences of unwanted sexual attention.
Esacove AW
Prevention Division, Seattle-King County Department of Public Health, WA 98104, USA.
The health effects of everyday occurrences of unwanted sexual attention (such as looks,
whistles, and comments) were explored in semistructured interviews with 8 women in
Seattle, WA. Participants described the strategies they used for avoiding and dealing with
unwanted sexual attention, as well as the effects the attention had on their health and sense
of self. The women in this study were affected both physically and emotionally by their
experiences and their perceived ineffectiveness in dealing with them.

[F] High Court docket includes key school cases
Walsh, Mark
Education Week.v. 18 no6 (Oct. 7 1998) p. 24.
The U.S. Supreme Court is due to decide on some key school cases this term. Among the
issues the Court must decide are school district liability for peer sexual harassment and
whether a district must pay for continuous one-on-one nursing services for medically
fragile students.

[F] Hosp Law Newsl 1995 Apr;12(6):1-6
Summary judgment in sexual harassment action overturned. Kopp v. Samaritan
Health System, Inc.
Hershey N

[F] How the victim pays the price
Murphy, Sharon Scribner
RN.v. 49 Oct. 1986 p. 48-9.

[F] J Adv Nurs 1997 Jan;25(1):163-9
Sexual harassment in nursing.
Robbins I, Bender MP, Finnis SJ
North Devon District Hospital, Barnstaple, England.
Sexual harassment is a problem faced by women in the workplace which can lead to
adverse psychological consequences as well as impaired work performance. Interventions
need to be aimed at both individual and organizational levels if there is to be a prospect of
reducing a major occupational stressor for nurses.

[F] J Am Acad Psychiatry Law 1999;27(1):51-63

Effects of practitioners' sexual misconduct: a follow-up study.

Luepker ET

School of Social Work, University of Minnesota, Minneapolis, USA.

A clinic population presenting with problems related to practitioner sexual misconduct was surveyed to describe their characteristics, distinguish the impact of the sexual misconduct from preexisting problems, and identify factors helpful in recovery. Most respondents reported substantial (at least 100 hours over the course of three or more years) use of professional mental health services. Many women who seek treatment following practitioner sexual misconduct can be expected to exhibit significant symptoms of mental illness and functional impairment. They require both intensive and extensive subsequent treatment, yet are vulnerable to professional revictimization.

[F] J Am Geriatr Soc 1997 Jan;45(1):76-8

Sexual violence, post-traumatic stress disorder and dementia.

McCartney JR, Severson K

Miriam Hospital, Providence, RI 02906, USA.

Little is known of Post-Traumatic Stress Disorder (PTSD) in older people. No literature exists on this disorder in older women exposed to sexual assault. A case of apparent PTSD in a demented woman raises questions of the anatomy and phenomenology of this disorder. Difficulties in diagnosis in a demented population may cloud the issues or prevent a proper therapeutic outcome.

[F] J Appl Psychol 1997 Aug;82(4):578-89

Antecedents and consequences of sexual harassment in organizations: a test of an integrated model.

Fitzgerald LF, Drasgow F, Hulin CL, Gelfand MJ, Magley VJ

Department of Psychology, University of Illinois at Urbana-Champaign, USA. lfitzger@s.psych.uiuc.edu

Sexual harassment of women in organizational settings has recently become a topic of interest to researchers and the general public alike. Although numerous studies document its frequency, the development of conceptual models identifying antecedents and consequences of harassment has proceeded at a slower pace. In this article, an empirical test of a recently proposed conceptual model is described. According to the model, organizational climate for sexual harassment and job gender context are critical antecedents of sexual harassment; harassment, in turn, influences work-related variables (e.g., job satisfaction); psychological states (e.g., anxiety and depression); and physical health.

[F] J Appl Psychol 1997 Jun;82(3):401-15

Job-related and psychological effects of sexual harassment in the workplace: empirical evidence from two organizations.

Schneider KT, Swan S, Fitzgerald LF

Department of Psychology, University of Texas at El Paso 79968, USA.
kschneid@mail.utep.edu
Previous evidence regarding the outcomes of sexual harassment in the workplace has come mainly from self-selected samples or analogue studies or those using inadequate measures. Results suggest that relatively low-level but frequent types of sexual harassment can have significant negative consequences for working women.

[F] J Appl Psychol 1999 Jun;84(3):390-402
Outcomes of self-labeling sexual harassment.
Magley VJ, Hulin CL, Fitzgerald LF, DeNardo M
Department of Psychology, University of Illinois at Urbana-Champaign, USA.
vmagley@wppost.depaul.edu
The authors propose that the issue of why it is that women who report such experiences generally do not indicate that they have been sexually harassed is an important psychological question, and may provide a path through the nested meanings of workplace harassment. The authors argue for the value of moving beyond a descriptive approach to this issue by examining the effects of self-labeling on the psychological, health, and work-related outcomes of unwelcome, sex-related experiences.

[F] J Occup Health Psychol 1998 Jan;3(1):19-32
Stressors and adverse outcomes for female construction workers.
Goldenhar LM, Swanson NG, Hurrell JJ Jr, Ruder A, Deddens J
National Institute for Occupational Safety and Health, Cincinnati, Ohio 45226, USA.
The authors examined the impact of a number of job stressors, including sexual harassment and gender-based discrimination, on female construction workers' level of job satisfaction and psychological and physical health. Perceptions of overcompensation at work and job uncertainty were positively associated with self-reports of insomnia. Finally, sexual harassment and gender discrimination were positively related to reports of increased nausea and headaches.

[F] J Psychol 1996 Jul;130(4):429-46
Emotional and psychological consequences of sexual harassment: a descriptive study.
Thacker RA, Gohmann SF, Jhacker RA
College of Business, Ohio University, Athens, OH 45701, USA.
The emotional and psychological consequences of sexual harassment were investigated. On the basis of previous empirical evidence concerning the correlates of sexual harassment, the role of the working relationship between harasser and target, type of harassment, gender composition of the work group, duration of the harassment, and gender were examined in relation to two psychological states: feelings about work and emotional/physical condition.

[F] Kelly, Liz.
Surviving sexual violence / Liz Kelly.
Minneapolis : University of Minnesota Press, c1988.

xi, 273 p. ; 23 cm.
LC Call No.: HV6561 .K45 1988
ISBN: 0816617511 : $45.00
0816617538 (pbk.) : $14.95
Includes index bibliography: p. [266]-267.
Subjects: Rape victims -- United States -- Psychology. Rape -- United States. Sex crimes -
- United States. Sexual harassment of women -- United States.
Source: DLC DLC

[F] Law Hum Behav 1997 Feb;21(1):71-93
Perceptions of sexual harassment: the effects of gender, legal standard, and ambivalent
sexism.
Wiener RL, Hurt L, Russell B, Mannen K, Gasper C
Department of Psychology, Saint Louis University, MO 63103, USA.
WIENERRL@SLUVCA.SLU.EDU
This research tests the possibility that the reasonable woman as compared to the
reasonable person test of hostile work environment sexual harassment interacts with hostile
and benevolent sexist beliefs and under some conditions triggers protectionist attitudes
toward women who complain of sexual harassment. The results are discussed from the
perspectives of law and psychology.

[F] Mil Med 1998 Feb;163(2):63-7
Psychological effects of sexual harassment, appraisal of harassment, and organizational
climate among U.S. Army soldiers.
Rosen LN, Martin L
Walter Reed Army Institute of Research, Department of Military Psychiatry,
Washington, DC 20307-5100, USA.
This study examines the effects of three types of unwanted sexual experiences in the
workplace on the psychological well-being of male and female U.S. Army soldiers, and the
mediating or moderating roles of appraisal of sexual harassment, organizational climate,
and the sociodemographic profile of victims. Unwanted sexual experiences were found to
be significant predictors of psychological symptoms for male and female soldiers.

[F] Nurs Times 1999 Mar 3-9;95(9):64-6
High time for justice.
Sayce L
Lambeth, Southwark and Lewisham Health Action Zone, London.

[F] Overview of State and Federal Law on Sexual Harassment. Staff Brief 92-9.
This Staff Brief provides background information on state and federal
laws and regulations, relevant proposals recently considered by the Wisconsin
Legislature and laws and proposals of selected other states relating to sexual
harassment.

[F] Perception of harassing communication as a function of locus of control, work force participation, and gender
Booth Butterfield, Melanie
Communication Quarterly.v. 37 Fall 1989 p. 262-75.

[F] Psychiatry chair ousted amidst schism at UCSF
Augmented title: Sam Barondes
Barinaga, Marcia
Science.v. 262 Dec. 10 1993 p. 1639-40.
Sam Barondes has agreed to resign from his position as chair of psychiatry at the University of California, San Francisco (UCSF). Barondes, who arrived in San Francisco in 1986 with a national reputation as a neuroscience researcher from UC San Diego, was reshaping UCSF to be a hotbed of cutting-edge research on the biological underpinnings of psychiatric disorders. Based on interviews with department members, however, there was widespread resentment among the more traditional faculty, who believed that Barondes ignored their needs and openly disdained their science. In addition, there were 2 lawsuits against Barondes, who was charged with being unfair to women in both his hiring practices and his handling of sexual harassment claims.

[F] Psychology in crisis?
Holden, Constance
Science.v. 265 July 22 1994 p. 476.
Dorothy Cantor, a private practitioner, became the first-ever non-Ph.D. president-elect of the American Psychological Association (APA) in July, indicating a possible shift from a scientific society to a more professional guild. The election also formed a battleground for the APA and the former head of its science directorate Louis Lipsitt, who ran for reelection after being forced to resign early because of charges of sexual harassment. This internal feuding may lead to further unrest within the association that would bode ill for the future of academic psychology within the APA.

[F] Psychology of women : a handbook of issues and theories / edited by Florence L. Denmark and Michele A. Paludi ; foreword by Leonore Loeb Adler.
Westport, Conn. : Greenwood Press, 1993.
xix, 760 p. : ill. ; 25 cm.
LC Call No.: HQ1206 .P747 1993
ISBN: 0313262950 (alk. paper)
Includes bibliographical references (p. [723]-728) and index.
Foreword / Leonore Loeb Adler -- Acknowledgments -- Introduction / Florence L. Denmark and Michele A. Paludi -- Historical development of the psychology of women / Florence L. Denmark and Linda C. Fernandez -- Feminist perspectives on research methods / Vita Carulli Rabinowitz and Jeri A Sechzer -- Meta-analysis in the psychology of women / Janet Shibley Hyde and Laurie A. Frost – Gender stereotypes / Kay Deaux and Mary Kite -- Sexism : an integrated perspective / Rhoda Unger and Saundra --

Developmental psychology of women : conception to adolescence / Pamela T. Reid and Michele A. Paludi -- Women in the middle and later years / Clair Etaugh -- Theories of female personality / Phyllis A. Katz, Ann Boggiano, and Louise Silvern -- Women and health / Cheryl Brown Travis -- Psychology of menstruation and premenstrual syndrome / Mary Brown Parlee -- Women and mental health / Nancy Felipe Russo and Beth L. Green -- Pregnancy / Bonnie Seegmiller. -- Recovering ourselves : the frequency, effects, and resolution of rape / Mary P. Koss and Takayo Mukai -- Research on battered women and their assailants / Maureen C. McHugh, Irene Hanson Frieze, and Angela Browne -- Breaking silence : the sexual harassment of women in academia and the workplace / Louise F. Fitzgerald and Alayne J. Ormerod -- Women and the psychology of achievement : a view from the eighties / Martha T. Mednick and Veronica G. Thomas -- Women's career development / Nancy Betz -- Work and family roles : selected issues / Beth L. Green and Nancy Felipe Russo -- Epilogue / Bernice Lott.
Subjects: Women -- Psychology. Feminist psychology.
Other authors: Denmark, Florence and Paludi, Michele Antoinette.
Source: DLC DLC EYE NLM UKM MTH

[F] Public/private rules
Stein, Nan D
Education Week.v. 18 no22 (Feb. 10 1999) p. 36.
The writer notes the parallels between the sexual harassment court case Davis v. Monroe County, Ga., School District and the impeachment trial of President Clinton in the Senate, describes how she thinks sexual harassment should be dealt with in schools.

[F] Quina, Kathryn.
Rape, incest, and sexual harassment : a guide for helping survivors / Kathryn Quina and Nancy L. Carlson.
New York : Praeger, 1989.
xii, 263 p. ; 24 cm.
LC Call No.: RC560.R36 Q56 1989
ISBN: 0275925331 (alk. paper)
Includes indexes and bibliography: p. [233]-251.
Subjects: Rape victims -- Mental health. Incest victims -- Mental health. Sexual harassment -- Psychological aspects. Counseling.
Source: DLC DLC VET MTH

[F] Research advances in sexual harassment: a Special issue of Basic and Applied Social Psychology/ edited by John B. Pryor and Kathleen McKinney
Mahwah, NJ: Lawrence Erlbaum, 1996
421-614p; 23cm
Subjects: Sexual harassment

[F] Researching sexual violence against women : methodological and personal perspectives / Martin D. Schwartz, editor.

Thousand Oaks : Sage Publications, c1997.
xvii, 222 p. : ill. ; 24 cm.
LC Call No.: HV6558 .R47 1997
ISBN: 0803973691 (cloth : acid-free paper)
0803973705 (pbk. : acid-free paper)
Includes bibliographical references (p. 193-208) and index.
Subjects: Rape -- Research. Rape -- Research -- Psychological aspects. Dating violence --
Research. Sexual harassment of women -- Research. Women -- Crimes against --
Research.
Source: DLC DLC AMH

[F] Responding effectively to sexual harassment: victim advocacy, early intervention, and
problem-solving
Hippensteele, Susan; Pearson, Thomas C
Change.v. 31 no1 (Jan./Feb. 1999) p. 48-53.
Students, faculty, and staff are being sexually harassed on campus to an epidemic degree.
Information reflected in studies over the last decade consistently shows that between 25 to
30 percent of undergraduate students are sexually harassed in a given year. During this
time, there have been great steps forward in studies of the incidence and effect of this
harassment on college campuses. As academic communities come to better comprehend the
complexities of the issue, their strategies keep evolving. One clear lesson is that if a
university's goal is to respond effectively to problems of sexual harassment on campus, an
all-embracing, proactive program must be in place.

[F] Sabbath's theater (book review)
Roth, Philip; Bellow, Janis Freedman, reviewer
Partisan Review.v. 62 Fall 1995 p. 699-708+.
In Sabbath's Theater, Philip Roth invites readers to inhabit a world bereft of love where all
real feeling is with the dead. It is a book about the end of things, where grief, malice, and
the itch for a fight is all that is left. We are introduced to a "hero" who has turned his
longtime mistress into a whore; been "publicly disgraced for the gross sexual harassment
of a girl forty years his junior"; and all the while sponged on his wife, driving her to drink
and eventually into a psychiatric institution.

[F] Sex scandal takes its toll
Augmented title: Simon Fraser University president resigns amidst controversy over
handling of sexual harassment case involving swimming coach
Fine, Philip
The Times Higher Education Supplement.no1314 (Jan. 9 1998) p. 11.
John Stubbs, president of Simon Fraser University, has resigned after a highly-publicized
sex harassment case involving a swimming coach and a student. Varsity swimming coach
Liam Donnelly was fired in May 1997 after a student alleged she had been date-raped by
him. However, Donnelly was subsequently rehired when it was discovered that the
investigative hearing procedure had been flawed. Stubbs resigned his post as president in

December 1997, following almost six months of leave for depression, which many believe was due to the pressure of the sexual harassment case.

[F] Sexual assault in school, mental health and suicidal behaviors in adolescent women in Canada
Bagley, Christopher; Bolitho, Floyd; Bertrand, Lorne D
Adolescence.v. 32 (Summer 1997) p. 361-6.
Adolescent women (N = 1,025) in grades 7 through 12 in a stratified random sample of Alberta high schools completed measures of emotional problems and suicidal behavior in the past six months, and of frequency and type of sexual assault (including sexual harassment) experienced in school.

[F] Sexual harassment on campus (book review)
Booth Butterfield, Melanie, reviewer
Communication Education.v. 47 no4 (Oct. 1998) p. 385-7.

[F] Teacher-on-student sexual harassment: monkeying around?
Augmented title: Gebser v. Lago Vista Independent School District
Zirkel, Perry A
Phi Delta Kappan.v. 80 no2 (Oct. 1998) p. 171-2.
Following the discovery of a relationship between student Alida Gebser and teacher Frank Waldrop, the Lago Vista Independent School District, Texas, sacked Waldrop and the state education department revoked his license. Given that the district had not adopted and issued a formal antiharassment policy or an official grievance procedure for sexual harassment under Title IX, Alida and her mother filed suit in November 1993. The federal trial court granted summary judgment in favor of the school district, and the Fifth Circuit Court of Appeals affirmed this decision. On June 22, 1998, the Supreme Court also affirmed the dismissal of the Title IX claim.

[F] The effects of sex and feminist orientation on perceptions in sexually harassing communication
Berryman Fink, Cynthia, 1952 ; Riley, Kimberly Vanover
Women's Studies in Communication.v. 20 Spring 1997 p. 25-44.
An examination of the effects of sex and feminist orientation on perceptions of sexually harassing communication. Two hundred respondents completed three measures of feminist orientation, assessed 18 situational incidents for the extent of sexual harassment and the offensiveness of behaviors contained in the incidents, and spontaneously produced alternative labels to sexual harassment. Women viewed more behaviors as sexual harassment and rated sexual behaviors as more offensive than did men. Feminists noted more sexual harassment than did non-feminists. This essay explores the types of alternative labels provided by men and women and offers sex role socialization and hegemony explanations for discursive reframing practices.

[F] The morning after (book review)

Roiphe, Katie; Wood, Julia T., reviewer
The Quarterly Journal of Speech.v. 82 May 1996 p. 171-85.
In The Morning After: Sex, Fear, and Feminism, Katie Roiphe asserts that "feminist preoccupation with rape and sexual harassment" has led to viewing "bad nights" as rape. Representing herself as typical of women, Roiphe does not recognize decisively different circumstances experienced by people less economically and educationally privileged than she and others who attend prestigious schools.

7) HEALTH CARE

[G] A professional disgrace
Lancet (North American edition).v. 342 Sept. 11 1993 p. 627-8.
Women doctors have recently raised the issue of sexual harassment of women in medicine,
but the response of the profession has been limp. The U.K. procedure for confidential
notification of a doctor's mental or physical disability should be extended to include
notification of sexual harassment. Such a scheme would not end sexual harassment of
women doctors immediately, but it would represent a more determined attempt to purge the
medical profession of this disgraceful conduct.

[G] AAOHN J 1996 Feb;44(2):73-7
Violence and sexual harassment: impact on registered nurses in the workplace.
Williams MF
This study sought to determine the prevalence and impact of violence and sexual
harassment experienced by registered nurses (RNs) in their workplaces in Illinois. About
one third of those who indicated they had been sexually harassed also had been physically
assaulted. Patients/clients were the most frequent perpetrators of sexual harassment and
physical assault, while physicians committed over half of the sexual assaults. Results
demonstrate that nurses need to take and active role in fostering a work environment free
from violence and sexual harassment. They should be knowledgeable about institutional
policies and, where none exist, they should work with administrators to develop them.
Prevention and intervention programs should be developed for both student and registered
nurses.

[G] AAOHN J 1997 Jul;45(7):366-7
Sexual harassment: what every occupational health nurse needs to know.
Calfee BE
Calfee & associates, huntsburg, ohio, USA.

[G] Acad Med 1996 Oct;71(10 Suppl):S25-7
Residents' and medical students' reports of sexual harassment and discrimination.
Baldwin DC Jr, Daugherty SR, Rowley BD
Rush Primary Care Institute, Chicago, IL 60612, USA.

[G] Acad Med 1997 Dec;72(12):1026-7
Eradicating sexual harassment during medical training.
Feldman P, Jones S, Shrier I

[G] Addiction 1996 Mar;91(3):391-403
Perceived workplace harassment experiences and problem drinking among physicians:
broadening the stress/alienation paradigm.
Richman JA, Flaherty JA, Rospenda KM
Department of Psychiatry, University of Illinois at Chicago 60612, USA.
Sociologists who embrace the stress or alienation paradigms generally focus on explaining
problem drinking in low status occupations. By contrast, this paper argues that a
broadened conceptualization of stress and alienation which incorporates abusive work
relationships has utility for explaining male and female drinking outcomes in both high and
low status occupations. We provide empirical data on the relationship between perceived
abusive experiences and drinking outcomes in a cohort of male and female physicians in
their internship year of training. The data show that perceived sexual harassment,
discriminatory treatment and psychological humiliation relate to various drinking outcomes
in men and women, controlling for drinking prior to the internship year. The implications
of these results for the design of future alcohol-related work-place studies are discussed.

[G] Ala Med 1994 Dec;64(6):18-9
The implications of sexual misconduct in a physician's practice.
Lightfoot WM, Summer GL

[G] Ala Med 1994 Dec;64(6):7-12
Psychotherapists who transgress sexual boundaries with patients.
Gabbard GO
Menninger Clinic, Topelea, KS 66601-0829.
The causes of therapist-patient sex are complex and multidetermined. Efforts to
understand why psychotherapists transgress sexual boundaries are hampered by the lure of
reductionism and oversimplification. Most of those who examine this issue would prefer to
categorize all such therapists as "bad" and "corrupt" as away of distancing themselves and
disavowing any similarities between these therapists and themselves. The pathology of
therapists who commit sexual boundary violations generally falls into four broad
categories: (1) psychotic disorders, (2) predatory psychopathy and paraphilias, (3)
lovesickness, and (4) masochistic surrender. Although a variety of individual
psychodynamic factors are involved within each group, this classification is highly useful
for informed treatment planning.

[G] Am J Crit Care 1994 Nov;3(6):409-15
Sexual harassment of critical care nurses: a costly workplace issue.
Kaye J, Donald CG, Merker S, University of Louisville, Ky.
Sexual harassment in the workplace is a prevalent form of impermissible sex
discrimination in employment. The high profile of this issue in the media, together with
laws prohibiting sexual harassment, have not prevented this problem for working nurses.
Objectives: To describe and determine the extent of sexual harassment incidents
experienced by nurses working in critical care areas, and to determine attitudes about, and

presence of policies regarding, sexual harassment in hospitals. For this descriptive study the federal government's definition of sexual harassment and a list of sexually harassing behaviors was mailed with a survey to 188 critical care nurses. These results suggest that many critical care nurses are harassed and that relatively few hospitals have sexual harassment policies known to employees. They also indicate that sexual harassment training, policies, and procedures are needed to provide a safe, healthy work environment for critical care nurses.

[G] Am J Obstet Gynecol 1997 Jun;176(6):1340-6; discussion 1346-8
Evaluation of sexual misconduct complaints: the Oregon Board of Medical Examiners, 1991 to 1995.
Enbom JA, Thomas CD
Oregon Board of Medical Examiners, Portland 97201, USA.
In 1991 the Oregon Board of Medical Examiners initiated a separate category for the complaint of sexual misconduct. Investigated complaints of sexual misconduct brought to the Oregon Board of Medical Examiners were analyzed for the years 1991 to 1995 to serve as a baseline. Comparison was made to the Federation of State Medical Boards sexual misconduct data for 1991 and 1992. Oregon has a higher percentage of sexual misconduct complaints than the average for 42 states reporting to the Federation of State Medical Boards for the years 1991 and 1992. Analysis of the Oregon Board's experience for the study years will provide a baseline for future evaluation and as an educational resource for the Oregon Board of Medical Examiners and professional and specialty societies. Ethical standards, the reporting and investigative processes, and the legal framework are in place and lessen the incidence of sexual misconduct and work toward zero tolerance.

[G] Am Pharm 1994 Dec;NS34(12):49-53, 58
Drawing the line: a case study in sexual harassment. Report of the American Pharmaceutical Association.
Weinstein BD
Center for Health Ethics and Law, West Virginia University, Morgantown.
Publication Types: Guideline

[G] AORN J 1996 Feb;63(2):443-6, 448-9
Sexual harassment and hostile environments in the perioperative area.
Kaye J
University Hospital, Augusta, GA, USA.
Nursing has dealt with sexual harassment since the era of Florence Nightingale. Despite legislation and increased media attention, perioperative nurses continue to experience frustration, embarrassment, and psychological and economic repercussions because of sexual harassment. Prevention of sexual harassment must encompass individuals, employers, and the health care profession as a whole. Awareness and prevention are the first steps to establishing and maintaining healthy workplaces that are free of sexual harassment.

[G] Arch Intern Med 1998 Feb 23;158(4):352-8
Prevalence and correlates of harassment among US women physicians.
Frank E, Brogan D, Schiffman M
School of Medicine, Emory University, Atlanta, Georgia, USA.
efrank@fpm.eushc.org
Despite concerns about its prevalence and ramifications, harassment has not been well quantified among physicians. Previous published studies have been small, have surveyed only 1 site or a convenience sample, and have suffered from selection bias. Women physicians commonly perceive that they have been harassed. Experiences of and sensitivity to harassment differ among individuals, and there may be substantial professional and personal consequences of harassment. Since reported rates of sexual harassment are higher among younger physicians, the situation may not be improving.

[G] Aust Health Rev 1996;19(3):14-27
Australian registered nurses and sex-based harassment in the health care industry.
Madison J, Gates R
Department of Health Studies, University of New England.
This paper discusses sex-based harassment in the nursing profession in Australia. The paper generates industry-specific hypotheses which may provide insights into sex-based harassment in the Australian context. A good understanding of sex-based harassment in health care is essential for reducing and eliminating the problem and its toxic sequelae.

[G] Aust Health Rev 1997;20(2):102-15
Australian registered nurses describe the health care workplace and its responsiveness to sexual harassment: an empirical study.
Madison J
Department of Health Studies, University of New England.
This report is a summary of findings from a 1995 study of Australian registered nurses and their perceptions of their health care workplaces, especially as it relates to sexual harassment. As the major employer of registered nurses, hospitals and health care facilities need to be concerned about employees' perceptions of the workplace.

[G] Aust J Adv Nurs 1997 Jun-Aug;14(4):29-37
RN's experiences of sex-based and sexual harassment--an empirical study.
Madison J
Department of Health Studies, University of New England, New South Wales.
A survey of 317 registered nurses enrolled in tertiary post-registration courses found that two thirds of the 197 respondents had encountered sexual harassment in the work place. A quarter of these nurses identified medical officers and 22.1% identified co-workers as their harassers.This paper identifies the harassing behaviours the respondents experienced, their responses to the behaviour and the effects the harassment had on them.

[G] Br J Gen Pract 1996 Nov;46(412):692

Sexual harassment of doctors.
Fordham S

[G] Bull Menninger Clin 1996 Winter;60(1):52-61
Helen Bramson: treatment after sexual abuse by a mental health practitioner.
Wohlberg JW, Reid EA
Patients who have had sexual contact or sexualized relationships with previous therapists
present a unique set of subsequent treatment challenges. From the patient's perspective, the
breach of trust experienced in the previous therapy has likely made the formation of a new
therapeutic alliance both threatening and compelling. It is also likely that whatever caused
the patient to enter therapy in the first place has never been adequately treated.

[G] Callan, Susan Rose.
Sexual exploitation in the treatment setting : a study of female survivors : a project based
upon an independent investigation / Susan Rose Callan. 1987.
iii, 137 leaves : ill. ; 28 cm.
Local Call No: SSW05 .C132 1987
Thesis (M.S.)--Smith College School for Social Work, 1987.
Bibliography: leaves 112-113.
Subjects: Sexual harassment of women. Sex between psychotherapist and patient.
Femininity.
Source: SNN SNN

[G] Can Fam Physician 1996 Jan;42:73-8
Sexual harassment of female physicians by patients. What is to be done?
Phillips S
Department of Family Medicine, Queen's University, Kingston, Ont.
Objective: To determine the responses of female physicians who have been sexually
harassed by patients, as a means of answering the question, "What is to be done?" As part
of a larger study on the topic, randomly selected participants were mailed a questionnaire
requesting information about the nature and extent of sexual harassment by patients and
about resulting feelings, actions, and suggestions for prevention. There is no single
effective response to sexual harassment, but understanding its source as an abuse of the
power of gender* (perhaps to overcome the powerlessness felt as a patient) could enable
female physicians to act in protective and effective ways.

[G] Can J Med Radiat Technol 1995 Mar;26(1):5-9, 11-6
Sexual harassment in health care: implications for medical radiation technology training
programs.
Knox M
Cross Cancer Institute, Edmonton, Alberta.
In May 1993, the Council on Education--Radiation Therapy of the Canadian Association
of Medical Radiation Technologists (CAMRT) decided to include two new items in its
curriculum guide: components of sexual abuse prevention; and legal requirements of

consent to treatment and specific procedures (especially those related to gender-sensitive procedures). This article attempts to give an overview of the literature as well as the author's recommendations on the format and content for presenting this subject to students. A summary of the students' comments is also included.

[G] Caring 1996 May;15(5):78-80, 84-6, 88-9
"Can't you take a joke?" Sexual harassment in health care.
Collin DW
Legal Nurse Network, Denver, CO, USA.

[G] CMAJ 1997 Jun 1;156(11):1577-9
Harassment issues should be dealt with before they become problems.
Capen K
Sexual and other forms of harassment are common in the medical work environment. Physicians who are employers and medical educators as well as clinicians should be aware they may be held responsible for the harassing conduct of colleagues, employees and others unless measures are in place in the workplace that show reasonable efforts have been made to prevent the behaviour and deal with it appropriately when it occurs. This article uses a US case to illustrate the evolution of a sexual-harassment complaint over several years.

[G] Emergency-room sex condemned in Canada
Kondro, Wayne
Lancet (North American edition).v. 350 Sept. 27 1997 p. 942.
Ontario Health Minister Jim Wilson has warned emergency room doctors in Canada to refrain from having sexual relations with their patients. The warning follows a study published last week (Can. Med. Assoc. J. 1997;157:663-9) indicating that 6 percent of 599 surveyed emergency room physicians across Ontario have had sex with a patient and that 9 percent of the doctors knew of an emergency room colleague who had sex with a patient. Patient abuse groups are demanding stricter guidelines regulating the relationship between patients and emergency room doctors, who apparently are not governed by guidelines for other physicians.

[G] Handling inappropriate sexual behavior with confidence
Zook, Ruth
Nursing 97.v. 27 Apr. 1997 p. 65.
Advice on how a nurse should deal with a patient who exhibits inappropriate sexual behavior is provided. This behavior can take the form of nonverbal, verbal, or physical actions. When dealing with this kind of patient, a nurse needs to set limits and stand by them to ensure that the patient knows she will not tolerate inappropriate sexual behavior and that he will have to take responsibility for his actions. Nine ways to help deal with and put a stop to a patient's inappropriate sexual behavior are discussed.

[G] Health Care Manage Rev 1995 Winter;20(1):47-53

Sexual harassment in the hospital industry: an empirical inquiry.
Kinard JL, McLaurin JR, Little B
Department Head of Management, Western Carolina University, Cullowhee, NC, USA.
A 1994 survey of hospital HRMs has revealed that charges of sexual harassment within the health care industry are increasing at an alarming rate. Most charges are filed by women who claim they were victims of "hostile environments." Nurses levy the largest number of complaints, followed by clerical/secretarial personnel, technicians, custodial workers, food service personnel, and therapists. Most charges are filed against coworkers. Approximately 10 percent of all charges of sexual harassment in hospitals are brought against physicians.

[G] Health Care Superv 1997 Sep;16(1):1-14
Sexual harassment in health care: a major productivity problem.
Decker PJ
School of Business & Public Administration, Univ. of Houston Clear Lake, TX, USA.
Sexual harassment in health care is a problem because of exorbitant legal costs, lost productivity, poor morale, and nonproductive absenteeism or turnover. Sexual harassment is more prevalent in health care. Health care organizations often do little to prevent it and do not respond properly when it occurs. In this article, legal precedents are reviewed, and a model of sexual harassment is developed to illustrate the phenomenon and identify interventions. It is argued that reduction of sexual harassment in health care is important because it is a major productivity issue.

[G] Health Serv Manage Res 1996 Nov;9(4):243-53
Sexual harassment of female nurses in a hospital in Turkey.
Kisa A, Dziegielewski SF
School of Public Health & Tropical Medicine, Tulane University, New Orleans, LA 70112, USA.
Sexual harassment has been identified as a universal factor that can affect nursing performance and work productivity in any type of health care facility. Few studies in the area of sexual harassment have been conducted in developing countries, and this is the first study of its type to be conducted in the country of Turkey. The general purpose of this study is to examine whether the problem of sexual harassment truly is "universal' and to begin to address whether it exists among female nurses in Turkey. In general, these findings suggest that sexual harassment of female nurses remains a disturbing problem in this developing country. Based on the findings, implications for policy and further study are suggested.

[G] Hosp Health Netw 1994 Dec 5;68(23):11
Sexual harassment. Study says it 'comes with the territory' in nursing profession.

[G] Hosp Health Netw 1995 Jan 20;69(2):54-7
Sexually harassed.
Sherer JL

When neurosurgeon Frances Conley resigned her Stanford University Medical School professorship over sexual harassment, her case received widespread notoriety. But Conley is far from alone in health care.

[G] Hosp Health Serv Adm 1993 Summer;38(2):167-80
Sexual harassment at work: issues and answers for health care administrators.
Robinson RK, Franklin GM, Fink RL
Department of Management and Marketing, University of Mississippi, University 38677. Sexual harassment is not new to the health care industry. What is new is that recent media attention has heightened awareness that sexual harassment is illegal. This fact, coupled with the substantial liability that employers may incur if they fail to control sexual harassment, mandates the need for outlining the major issues relative to sexual harassment in today's health care setting. This article gives particular emphasis to the fact that sexual harassment can be prevented by taking a proactive stance.

[G] Hosp Secur Saf Manage 1999 Mar;19(11):12-4
Hospital liability for negligent hiring and supervision.

[G] In his dreams
Augmented false accusations of sexual assault by a mentally ill patient
Nursing 98.v. 28 no11 Nov. 1998 p. 18+.
Advice is given to a nurse facing a false accusation of sexual assault from a mentally ill nursing home resident who expressed his intention to sue. The nurse is advised to ask her unit head to arrange a psychiatric consult for the resident and to keep documentation of all meetings regarding him and the responses received from management. The nurse should also consider requesting a transfer to another area.

[G] Int J Gynaecol Obstet 1995 Feb;48(2):239-42
ACOG committee opinion. Sexual misconduct in the practice of obstetrics and gynecology: ethical considerations. Number 144--November 1994. Committee on Ethics. American College of Obstetricians and Gynecologists.

[G] Issues 1995;16(2):6, 14-5
Professional sexual misconduct: should nurses be concerned?

[G] Issues 1996;17(2):11-3
Raising awareness of professional boundaries and sexual misconduct. Nursing faculty are encouraged to take a proactive role.

[G] J Am Acad Psychiatry Law 1998;26(4):563-78
Addressing bias in the forensic assessment of sexual harassment claims.
Gold LH
Dept. of Psychiatry, Georgetown University School of Medicine, Washington, DC, USA. This article addresses unique biases that arise in the assessment of sexual harassment

claims by forensic psychiatrists. These include gender biases, diagnostic biases, sociopolitical biases, and bias that arises from lack of knowledge regarding sexual harassment or lack of formal psychiatric training.

[G] J Am Acad Psychiatry Law 1999;27(1):51-63
Effects of practitioners' sexual misconduct: a follow-up study.
Luepker ET
School of Social Work, University of Minnesota, Minneapolis, USA. A clinic population presenting with problems related to practitioner sexual misconduct was surveyed to describe their characteristics, distinguish the impact of the sexual misconduct from preexisting problems, and identify factors helpful in recovery.

[G] J Am Med Womens Assoc 1995 Nov-Dec;50(6):207-11
Harassment of women physicians.
Schiffman M, Frank E
Department of Family and Preventive Medicine, Emory University School of Medicine, Atlanta, Georgia, USA.
This paper reviews current knowledge about the prevalence, characteristics, and costs of sexual harassment of women medical students and physicians. It also addresses the limited research on other forms of physician and student harassment, and notes the kinds of information that are still needed.

[G] J Emerg Med Serv JEMS 1999 Apr;24(4):80
Update: sexual harassment & EMS.
Wirth SR

[G] J Health Hosp Law 1996 Jul-Aug;29(4):230-7
A policy approach to sexual harassment in medicine.
Silfen E
Reston Hospital Center, VA, USA.

[G] J Health Hum Serv Adm 1995 Fall;18(2):163-77
Sexual harassment among nursing professionals: evidence and prescriptions for administrators.
West CT Jr, Holoviak SJ, Figler RA
University of Akron, OH, USA.
The results of this study indicate that the experience of sexual harassment among nursing professionals may be more widespread than previously reported. To lower the risk of liability from claims of both victims and the accused, harassment and discrimination policies should be aggressive, proactive, fair, and thorough.

[G] J Healthc Prot Manage 1995 Summer;11(2):74-7
Healthcare security and sexual harassment: management issues and answers.

Gonzalez JC
Successful Negotiations, Inc., Palo Alto, CA, USA.

[G] J Nurs Adm 1999 Feb;29(2):10-3
Protecting your healthcare organization from liability for sexual harassment by
employees and non-employees.
Moore HL, Whitehead R Jr
University of Central Arkansas, Conway, USA. herfm@mail.uca.edu

[G] JPMA J Pak Med Assoc 1996 Jun;46(6):131-2
Harassment in medical profession--myth or reality in Pakistan.
Shaikh MA
Pakistan Medical Research Council, Islamabad.

[G] Lakartidningen 1995 Jan 4;92(1-2):39-41
[Sexualization of the physician-patient relation. Betrayal of confidence has very negative
effects].
[Article in Swedish]
Persson G, Holmberg MB
Institutionen for klinisk neurovetenskap, omradet for psykiatri, Sahlgrenska
sjukhuset, Goteborg.

[G] Louder than words
Nursing 88.v. 18 Jan. 1988 p. 23.

[G] Male nurse: two strikes
Nursing 92.v. 22 May 1992 p. 18.

[G] Mater Manag Health Care 1995 Feb;4(2):52
Sexual harassment: health care's costly little secret.
Sherer JL

[G] Medsurg Nurs 1996 Jun;5(3):199-200
Sexual harassment: a practical guide for nurses.
Pfeiffer M

[G] Mich Med 1995 Feb;94(2):30-2
Sexual harassment in the medical workplace.
Werbinski J

[G] N Y State Dent J 1995 Oct;61(8):48-52
Sexual harassment in the dental office. A model policy.
Plunkett L

[G] N Z Med J 1998 Feb 27;111(1060):53-5
General practitioner attitudes toward mandatory reporting of doctor-patient sexual abuse.
White GE, Coverdale J
Department of Nursing and Midwifery, Massey University at Albany.
AIM: To explore general practitioner attitudes toward mandatory reporting of doctor-patient sexual abuse. CONCLUSION: There was a lack of strong consensus on mandatory reporting of doctor-patient sexual abuse.

[G] Nurs Adm Q 1995 Winter;19(2):48-55
Ending the silent conspiracy: sexual harassment in nursing.
King CS
Sexual harassment in health care institutions presents a formidable challenge for nurse leaders as solutions and accountabilities get mired in power, politics, and a historical tradition of secrecy and silence. Harassment is devastating to all individuals, but especially to women because it blatantly violates the victim's personal autonomy and individual sense of equality. Nurse executives must learn the subtle complexities surrounding harassment, voice strong opposition against harassment, and take swift and comprehensive action to prevent sexual harassment.

[G] Nurs Manage 1999 May;30(5):16-8
When sexual harassment hits home.
Fiesta J
Legal Services/Risk Management Dept., Lehigh Valley Hospital, Allentown, Pa., USA.
Sexual harassment cases illustrate the problems facing employees, including nurses' abusive experiences with both physicians and patients. Learn how to give employees the support they need and lower your liability.

[G] Nurse abuse: handling your harasser
Salladay, Susan A
Nursing 95.v. 25 June 1995 p. 73.
A sexually harassed nurse wonders how best to deal with the offending patient. The nurse is advised to file formal reports of each incident, to inform her nurse manager and the patient's physician of the situation, and to ensure that she is never left alone with the patient. The nurse can also confidentially discuss the issue with her hospital's human resources representative if she feels she does not receive enough support from closer quarters.

[G] Nursing 1994 Oct;24(10):48-50
Confronting sexual harassment.

[G] Nursing 1998 Sep;28(9):82
Protesting sexual harassment. Was this a hostile work environment.

[G] Ohio Nurses Rev 1996 Aug;71(7):4, 13
Sexual harassment and registered nurses.
Petroff J

[G] Perspect Psychiatr Care 1997 Oct-Dec;33(4):5-13
The psychiatric advanced practice nurse's role as sexual harassment ombudsman.
Spratlen LP
University of Washington, Seattle, USA.
Topic: The psychiatric advanced practice nurse's role as sexual harassment ombudsman.
Goal: To describe the role of ombudsman for sexual harassment and its fit with nursing as
seen in the Price Spratlen Ombudsing Model. An ombudsman for sexual harassment can
play a significant role in the continuing problem of sexual harassment in the workplace.
Managing grievances requires a client-centered approach, environmental assessment and
sensitivity, flexibility in programs, and cost-effectiveness. Nurse's duty to guard against
sexual predators on staff.
Tammelleo AD

[G] Phys Ther 1997 Jul;77(7):739-44
Patient sexual behaviors and sexual harassment: a national survey of physical therapists.
deMayo RA
Graduate School of Education and Psychology, Pepperdine University, Culver City, CA
90230, USA.
The objective of this study was to describe the extent to which physical therapists have
experienced patient sexual behaviors and sexual harassment. The results support the
findings of previous investigators who concluded that patient sexual behavior and sexual
harassment is an important issue that needs to addressed in training programs.

[G] Physician-patient relationships: patients as friends and patients who harass.
Phillips S
Publication Types: Comment Letter
Comments: Comment in: Can Med Assoc J 1995 Nov 1;153(9):1241-5

[G] Physiother Res Int 1999;4(1):28-42
Inappropriate sexual behaviours of patients towards practising physiotherapists:
a study using qualitative methods.
O'Sullivan V, Weerakoon P
Faculty of Health Sciences, University of Sydney, Australia.
Recent research recognizes the occurrence of inappropriate sexual behaviour (ISB) by
patients towards health professionals. The objective of this study was to explore in-depth
the clinical context and effect of incidents of ISB towards practising physiotherapists. The
findings are discussed in the context of theory pertaining to boundaries and issues of
transference and counter-transference. This emphasized the need for effective
communication skills training of both undergraduate and graduate physiotherapists in the
prevention and management of ISB from patients.

[G] Protecting your healthcare organization from liability for sexual harassment by employees and non-employees.
Moore HL, Whitehead R Jr
University of Central Arkansas, Conway, USA. herfm@mail.uca.edu

[G] Revolution 1995 Fall;5(3):68-76
"Can't you take a joke?" Sexual harassment in healthcare.
Collins DW

[G] Revolution 1998 Spring;8(1):23-8
Fighting the good fight--legal issues and legislative update for nurses.
Stearley H

[G] Sexism charged by Stanford physician
Barinaga, Marcia
Science.v. 252 June 14 1991 p. 1484.
Neurosurgeon Frances Conley of the Stanford University School of Medicine resigned from her faculty position on May 23, 1991, citing sexual harassment. Conley states that surgeon Gerald Silverberg, who has been recommended for a promotion, undermined her authority with demeaning treatment and called her "honey" in front of her surgical team. She says that she decided to make her charges public in the San Francisco Chronicle after a medical school faculty senate meeting, in which she discovered that other women at the school were experiencing similar problems.

[G] Sexual abuse in the doctor/patient relationship
Coney, Sandra
Lancet (North American edition).v. 344 Sept. 17 1994 p. 811.
The Medical Council of New Zealand has issued new comprehensive guidelines on sexual misconduct by physicians. The guidelines cover the expected behavior of physicians toward their patients and a separate pamphlet for patients that explains the boundaries that physicians should adhere to and how patients can make complaints. The council has the power to deregister offending doctors, but the maximum fine possible is a mere NZ$1,000. The new guidelines have been well received by professional groups.

[G] Sexual harassment in medical training
Komaromy, Miriam; Bindman, Andrew B; Haber, Richard J
The New England Journal of Medicine.v. 328 Feb. 4 1993 p. 322-6.

[G] Sexual harassment: an updated picture
Lippman, Helen
RN.v. 56 Feb. 1993 p. 61-2+.
Sexual harassment; Nurses Attitudes.

[G] Sexual harassment: identifying it in dentistry
Weinstein, Bruce D
Journal of the American Dental Association.v. 125 July 1994 p. 1016-21.
The problem of sexual harassment in dentistry is discussed. Case studies are used to explain what sexual harassment is, why it is unethical and illegal, and how it can be reduced or eliminated from dental practice. If the suggested measures to deal with this problem were taken seriously, it would help to make the dental office a comfortable and respectful environment for everybody.

[G] Sexual harassment: you can do something about it
Arbeiter, Jean S
RN.v. 49 Oct. 1986 p. 46-51.

[G] Sexual harrassment of female doctors by patients
Phillips, Susan P; Schneider, Margaret S
The New England Journal of Medicine.v. 329 Dec. 23 1993 p. 1936-9.
The sexual harassment of female doctors by patients was examined. A random sample of 599 of the 1,064 licensed female family physicians in Ontario, Canada, received questionnaires in the mail. More than 75 percent of the respondents reported some sexual harassment by a patient at some stage during their careers. As sexual harassment of female doctors appears to be a frequent occurrence, it is important to address this issue in medical school and during professional development.

[G] Sexual taunts: just say no
Nursing 96.v. 26 Mar. 1996 p. 26.
Hospitals and physicians have a duty to protect staff from the offensive behavior or sexual taunts of patients. Failure to respond to the complaints of staff members could lead to lawsuits being brought against the hospital and physician in question. An offensive patient should be informed that his conduct is inappropriate by the nurse-manager and the relevant physician, and the staff should implement a course of action to discourage objectionable behavior and reinforce appropriate behavior. A psychiatric consultation may be necessary if these actions fail to have the desired effect.

[G] Soc Sci Med 1997 Sep;45(5):669-76
A qualitative study of sexual harassment of female doctors by patients.
Schneider M, Phillips SP
Department of Applied Psychology, Ontario Institute for Studies in Education, University of Toronto, Ontario, Canada.
This paper reports the qualitative data from a study of sexual harassment of female family physicians by patients. In addition to the everyday harassment that any woman might encounter in a work setting, the physicians in this study also reported types of harassment which are unique to the practice of medicine. The findings are discussed in the context of theory pertaining to contrapower harassment. It is concluded that for some patients the

gender of the physician takes precedence over her occupational status and, this combined with the unique characteristics of the doctor/patient relationship, can make the practice of family medicine more conductive to sexual harassment than other professions.

[G] Touchy subject
Augmented title: surgeon harasses nurses
Miya, Pamela A
American Journal of Nursing.v. 94 Sept. 1994 p. 56.
Nurses are advised on how to deal with sexual harassment. Sexual harassment can affect quality nursing care, and the harassed individual should assert her rights. The nurse should firmly object to the offender's behavior and make written notes on each episode of harassment. If the behavior continues, the nurse is advised to inform her supervisor or the hospital's office of affirmative action or human resources.

[G] Toward a more perfect world- eliminating sexual discrimination in academic medicine
Conley, Frances K
The New England Journal of Medicine.v. 328 Feb. 4 1993 p. 351-2.
Sexual harassment; Interns.

[G] Va Med Q 1995 Summer;122(3):198-9
Allegations of sexual abuse and chaperones in the examination room.

[G] When sexual harassment hits home.
Fiesta J
Legal Services/Risk Management Dept., Lehigh Valley Hospital, Allentown, Pa., USA.
Sexual harassment cases illustrate the problems facing employees, including nurses' abusive experiences with both physicians and patients. Learn how to give employees the support they need and lower your liability.
ERIC Clearinghouse on Educational Management, Eugene, Oreg.

SUBJECT INDEX

A

Aberdeen Proving Ground · 78
abortion · 11, 82, 85, 93
affirmative action · 17, 46, 101, 102, 106, 116, 165
Aggressors · 22
AIDS · 8, 119
ambivalent sexism · 145
American Graduate Council · 138
American Medical Association · 115
American Psychological Association · 26, 146
American School Board · 93, 99, 109, 123, 132, 134, 138
Americans with Disabilities Act · 42, 54, 84, 116
Anita Faye Hill · 29, 91
Anita Hill · 3, 4, 7, 10, 12, 22, 26, 27, 28, 30, 38, 40, 42, 43, 46, 48, 50, 58, 87, 91
Anita Hill/Clarence Thomas hearings · 3
anorexic logic · 13
Armed Forces · 75, 77, 78, 80
Assertive-empathic communication · 139
attorney-client privilege · 42
Australia · 18, 108, 154, 162

B

Brown University · 101

C

California Education Code · 105
case study · 40, 57, 103, 153
Chapel Hill · 27, 98, 132
child abuse · 12, 14, 133
Child Abuse · 17
Child molesting · 20
Child Welfare · 103
Chinese University of Hong Kong · 101
Christianity · 3, 35

Church · 3, 40
citizenship education · 104, 105
Civil rights · 44, 81, 95
Civil Rights · 59, 84, 85, 89, 90, 91, 92, 95, 99, 129, 130, 131, 137, 138
Civil Rights Act · 59, 85, 89, 90, 91, 99, 130, 137
Clarence Thomas · 12, 27, 28, 30, 38, 42, 43, 46, 48, 50, 58, 64, 67, 70, 83, 91
classroom · 31, 81, 97, 98, 102, 133
clergy · 35
College teachers · 106
colleges · 38, 44, 71, 81, 84, 94, 104, 106, 107, 108, 109, 112, 117, 118, 119, 120, 121, 126, 127, 129, 133
computer industry · 4
confidentiality · 35
contrapower harassment · 164

D

dental practice · 71, 164
Dentistry · 28, 63
Department of Defense · 75, 78
Department of Education · 92, 95, 108, 109, 113, 130, 167
Department of Military Psychiatry · 76, 78, 145
Dept. of Public Health · 113
developing countries · 157
discrimination · 1, 4, 14, 15, 36, 54, 55, 57, 61, 62, 63, 67, 69, 70, 71, 73, 82, 84, 85, 87, 88, 89, 97, 99, 100, 101, 102, 104, 109, 115, 117, 122, 123, 124, 126, 132, 136, 137, 139, 144, 151, 152, 159, 165
domestic violence · 17, 68

E

EEOC · 56, 59, 84, 90
E-mail · 13
emergency room · 156
EMS · 159

Equal Employment Opportunity · 59, 71, 72
Equal Protection Clause · 132
Equality · 12, 15, 83

F

Family violence · 17, 33, 45
federal guidelines · 95
Feminist theory · 1, 13, 16, 18, 31, 33, 47, 117
Florida school districts · 113, 129
Fourteenth Amendment · 84, 92, 132

G

gay students · 117
Gay Young · 9
Gebser v. Lago Vista · 86, 121, 123, 130, 131,
    138, 149
gender · 1, 2, 4, 8, 9, 10, 16, 17, 22, 29, 31, 34,
    35, 38, 39, 40, 46, 53, 57, 59, 61, 62, 65, 75,
    79, 87, 91, 93, 94, 97, 99, 100, 104, 110, 117,
    122, 125, 133, 136, 143, 144, 145, 146, 155,
    159, 165

H

Hate crimes · 37
Heterophobia · 20, 117
Hill, Anita · 4, 7, 12, 28, 30, 42, 43, 50, 83, 87,
    91, 94
HIV-positive · 35
homophobia · 114
Hospitals · 29, 164
hostile environments · 153, 157

I

Internet · 13, 21
Interns · 165

L

labor laws · 88
Law Enforcement · 68
Line Veto Act · 42

M

Manhattan Project · 71
mass media · 141
medical school · 115, 117, 163, 164
Medical students · 115
medical training · 116, 126, 138, 151, 163
mental health · 36, 49, 67, 143, 147, 149, 155
mentally ill · 158
Military law · 77
Monica Lewinsky · 2

N

National Advisory Council · 136
Navy · 41, 75, 76, 77, 80
non-assertive communication · 139
non-consensual · 6
nurse · 35, 59, 66, 92, 114, 151, 156, 158, 160,
    161, 162, 165

O

Oak Ridge National Laboratory · 71
Occupational Safety · 61, 144

P

patient · 27, 35, 70, 155, 156, 158, 161, 162,
    163, 164, 165
pedophilia · 112
peer harassment · 31, 86, 104, 127
peer sexual harassment · 36, 83, 88, 92, 95, 103,
    134, 142
performing arts · 131
Persian Gulf War · 76, 79
Police · 13, 122
pornography · 1, 11, 13, 14, 16, 41, 82, 85
post-traumatic stress disorder · 70, 143
Post-Traumatic Stress Disorder · 143
President Clinton · 3, 16, 37, 39, 82, 147
preventive management · 61
priests · 36, 112
prison · 8, 20, 29
Prison deaths · 29
protectionist attitudes · 145
psychological consequences · 59, 142, 144
psychological effects · 60, 143

public space · 8

Q

R

race · 2, 30, 38, 40, 48, 49, 79, 87, 101, 103, 117
rape · 12, 13, 14, 16, 33, 41, 44, 46, 56, 66, 85,
    102, 107, 113, 136, 147, 150
reasonable person · 66, 145
reasonable woman · 22, 66, 145
reasonable woman standard · 22
risk factors · 5
Robinson v. Jacksonville Shipyards · 56, 84

S

Salk Institute · 32
Same-sex · 91
School Counseling · 111, 123
School nurses · 114
School safety · 134
schools · 41, 86, 88, 89, 91, 97, 99, 103, 104,
    105, 106, 107, 111, 112, 113, 114, 116, 117,
    119, 122, 123, 127, 128, 131, 132, 133, 134,
    135, 138, 147, 149, 150
secondary schools · 113, 115, 119, 124
Section 1983 · 132
segregation · 57
Senator Robert Packwood · 43
Sex discrimination · 14, 15, 16, 34, 47, 48, 55,
    57, 58, 62, 65, 67, 69, 70, 72, 75, 84, 85, 87,
    89, 90, 115, 117, 125, 126, 128, 129
sex education · 107, 124
sexual assault · 16, 24, 41, 53, 69, 77, 113, 120,
    143, 149, 151, 158
Sexual ethics · 37, 105
Sexual Harassment Attitudes Scale · 62
Simon Fraser University · 98, 125, 148
social welfare · 17
South Africa · 87, 89
Stanford University · 59, 99, 131, 158, 163
State University of New York · 10, 112, 117,
    124, 129, 133, 134
substantial liability · 158
Substantive Due Process Clause · 92
Supreme Court · 12, 28, 30, 38, 42, 43, 46, 48,
    50, 55, 59, 64, 67, 68, 71, 81, 82, 83, 84, 85,
86, 88, 89, 90, 91, 93, 94, 95, 99, 103, 104,
    105, 110, 116, 123, 130, 131, 133, 138, 142,
    149
Systemic violence · 133, 134

T

Tailhook · 41, 75, 77, 79
Thomas, Clarence · 7, 12, 28, 30, 42, 43, 50, 83,
    91, 94
Title IX · 83, 86, 89, 91, 92, 95, 99, 103, 104,
    105, 122, 124, 127, 130, 132, 134, 149
transit system · 8
Transsexual · 137

U

United States Army · 78
universities · 21, 38, 44, 94, 98, 100, 102, 106,
    107, 108, 109, 112, 117, 118, 119, 121, 123,
    125, 126, 129
University of California · 17, 20, 71, 97, 102,
    146
Utley, Alison · 111

V

verbal harassment · 114, 117
veterinary · 59
Vietnam veterans · 76
violence · 12, 14, 16, 18, 26, 33, 41, 48, 49, 53,
    71, 85, 89, 107, 113, 114, 119, 122, 133, 134,
    143, 144, 147, 151
Virginia Military Institute · 78

W

women physicians · 64, 154, 159
women professors · 68, 139

Z

zero tolerance · 99, 100, 108, 153

AUTHOR INDEX

A

Aase, KA · 71
Abel, GG · 29
Adams, RS · 114
Adelson, Melissa · 4
Aggarwal, Arjun P. · 54
Alger, Jonathan R. · 89
Allen, Robert L. · 12
Alston, Kal · 108
Altman, Andrew · 89
Alvarez de los Heros, JI · 5
Anderson, A.J. · 103
Angier, Natalie · 30, 35
Arbeiter, Jean S. · 164
Arthur, John · 102
Ash, A. · 100
Atkinson, Camille · 57
Au, KC · 101

B

Baca, M. Carlota · 118
Backes, John S · 127
Badenhausen, Richard · 39
Bagley, Christopher · 149
Bailey, Joe · 127
Baker Fletcher, Karen · 38
Baldwin, DC Jr. · 100, 151
Bannerji, Himani · 40
Bargh, JA · 22
Barickman, Richard B. · 69, 117
Barinaga, Marcia · 146, 163
Barling, J. · 62
Barnett, KH · 116
Barnett, RC · 100
Barrett, Paul · 81
Barstow, Anne L. · 5
Bateson, Melissa · 23
Beauregard, Audra Rae · 141
Beauregard, Terri Kinion · 69, 130

Beletsky, Les D. · 45
Bell, EA · 76
Bell, PA · 66
Bellow, Janis Freedman · 32, 148
Bender, MP · 59, 142
Bendixen, M. · 136
Bennett, L. · 36
Benokraitis, Nijole V. · 37
Bensko, NL · 66
Berdahl, JL · 23
Bergen, M. · 99
Berger, Gilda · 54
Berhane, Y. · 107
Berlant, Lauren · 40
Berlin, Lois F. · 105
Bertrand, Lorne D. · 149
Beyer, CE · 113
Bier, John Allan · 28
Bikel, Ofra · 50
Bindman, Andrew B. · 163
Bingham, Shereen G. · 10
Birks, Sharon M. · 45
Black, PN · 113
Blumenthal, JA · 22
Boisnier, AD · 100
Bolitho, Floyd · 149
Bollag, Burton · 123
Boot, William · 70
Booth Butterfield, Melanie · 146, 149
Bordo, Susan · 7, 34
Borrowdale, Anne · 14
Boureau, Alain · 6
Bracey, Gerald W · 135
Brady, Barbara · 59
Brake, Deborah L · 92
Brandenburg, Judith Berman · 10, 104
Brant, Clare · 31
Brock, David · 7
Brogan, Donna · 64, 154
Brooks, Geraldine S. · 55
Brown, Cindy M. · 37
Brown, JB · 11
Brown, Lisa A. · 132
Brown, LM · 22

Brown, SC · 113
Bruner, Belinda · 15
Bryant, M. · 29
Buchwald, Emilie · 41
Budhos, Marina Tamar. · 70
Burda, D. · 25
Bursztajn, HJ · 4
Bushnell, Dana E. · 1
Buss, David M. · 33

C

Calfee, Barbara E. · 88, 151
Callan, Susan Rose · 155
Calleja, Garcia E. · 5
Cancelo-Hidalgo, MJ · 5
Cantu Weber, Josie · 109
Capek, Mary Ellen · 36
Capen, K. · 156
Carlson, Eric Stener · 76
Carlson, Karen J. · 141
Carlson, Nancy L. · 147
Carpenter, Linda Jean · 95
Carr, P. · 100
Cashin, JR · 112
Cericola, SA · 64
Chamallas, Martha · 44
Chan, Anja Angelica. · 82
Chance, Jean · 69
Cheung, FM · 101
Chizuko, Ueno · 32
Chliwniak, Luba · 110
Choi, PK · 101
Chrisman, Robert · 12
Ciresi, Rita · 8
Clark, Robert · 13
Clarke, Adele E. · 49
Clode, Dianne · 8
Cochrane, Lydia G. · 6
Coffman, Sandra · 63
Cohen, M. · 73
Cohen, Patricia Cline · 24
Cole, Elsa Kircher · 128
Collier, Rohan · 55
Collins, DW · 156, 163
Coney, Sandra · 163
Conley, Frances K. · 165
Connell, DS · 56, 84
Conway, J. · 21
Conway, S. · 21
Cook, Ellen Piel, · 57
Cook, S.E. · 23
Cornell, Drucilla · 11, 82

Cornwell, Tim · 116
Costello, R. · 21, 60
Cotton, Paul · 19
Coverdale, J. · 161
Coxell, A. · 6
Creamer, Elizabeth · 34
Crisci, George S. · 138
Crouse, Lindsay. · 102
Curcio, Joan L. · 105
Cutting, JoAnn C. · 121
Cuzydlo, C. · 24

D

Dalton, Rex · 32
Danforth, John C. · 83
Daniluk, Judith C. · 55
Daugherty, SR · 100, 151
Davidhizar, R. · 90
Davis, Donald F. · 53
Davis, Sue · 132
Decker, PJ · 157
Deddens, J. · 61, 144
Dekker, I. · 62
deMayo, RA · 162
Denniston, Lyle · 94
Dickerson, Bette J. · 9
Diehl, Lesley A. · 31
Donald, CG · 152
Donis, FJ · 62
Donnelly, Liam · 98, 125, 148
Dowd, S. · 90
Dowell, Susan · 14
Downing, Paul R. · 84
Drake, Larry · 73
Drasgow, F. · 143
Drum, ML · 67
Duffy, Angela · 103
Dupper, DR · 103
Dziech, Billie Wright · 37, 105, 105, 106, 127
Dziegielewski, SF · 157

E

Eastland, Terry · 38
Easton, AN · 113
Einarsen, S. · 73
Eisaguirre, Lynne · 14, 15
Eisenstat, Stephanie A. · 141
Elliott, Cathy · 34, 69
Emerson, Thomas I. · 62

Enbom, JA · 153
Enloe, Cynthia · 78
Epp, Juanita Ross · 133, 134
Erdel, S. · 90
Erickson, Chris D. · 139
Erickson, J. Bianca. · 106
Esacove, AW · 142
Essex, Nathan L. · 123

F

Farley, Lin · 57
Fatunde, Tunde · 125
Fear-Fenn, Marcia · 93
Fekete, John · 100, 107
Feldman, P. · 151
Feldman-Schorrig, S. · 4, 7
Fendrich, M. · 67
Fiesta, J. · 161, 165
Figler, RA · 159
Fine, Philip · 125, 148
Fineran, S. · 36
Fink, RL · 158
Finnis, SJ · 59, 142
First, Patricia F. · 105
Fitzgerald, LF · 23, 60, 143, 144
Flaherty, JA · 67, 152
Flatow, Gail M. · 37
Fletcher, Pamela R. · 41
Flowers, Ronald B. · 16
Flynn, Andrea Feltus · 127
Fontana, Alan · 76
Ford, CA · 62
Ford, Laura Christian · 17
Fordham, S. · 155
Fortune, Marie M. · 112
Fosson, SE · 99
Fox Genovese, Elizabeth · 31
Francis, Leslie P. · 107
Frank, E. · 68, 154, 159
Frank, Erica · 64
Franke, Ann H. · 10, 94
Franklin, GM · 158
Franklin, Phyllis · 126
Fraser, Nancy · 67
Fredrick, Candice · 57
French, Stanley G. · 44
Friedman, RH · 100
Fuehrer, Ann · 128
Fuertes, Monica · 122

G

Gabbard, GO · 152
Gallop, Jane · 15, 107
Gardner, Carol Brooks · 17
Garment, Suzanne · 46
Garner, Helen, · 18, 108, 135
Gasper, C. · 145
Gates, MM · 60
Gates, R. · 154
Gehring, Donald D. · 127
Gelfand, MJ · 143
Gerardi, Robert J. · 26
Gilbert, JA · 63
Gold, LH · 158
Goldenhar, LM · 61, 144
Goldstein, Leslie Friedman · 85
Gomez, N. · 5
Gomez-Preston, C. · 27
Gordon, D. · 6
Gose, Ben · 101
Gottlieb, Naomi · 63
Gould, Carol C. · 18
Green, Jason · 101
Grierson, R.D. · 97
Grossman, Wendy M. · 3
Grundhuber, L. · 17
Gumley, N. · 55
Gutek, Barbara A. · 58

H

Haber, Richard J. · 163
Hajdin, Mane. · 23
Halleck, SL · 27
Hallgarth, Susan A. · 36
Hamilton, Linda H. · 41, 131
Hanmer, Jalna · 48
Hartel, Lynda Jones · 19
Hastings, Susan C. · 127
Hawkins, C.E. · 117
Hawkins, Michael W · 127
Haworth, Karla · 98, 120
Hayes, Richard L. · 111
Hebel, Sara · 133
Heimann, Sue · 104
Helmlinger, Connie · 54
Hendrickson, Robert M. · 87
Hendrie, Caroline · 131
Hendrix, BB · 25

Herbert, Carrie M. H. · 20, 58, 109, 110, 127, 134
Hershey, N. · 142
Herzog, Kristin · 69
Heywood, Leslie · 14, 20
Hickson, Mark · 97
Hill, Anita Faye · 29, 91
Hippensteele, Susan · 121, 148
Hoff, David J. · 108
Hogan, K. · 24
Holden, Constance · 131, 146
Holmberg, MB · 160
Holmes, Robert L. · 126
Holoviak, SJ · 159
Hood, Clifton · 8
Hooks, Bell · 56
Horn, HR · 113
Horning, Beth · 71
Horosko, Marian · 39
Horsley, Jack E. · 56
Hotelling, Kathy · 130
Houghton-James, Hazel · 87
Hovland, DL · 60
Howard Hamilton, Mary F. · 116
Howard, Melanie · 70
Howard, Susan · 137
Hughes, William · 130
Hulin, CL · 143, 144
Hurrell, JJ Jr. · 61, 144
Hurt, L. · 145
Hyslop, Jonathan · 87

I

Irons, Nicholas H. · 68
Irons, RR · 61

J

Jacob, SK · 99
Jacobs, C. · 99
Jacobs, Jennifer W. · 95
Jameson, V. · 113
Johnson, TP · 67
Jones, Rebecca · 99, 132
Jones, S. · 151
Jordan, Emma Coleman · 29, 91
Jordan, Timothy R. · 114
Juster, Susan · 2

K

Kadue, David D. · 62, 89
Kaplan, Rochelle K. · 71
Kaplan, RS · 82
Kassaye, M. · 107
Kaye, J. · 152, 153
Keaveney, Madeline M. · 9
Keim, Jeanmarie S · 139
Kelly, Liz · 144
Kikotho, Wachira · 125
Kinard, JL · 157
King, CS · 161
King, Keith A. · 123
King, M. · 6
King, RE · 75
King, Robert L. · 42
Kinoshita, June · 139
Kiok, Jennifer · 114
Kirtley, Jane · 82
Kirtz, William · 16
Kisa, A. · 157
Kitzinger, Celia · 34
Klein, J. · 4
Klein, Susan Shurberg · 124
Knowles, Norman · 40
Knox, M. · 155
Kokkonen, Jorma · 115
Komaromy, Miriam · 163
Kondro, Wayne · 156
Kopels, S. · 103
Koss, Mary P. · 26
Krolokke, Charlotte · 139
Kuhlmann, Ellen · 22
Kulisch, W. Anthony · 105

L

LaMarche, Gara · 36
Lambert, Cheryl · 48
Lane, Ann J. · 97
Larsen, Kristine M. · 139
Lasater, NE · 81, 95
Lawrence, Jennifer · 3
Layman, Nancy S. · 115
Leatherman, Courtney · 97, 132, 133
Lebrato, Mary T. · 19
Lederman, Douglas · 84
Lee, Deborah · 137
Lee, Francis S. · 116

LeMoncheck, Linda · 23
Lengel, Gena · 131
Levesque, RJ · 5
Lewis, John F. · 127
Lindemann, Barbara · 62, 88
Linder, Barbara C. · 97
Lippman, Helen · 163
Little, B. · 157
Lock, RS · 113
Lorenzkowski, Barbara · 53
Lozada, Marlene · 108
Luce, EA · 29
Luepker, ET · 143, 159
Lumsden, Linda S. · 19
Lyncheski, JE · 11

M

Ma, Kenneth · 137
MacFarlane, Lisa · 2
MacGregor, Karen · 89
MacKinnon, Catharine A. · 62, 69
MacLeod, Christine · 39
Madison, J. · 54, 154
Magley, VJ · 143, 144
Malamuth, Neil M. · 22, 33
Mangus, R.S. · 117
Mann, Richard L. · 130
Mannen, K. · 145
Marcus, Jon · 119, 123
Marczely, Bernadette · 116
Mark, Y. · 24
Martin, L. · 76, 78, 145
Masako hensh¯u ky¯oryoku, Amano · 32
Mathis, Patricia A. · 68
Mattick, Paul · 27
Maynard, Mary · 48
Mazza, Cris · 23
McCaffrey, Kate S. · 134
McCaffrey, Susan · 31
McCarthy, Martha M. · 132
McCartney, JR · 143
McConaghy, Tom · 98
McConnell, Michael W. · 94
McCrory, E. · 54
McDaniel, Susan A. · 126
McDonald, JJ Jr. · 90
McEvoy, TJ · 81, 95
McGovern, PG · 45
McKinney, Kathleen · 147
McLaughlin, MA · 99
McLaurin, JR · 157
Meilman, PW · 112

Merker, S. · 152
Mezey, G. · 6
Michaelis, Karen L · 92
Miller, Anita · 42
Miller, Edward · 119
Miller, M.J. · 117
Minnich, Elizabeth · 120
Miya, Pamela A. · 165
Modleski, Tania · 25
Monaghan, Peter · 98
Monarch, K. · 64
Monroe, Bill · 22
Monte-Mercado, JC · 5
Mooij, Ton · 119
Moore, HL · 160, 163
Moore, Michele Johnson · 113, 129
Morewitz, Stephen John · 25
Morris, A. · 61
Morris, Celia · 26
Morrison, Toni · 30, 91
Moser, Rita M. · 10
Moskowitz, MA · 100
Moskowitz, Rachel · 73
Mrkwicka, L. · 64
Mulugeta, E. · 107
Munson, Naomi · 58
Murdoch, M. · 45
Murphy, Sharon Scribner · 142
Murrell, Patricia H. · 121
Muus, KM · 136
Myrsiades, Linda · 2

N

Nawyn, Stephanie J. · 67
Nelson, Cary · 136
NiCarthy, Ginny · 63
Nieto, Jose C. · 36
Nora, LM · 99
Nuutinen, Matti · 115

O

O'Donnell, Teresa Blankenbeker · 35
O'Donohue, W. · 5
O'Hare, EA · 5
O'Sullivan, Gerry · 64
O'Sullivan, V. · 162
O'Barr, Jean · 120
Ogletree, RJ · 113
Olesen, Virginia L. · 49

Oxley, Chris · 34, 69

P

Pacitti, Domenico · 21
Pack, Michael · 102
Paisley, Pamela O. · 111
Paludi, Michele Antoinette. · 12, 69, 112, 116,
    124, 147, 129, 146
Paranjpe, R. · 24
Patai, Daphne · 20, 117
Peach, Larry · 99
Pearson, Thomas C. · 121, 148
Perlstein, Daniel · 122
Perry, Linda A.M. · 10
Persson, G. · 160
Peters, Cara · 64
Petrocelli, William · 90
Petroff, J. · 162
Pfeiffer, M. · 160
Phelps, Rosemary E. · 111, 116
Phelps, Timothy M. · 28
Phillips, Susan P. · 155, 162, 164
Pierce, Christina · 33
Pierce, Patricia A. · 35
Piotrkowski, CS · 61
Piskorski, TJ · 56
Pitman, Andrew · 67
Plunkett, L. · 160
Podhoretz, Norman · 1
Presley, CA · 112
Preston, SH · 24
Price, James H. · 114, 123
Pringle, Rosemary · 65
Prizer, John · 102
Prochaska, SJ Jr. · 27
Prokop, Ruth T. · 68
Pryor, JB · 22
Pryor, John B. · 147
Purdy, Laura M. · 45

Q

Quick, JC · 61
Quina, Kathryn. · 147

R

Radwan, Jacek · 27
Ragan, Sandra L. · 94

Raknes, BI · 73
Ranney, Frances · 90
Raymond, P. · 22
Reddick, Thomas L. · 99
Reed, Carole Ann · 109
Reid, EA · 155
Reisfeld, R. · 27
Repa, Barbara Kate · 90
Resnick, Rosalind · 20
Rice, Suzanne · 135
Rich, Vera · 114
Richardson, L. Anita · 42
Richman, Judith A. · 67, 152
Rienzo, Barbara A. · 129
Riggs, Robert O. · 121
Robbins, I. · 59, 142
Robinson, RK · 158
Rogers, Michael · 83
Roiphe, Katherine · 122
Roiphe, Katie · 150
Rosen, LF · 71
Rosen, LN · 76, 78, 145
Rosenfeld, Rachel · 120
Rosenheck, Robert · 76
Rosman, JP · 90
Rospenda, Kathleen M. · 67, 152
Roth, MA · 76
Roth, Martha · 41
Roth, Philip · 32, 148
Rouleau, JL · 29
Rowley, BD · 100, 151
Rubin, Paula N. · 44, 95
Ruder, A. · 61, 144
Ruenzel, David · 117
Ruiz, Diana D. · 5
Russell, B. · 145
Russell, Diana E.H. · 66
Russo, Peggy Anne · 27
Ruzek, Sheryl Burt · 49

S

Sabato, Larry J. · 40
Sage, Lorna · 135
Salladay, Susan A. · 161
Sankar, Andrea · 48
Saperstein, Aron · 21
Sarrion Mora, Adelina · 36
Sayce, L. · 27, 145
Schei, B. · 136
Schiffman, M. · 154, 159
Schiffman, Melissa · 64
Schilb, John · 15

Schilling, Karen Maitland · 128
Schmidt, JL · 99
Schneider, Alison · 81, 119, 137
Schneider, JP · 61
Schneider, KT · 60, 143
Schneider, M. · 164
Schneider, Margaret S. · 164
Schulhofer, Stephen J. · 92
Schwartz, Linda Spoonster · 76
Schwartz, Martin D. · 147
Scott, S. · 113
Segrave, Kerry, · 66
Selingo, Jeffrey · 87, 99, 101, 142
Sendor, Benjamin · 134, 138
Severson, K. · 143
Sexton, Sarah · 53
Sfikas, EM · 8
Sfikas, Peter M. · 70
Shaikh, MA · 160
Shalit, Ruth · 135
Shapiro, Amy. · 102
Shaver, Susan · 31
Sheets, VR · 56
Shepard, Alicia C. · 3, 39
Shepherd, BW · 60
Sherer, JL · 58, 157, 160
Shrier, I. · 151
Siegel, Deborah L. · 36, 70
Siegel, PJ · 82
Silfen, E. · 159
Silverthorne, Jeanne · 28
Simon, Rita J. · 17, 84
Sjostrom, Lisa · 132
Skolnick, Andrew A. · 29
Smith, Kelly J. · 97
Smith, Patricia · 15
Smitherman, Geneva · 50
Smolla, Rodney A. · 81
Smuts, Barbara · 4
Solomon, Robert C. · 47
Sommers, Christina Hoff · 46
Spain, Valerie · 63
Spender, Dale · 50
Spratlen, LP · 162
Stamler, Virginia Lee · 107
Stan, Adele M. · 13
Stanley, Liz · 47
Stearley, H. · 92, 163
Stein, Nan D. · 124, 131, 147
Stein, Ronald H. · 118
Stepp, Carl Sessions · 38
Sterk, Helen M. · 10
Stetson, Dorothy M. · 93
Stevenson, David S. · 91

Stockdale, Margaret S. · 68
Stone, Gerald L. · 107
Stone, Graham N. · 15
Strack, F. · 22
Stratton, Stanley D. · 127
Strong, C. · 113
Strout, Elizabeth · 37
Sudmann, T. · 1
Summer, GL · 54, 100, 152
Summers, J. · 113
Sumrall, Amber Coverdale · 33
Swan, S. · 60, 143
Swanson, NG · 61, 144
Swisher, Karin L. · 33, 45
Szalacha, L. · 100

T

Tamelleo, AD · 91
Tang, CS · 101
Taylor, Dena · 33
Teays, Wanda · 45
Telljohann, Susan Kay · 114
Teruko, Inoue · 32
Thistlethwaite, Susan Brooks · 35
Thomas, Alison M. · 34
Thomas, CD · 153
Thompson, David P. · 95
Thompson, Janna · 47
Thompson, Martha · 48
Till, Frank J. · 136
Too, Yun Lee · 31
Torres, Vasti · 116
Totenberg, Nina · 42
Tribble, Joanne L. · 113, 123
Trix, Frances · 48
Turner, Lynn H. · 10

U

Uhari, Matti · 115
Utley, Alison · 111

V

Vaccaro, PL · 29
Van Bronkhorst, Erin · 64
Van Rossmalen, Erica · 126
Van Tol, Joan E. · 129
Vernon, Jennifer G. · 23

Viano, Emilio C. · 12
Vietenthal, P. · 32
Viney, W. · 66
Viuda de la Garcia, E. · 5
Voge, VM · 75
Vukovich, MC · 138

W

Wade, Brent · 45
Walby, S. · 57
Waldo, CR · 23
Wall, HP · 113
Wallace, PB · 113
Walsh Childers, Kim · 69
Walsh, Mark · 83, 86, 88, 93, 104, 110, 121, 142
Wasserman, Nora M. Fraser · 127
Watkinson, Ailsa M. · 133, 134
Weaver, Carolyn · 3
Weaver, Ellen Cleminshaw · 71
Weber, RD · 63
Weed, G. · 76
Weerakoon, P · 162
Weiner, Linda · 106
Weinstein, Bruce D. · 28, 153, 164
Weinstein, Laurie · 78
Weissenstein, E. · 25
Wekesser, Carol · 33
Wellbrock, Richard D. · 34
Werbinski, J. · 63, 160
West, CT Jr. · 159
Westerstahl, A. · 115
Weston, Ralph · 69
White, Christie C. · 78
White, GE · 161

Whitehead, R. Jr. · 160, 163
Whittenbury, Elizabeth R. Koller · 105
Wiener, RL · 145
Wilcox, Diane Michelfelder · 46
Wilcox, William H. · 47
Williams, KG · 89
Williams, MF · 53, 151
Williams, Verna L · 81, 92
Willis, Ellen · 44
Wilson, JF · 59
Wilson, Robin · 98, 118
Winternitz, Helen · 28, 29
Wirth, SR · 159
Wise, Sue · 47
Witzke, D. · 99
Wohlberg, JW · 155
Wolfe, Suzanne · 32, 59
Wolfson, Nicholas. · 95
Wood, Julia T. · 14, 46, 94, 150
Woody, WD · 66
Wylie, Herb · 40

Y

Yik, MS · 101
Yumiko hen, Ehara · 32

Z

Zimmerman, Jean. · 79
Ziporyn, Terra · 141
Zirkel, Perry A · 111, 138, 149
Zook, Ruth · 156